THE INSTITUTIONAL REVOLUTION

MARKETS AND GOVERNMENTS IN ECONOMIC HISTORY

A Series Edited by Price Fishback

The Institutional Revolution

Measurement and the Economic Emergence of the Modern World

DOUGLAS W. ALLEN

THE UNIVERSITY OF CHICAGO PRESS   Chicago and London

DOUGLAS W. ALLEN is the Burnaby Mountain Professor of Economics at Simon Fraser University.

The University of Chicago Press, Chicago 60637
The University of Chicago Press, Ltd., London
© 2012 by The University of Chicago
All rights reserved. Published 2012.
Printed in the United States of America

31 30 29 28 27 26 25 24   3 4 5 6

ISBN-13: 978-0-226-01474-6   (cloth)
ISBN-10: 0-226-01474-6   (cloth)

Library of Congress Cataloging-in-Publication Data

Allen, Douglas W. (Douglas Ward), 1960–
    The institutional revolution : measurement and the economic emergence of the
    modern world / Douglas W. Allen.
        p.   cm.—(Markets and governments in economic history)
    ISBN-13: 978-0-226-01474-6 (hardcover : alk. paper)
    ISBN-10: 0-226-01474-6 (hardcover : alk. paper)
        1. Public institutions—England—History.   2. Great Britain—History—Stuarts,
    1603–1714.   I. Title.   II. Series: Markets and governments in economic history.
    JN191.A554   2012
    331.25—dc22   2011012408

♾ This paper meets the requirements of ANSI/NISO z39.48-1992 (Permanence of Paper).

To A.D., C.H., T.B., and Y.B., for showing me that economics is about more than prices and quantities.

Contents

Preface

This book started with the television show *Masterpiece Theatre*. The three-part series was called *Sharpe, II,* which aired in the spring of 1995 (I had missed the two-part series *Sharpe, I,* which had aired in the 1993–1994 season). The program followed the adventures of Richard Sharpe, a common foot soldier in the Spanish campaign against Napoleon. In the earlier series, Sharpe bravely saved the Duke of Wellington, who then promoted him to lieutenant and placed him in charge of a rifle division. Over the course of the series Sharpe would lead his men from one adventure to another.

It was great entertainment, and as with most episodes of *Masterpiece Theatre,* the host, Russell Baker, would come on before and after the program to provide commentary and historical context. On one of these occasions he said the following: "Wellington in fact preferred that his officers be gentlemen . . . what he wanted in an officer was a well-rounded gentleman who had studied the past in the college library and the present on the grand tour of Europe." I had never heard of the "grand tour of Europe," but I ignored the remark when Baker went on to say something along the lines of "indeed, most officers during the Napoleonic Wars purchased their commissions and were not promoted through the ranks based on merit." I thought I heard incorrectly. Why would someone ever pay to be an officer? Wouldn't the Crown have to pay officers to fight? And should merit not have counted for something? It made no sense, and the economist in me had to look into it further.

I am not a professional historian. I am not even an economic historian. I love history, but my training is in the economics of organization, and so as a historian I'm a mere amateur. It was good for me that several real historians had documented the details of the military purchase system. It turned out that Russell Baker was right. For hundreds of years most military commissions were bought and sold among private individuals who ran their "companies" like Warren Buffett runs Berkshire Hathaway—always with an eye on the bottom line. It was not a system of pure laissez-faire capitalism, however. Rather, it was a rich and complicated system that involved the Crown, officers, and the general army apparatus. Most important to me, it was a system that had a beautiful economic logic. The purchase system actually solved a difficult problem for the Crown: how to develop an army of good fighters in a world where it was very difficult to measure performance. How this was accomplished is demonstrated in Chapter 6. In the meantime, as I examined the history of purchased commissions more closely, I discovered that officers in the navies during the age of fighting sail *never* purchased their commissions. Looking into this new riddle revealed an unusual world in terms of social conventions, formal rules, strange offices, and enormous penalties for nonperformance. One puzzle arose after another, and I believed there had to be some underlying economic reason to it all.

A quick survey of economic writings came up short. In the mid-1990s no one in my clan had paid much attention to the specific organizations I was interested in. There simply were no economic papers on dueling, purchased commissions, or a lack of public police. Of course, several economic historians had examined historical institutions: Avner Greif had looked at the Maghribi traders in the medieval Mediterranean; Douglass North had examined numerous market institutions throughout European history; and indeed, the theorist Daron Acemoglu had examined the success of nations and made institutional economics almost "sexy"—academically speaking. But no one had addressed the really odd institutions I was coming across. No one could tell me why lighthouses were privately owned or why the nobility had a passion for enormous parks.

The reason for these omissions in the economic analysis is not hard to discover. Generally speaking, modern economists have ignored the details of the odd institutions that existed prior to the Industrial Revolution. Economists have only given serious thought to institutions for a few years, and I suppose the institutionally interested just have not had time to go this far back in history. Of those who had, their work often focused on markets, trade, and transportation—areas economists traditionally feel comfortable in. Of course, a large economic history literature exists, but most of the ink spilled over my period of interest deals with the technical breakthroughs and growth in output during the Industrial Revolution, and rightly so. Unfortunately for me, most of this work is purely noninstitutional in nature—concerned with technological changes in production, rising output, and price movements. Traditional economic historians have begun to examine the role of institutions, especially within the context of gross domestic product (GDP) growth over the Industrial Revolution, but institutions in this literature are often thought of on a grand scale, such as "the rule of law" or "enforceable private property," and they often are treated as natural resources, like iron ore or good harbors. In the end, I found little written among my own tribe to help understand why Sharpe would have been the exception rather than the rule in Wellington's army.

I had better luck among historians, who have been documenting the details of institutions in this era for some time. For the most part, I found the *descriptions* of pre-modern institutions extremely well done. Yet in terms of *explanations* for why the world was once ruled this way, I found the historians lacking. To overgeneralize (and probably to be quite unfair), I found that many historians have viewed history through a Marxian, or social history, lens and see every institution as a mechanism for exploitation. Other historians are more Whiggish and see history as a steady pace of human progress. In both cases, the view of the pre-modern world is quite dismal. Either factory discipline was simply a cruel means of extracting rents from workers, or it was an early form of better organization that just needed a few bugs worked out. Venal offices—those which were sold to the highest bidder—were either a means by which the wealthy grew even wealthier, or they were mere corruption. So much time spent on passing judgment often replaced efforts to develop operational theories of why these institutions existed in the form they did.

It is easy to sympathize with the historians. After all, if given a choice, who would prefer to live in the pre-modern world over our own? And how could institutions that encouraged the sale of public office, promotion by social rank or family relations, or punishment by death be described as anything other than "old corruption" and exploitive? Perhaps the past was an evil that the modern world escaped from.

But, at least for a moment, I had to take a more optimistic point of view. This book is laced with the idea that institutions are "constrained efficient." By that is not meant that they are designed by an all-knowing social planner who uses his calculus to constantly determine that all decisions are made correctly. Nor does it mean that institutions achieve some global social utopian ideal, or that we cannot find examples in life—like North Korea—where bad institutions are clearly at work. Rather, it means that in the Darwinian struggle between nations, firms, and individuals, societies are driven to find institutions that get the job done best under the circumstances faced at the time. Institutions are arrived at in many ways, often by accident or by trial and error. When they work well relative to the competition, they tend to survive and the society prospers. There may be other institutional arrangements that might be technically feasible, but under the circumstances they are not economical.

For me, this seems like the right approach, at least for a broad look at the pre-modern world. All of the pre-modern institutions analyzed in this book existed for hundreds of years. Any time a country prospers under rules that last for hundreds of years, I believe it calls upon the scholar to pause, humble himself, and ask, "What problem was that rule solving?" Such was my goal, narrowly defined to military commissions, back in the summer of 1995.

I published my first paper on purchased commissions in 1998, and I have been working in this area ever since. In this book I compile and elaborate on my published work and take the opportunity to step back and look at the entire pre-modern institutional system. Over time, I have come to realize that between roughly 1780 and 1850, the world experienced what can only be called an "Institutional Revolution." By using the term "revolution," I do not claim that every organization prior to 1780 was different from what existed after 1850, any more than one could claim the France of 1788 was completely different from the France of 1790. Rather, I mean that there was a distinct change, especially in the sector of the economy we call the "public service." The economic world had been evolving, but during the period from 1780 to 1850 it reached an organizational tipping point. And the changes were, indeed, revolutionary. This revolution not only changed the way Western countries organized life, but as I speculate toward the end of the book, it may be the key to understanding why the other revolution—the industrial one—had the impact it did.

Although this book takes an institutional economic approach to history, it is written with a wider audience in mind. As an economist rooted in institutional analysis, I cannot help but think my colleagues in new institutional economics will find the material of interest. However, I hope that other economists, historians, and the proverbial interested layman will also find the book appealing. I have made every attempt to minimize jargon and explain the technical terms when the cost of using alternatives was just too high. There are no mathematical equations or graphs and only a few diagrams to save a thousand words. Finally, most endnotes are only references to my sources—although the academic in me cannot help mentioning the odd theoretical detour every now and then. This approach will undoubtedly be unsatisfactory to many. The historians will likely be appalled by my failure to elaborate on the nuances of change and my reluctance to qualify general statements. Economists will object to the lack of formal theory and quantitative tests. Specialists in particular battles or naval formations will accuse me of ignorance of any number of historical details. And given what I believe is the originality of my thesis, many will object to my monocausal, parsimonious conjecture and my unwillingness to consider alternative theories in the detail they deserve. Such is the cost of walking the fine line of a broad book trying to make an original academic argument. My goal is to show there is a common thread in the blanket of institutional history that has been mostly ignored. If there is merit in what I have done, others will elaborate, formalize, correct my faux pas, and formally test the theory.

Over the years, I have had to rely on a number of historians to calm down my wild tendencies as an economist to generalize. Special thanks go to my history colleague John Craig in this regard. I have also received assistance from historians Nicholas Tracey, N. A. M. Rodger, and William Doyle. My good friend, co-author on dueling, and former and only economic history teacher, Clyde Reed, has been a support throughout the entire journey, and I thank him for all of his comments. I have also tortured many economists and friends with historical episodes until they finally surrendered and confessed a few comments. Thanks to James Amegashi, David Andolfatto, Brian April, Cliff Bekar, Phil Curry, Greg Dow, Steve Easton, Bob Ellickson, Bruno Frey, Steve Globerman, Chris Hall, Doug Hay, David Jacks, Ron Johnson, Anke Kessler, Levis Kochin, Gary Libecap, Frank Lorne, Dean Lueck, Christoph Lülfesmann, John Lunn, Joel Mokyr, Krishna Pendakur, Eric Posner, Tom Ross, Desmund Sackey, Robert Stevens, Wing Suen, Chris Thornberg, and Gordon Tullock. Thanks to others, such as Thomas Allen, Yoram Bauman, Tracey Block, John Chant, Brian Crowley, Steve Fagan, Price Fishback, Milton Friesen, Joel Mokyr, Laura Nielson, Leanne Rancourt, Rick Szostak, and Justin Wiltshire, who provided yeoman's service in reading early versions of the manuscript and who corrected some of my major affronts to the English language, economic theory, and historical facts. Thanks to Vera Lantinova for her work on the index. I also thank the anonymous reviewers of the book who provided detailed criticism on every chapter. I apologize for accepting only most of their remarks. Of course, my editor, David Pervin, deserves special thanks for going through the manuscript with care . . . several times. Although I grew tired of his lament "plain English please!" most readers should be grateful for his efforts. Finally, I'd like to thank Yoram Barzel, who not only co-authored one of my historical papers and has read just about every word I have ever written, but to whom I owe an intellectual debt in terms of how to think about institutions.

CHAPTER ONE

Introduction

To my Lords in the morning, where I met with Captain Cuttance, but my Lord not being up I went out to Charing Cross, to see Major-general Harrison hanged, drawn, and quartered; which was done there, he looking as cheerful as any man could do in that condition. He was presently cut down, and his head and heart shown to the people, at which there was great shouts of joy.

SAMUEL PEPYS, *The Diary of Samuel Pepys,* October 13, 1660

If it were not for his remarkable diary and detailed records, Samuel Pepys would hardly rate a footnote in history as an able naval administrator. But he did write a literary gem of a diary, in which his personal accounts and keen observations of life in seventeenth-century London enjoyably take us back in time to a world much different than our own. Today many (though perhaps not that many) read the diary for a first-hand account of the Great Plague of 1665 or the Great Fire of London in 1666, or simply to feel nostalgia for days gone by in Freshman English. But even a casual reader cannot overlook some outlandish curiosities . . . like how it came to pass that a major-general was hanged, drawn, and quartered in public, much to the thrill of onlookers. Some readers are old enough to remember hanging as a capital punishment, but no one today has any experience with a public drawing and quartering.

There is more to Pepys's diary than gory dismemberment. By any account, Pepys was a successful man: chief secretary to the Admiralty, justice of the peace, member of Parliament, fellow and president of the Royal Society, and brother and master of Trinity House, to name only a few posts.[1] Some of these positions ring familiar, others less so, but a closer inspection of any single office reveals many strange things.

For example, Pepys got his start in the navy when his first cousin once removed, Sir Edward Montagu, was willing to act as his patron.[2]

A patron in Pepys's day was a person of influence who, with a word, could make or break a career. A patron was almost always necessary for any advancement in what we would now call the "public service," and Sir Edward had his own—a well-known character named King Charles II. Charles granted Montagu a number of titles, offices, and honors—including the 1st Earl of Sandwich—for his loyal service during the restoration of his Crown in 1660, and his positions allowed Montagu to influence the Admiralty to grant Pepys his first office, the clerk of the acts, in the navy. Pepys had no administrative experience or formal knowledge of the navy, but this hardly mattered at the time. Patronage appointments were given to people whom the patron could trust; ability was a distinctly secondary matter. What was also strange about Pepys's office, along with most others of the age, was that it became a matter of (mostly) private property once received. When Pepys became the clerk of the acts, he owned the office the way we now own our homes: he could sell, borrow against, and earn an income from it.

As a member of Trinity House, Pepys was part of an ancient monopoly organization that privately built lighthouses and actually charged ships for the service: no payment, no light. When he was elected to Parliament, it was first on behalf of a Lord Howard, and very few of his countrymen were allowed to vote—perhaps none of them freely, given the lack of secret ballots, the influence of sheriffs, and the ownership of many boroughs by high nobility. Though a justice of the peace, he received no salary for his efforts, and he openly accepted bribes at his naval office. His day-to-day life was very commonplace for a gentleman, but he also lived in quiet fear that someone might challenge him to a duel. Thus, Pepys provides a nice example of the paradox of life between the modern and the pre-modern world. On the one hand, Pepys's life was as ordinary as a human life could be: he worried about his supper and his gold, he was proud that his home had a spare bed for visitors, he pursued his mistresses, and he gossiped about his friends and co-workers. And yet, on the other hand, his life took place within the context of a set of social rules, norms, and organizations quite alien—and often offensive—to us today. In the West, patronage and bribes now imply corruption, duels are long gone, and universal suffrage with a secret ballot is a fundamental right. Indeed, it is this contrast in institutional context between the past and present that rivets students of history to the Pepys narrative.

In general, what often attracts us to history is the exotic within the context of the ordinary. We marvel at the spectacular military leader in an otherwise common battle. We are drawn to understand polygamy and arranged marriage among almost universal monogamous hetero-sexual marriage. Although we relate to, and sympathize with, the complaints of the eighteenth-century shipowner over excessive port taxes, we are more curious about the private "tax farmer" who paid the Crown for the right to collect the dues. And, of course, we are flabbergasted at the seventeenth-century diarist who unabashedly traded naval contracts for every form of payment from cow's tongue to sexual favors. If history did not have these exotic episodes, if the organization of life never changed, or if we could not relate to the individuals of the past, then history would make an unattractive study indeed. Fortunately, history has the common thread of humanity that makes it relevant. Doubly good is that its organizational detail changes over time and is therefore compelling and interesting.

Economics provides a useful tool for understanding the past because the human experience, over time, is connected through a common economic reality. At the most fundamental level, all people at all times have dealt with the problem of scarcity. There has never been enough, there will never be enough, and as a result people always have been driven to find better ways to increase their wealth and consumption. Scarcity has several universal implications: choices always have had to be made, trade-offs always have existed, actions always have had costs, and there always have been winners and losers. Modern readers recognize the signs of scarcity in our past and understand things like sibling rivalry—whether told through Cain and Abel, the daughters of King Lear, or Michael and Fredo Corleone in *The Godfather*. Humans have always used innovations to reduce the level of scarcity; thus technology, which is ever present in one form or another, has improved over time. Markets have also existed since antiquity, and life throughout history is a continuous attempt to get and produce more through exchange. The Romans had capital markets and interest rates. In many ways the baker of antiquity was similar to our baker on the corner because all bakers are simply trying to make a living.

What then, in a broad sense, is different? What captures our attention when we see a historical society different from our own? Economists naturally tend to focus on measures of well-being such as technology, incomes, height, or the absence of violence. This is an economic history of quantifiable averages. Output has increased over time, along with population and per capita incomes—on average. Health is better, people are taller, transportation is faster—on average. This is all well and good, but it often fails to capture what many sense to be a greater difference. Armies today are not just more deadly on average; they look different. They wear camouflage, do not fight in tight formations, are not composed of foreign mercenaries, and do not receive compensation through the spoils of battle. If we go back to our friend Samuel Pepys, we see that a middle-class administrator in the British navy today would have more possessions and live longer, but we are also aware that no one in the West today nonchalantly watches a man's heart get ripped out in a public square. So we realize that there is more to change over time than just a difference in averages.

Nevertheless, it is unfair to accuse economists of being completely focused on averages. Many have recognized that a major component of what differs over time are the rules we live by and how life is organized.[3] For the moment, call these rules "institutions." The more institutions differ over time, the more different the past appears. Today, in the West, the world is considered "modern." By that is meant a world governed by a series of secular institutions: the rule of law; well-enforced property rights; elected democratic governments; human rights; public provision of courts, health care, national defense, and education; professional services; regulated markets; concerns over social welfare and income distributions; and the concept of individual liberty within a modern state. We are comfortable with corporations producing food, with public police investigating our stolen automobiles, with money used as a unit of account for everything, with wage labor, with free mobility, and with individuals determining who they will marry and what occupation they will have. Perhaps above all, we expect to have equal social standing among our neighbors. Ours is a society based on a concept of merit, and those who work hard and produce much expect to be rewarded. The race may not always be to the swift, but the laborer is worthy of his hire, and we believe that, with effort and a little luck, anyone can reach the top of the social ladder. But it was not always so.

Not so long ago there was a strong social class structure where a large gulf separated ordinary people from the elite, and seldom did one cross over from one station to the other. Masters controlled servants, and both knew their place in the world. Merit was valued, but it was not the coin of the realm—personal connections, conduct, and birth mattered much more. Markets and prices existed for votes, state offices, and roads. There were jails where criminals were temporarily housed, but no penitentiaries for long-term incarceration and reform. There was money, but many payments were made in kind, with truck and barter, or through gleaning scraps off the workroom floor. There were watchmen but no police. The institutional landscape was shockingly different in the pre-modern world.

Amazingly, our Western world has been institutionally modern for only a short period. Institutions tend to last longer than any one person, and as a result, even a relatively young institution can feel old to the current generation. Communism, at the time of the fall of the Berlin wall, might as well have been an ancient form of government to the twenty- and thirty-somethings who pounded away at the concrete with sledgehammers in November 1989. The leaders were old, the state machinery was tired, the barbed wire was rusted, and everything about the system appeared outdated. Yet formal communist governments were just over 70 years old—mere infants in the life cycle of an institution.

It is because our world has been modern only since around the middle of the nineteenth century that we do not have to go far back in time before institutions become foreign to our modern senses.[4] Our local government administrations; systems of taxation; our widespread views on marriage, occupation, and social status; the practice of universal suffrage; and our sense of individualism, to name but a few, are all relatively recent institutional innovations. Institutionally speaking, if someone today could teleport back in time from modern America to late Victorian England, it would not be much different than traveling from Los Angeles to Christchurch—with apologies to the beautiful city of Christchurch. The traveler would notice some less functional plumbing and the absence of insulation, but the rules of the game would be basically the same. The traveler would be able to get by.

The same could not be said of traveling back to the middle of the eighteenth century, and it would involve more than noticing all the bad teeth and lack of cell phones. Much of the organization of life was different in the pre-industrial world, and a modern time traveler would be hard-pressed to fit in or understand it all. The institutional reality is that around 1850 the modern world—the world containing the modern institutions we are accustomed to—emerged. This is not to say there was no institutional overlap between the modern and pre-modern world—of course there was. There were elections in 1500 and 1900; there were banking, commerce, and coins; there were stocks, bonds, and interest rates; and there were families, firms, and churches. Some pre-modern institutions hardly changed at all over the course of the Industrial Revolution, but many changed in some manner, while others were completely transformed, discarded, or invented. Overall, and especially with respect to civil services, our modern world emerged out of a time organized far differently. Often the changes in the rules of life were so radical that we are now dismayed the old rules ever existed at all. Dueling? How barbaric! Lordship? How evil!

At some level, we are familiar with the historical organizations covered in this book. Almost everyone recognizes a picture of Queen Elizabeth II and knows something of the House of Lords—if only its existence. But few of us, except for fans of Jane Austen, are familiar with the institutional rules that governed the lives of the pre-modern aristocrats that allowed them to govern a nation for 300 years. Many have seen the movie version of *The Count of Monte Cristo*, where the wrongfully accused Edmond Dantès, after his revenge against his rivals, purposely shoots wide in an unanticipated duel with his son. Little do we realize that this type of behavior—shooting wide, not dueling— was not allowed and was equivalent to declining the duel in the first place. It is only by examining the details of pre-modern institutions that we appreciate the deep institutional changes that took place throughout the nineteenth century.

The institutions analyzed in this book are all of this sort—seemingly odd ones that either ended or were created over this transition period. They mostly span the time period I will call "pre-modern," that time after the fall of feudalism in England (c. 1500) until the Industrial Revolution was well on its way (c. 1850). In terms of English monarchs, the period spans from the first pre-modern ruler, Henry VIII, to the first modern one, Victoria. By the end of this time period there was what can only be described as a revolution in institutions. The Institutional Revolution was mostly—but not exclusively—centered on the changes that took place in the rules of public governance, and so the topics covered here include a host of institutions we now consider part of the public service: a nonexhaustive list includes the aristocrats, dueling, naval and army administration, lighthouses, private roads, taxation, factories, private police, and the evolution of criminal law.

Other institutions changed as well, and some contemporary writers such as Marx and Engels noticed what was going on:

> The bourgeoisie, wherever it has got the upper hand, has put an end to all feudal, patriarchal, idyllic relations. It has pitilessly torn asunder the motley feudal ties that bound man to his "natural superiors", and has left remaining no other nexus between man and man than naked self-interest, than callous "cash payment". . . . It has resolved personal worth

into exchange value, and in place of the numberless indefeasible chartered freedoms, has set up that single, unconscionable freedom—Free Trade.[5]

Although they clearly did not approve, Marx and Engels were on to something. They noticed a change was afoot; they recognized the past was not all bad; and they identified freedom to exchange as a key to the modern world.

My purpose here is to make the general claim that "measurement costs" are the common source behind the Institutional Revolution that troubled Marx and Engels. Free trade and the ability to socially interact with only "naked self-interest" and "callous cash payment" required the ability to measure what was being traded. Until this ability to measure materialized, communities required "patriarchal relations," "feudal ties," and "chartered freedoms" to get many things done. Which is not to say there was only a single source. Institutions arise and develop over several factors; I wish to highlight an important one that has been ignored.

I argue that many pre-modern institutions—at least the ones we find strange and fascinating—fall into two broad classes. In one class were those institutions based on what will be called "trust" between a patron/master and his servant. Although there were many trusting institutions, in this category I examine only a few exemplars: the aristocracy, dueling, and the patronage system. In the other class were institutions designed to exploit the entrepreneurial spirit of private incentives. Here an office was sold to its holder, and these were known as "venal" institutions. Here I examine the purchase of military commissions, the purchase of private offices, and the private investigations of crime.[6] The general claim is that the use of trust and private incentives were the Crown's two main institutional tools against improper behavior on the part of its servants within a world where measurement of many daily, basic things was difficult and/or often close to meaningless. These institutional weapons were used in both the great and minor offices of the state, and were replaced by modern bureaucratic institutions after the Industrial Revolution increased the ability to measure in a practical way.

On the one hand, a purpose of this book is to collect and analyze many of the strange and odd institutions of the pre-modern world. Their exotic characteristics, just by themselves, are enjoyable to read about. But on the other hand, and more important, I argue that these strange institutions had an economic logic. Their details were designed to solve incentive problems that arose in the pre-modern world; that is, to generate wealth through reduced shirking, pilfering, embezzlement, theft, dereliction of duty, cowardice, and the host of other bad behaviors that arise when people come together for one reason or another. The reason why the pre-modern world had institutions different from the modern world was simply because circumstances were different. The reason why the Western world went through an Institutional Revolution was because those circumstances changed. And the most important circumstance to change was the ability to measure basic fundamentals such as time or distance. This economic framework not only provides a unified theory for many pre-modern institutions and their transition to modern ones but explains the nitty-gritty institutional detail that separates the pre-modern world from our own.

A QUESTION OF RESPONSIBILITY

Measurement is necessary because we want to know things, and when interacting with other people what we often want to know is *whom to blame*. A fundamental problem in any life fraught with human interaction is this: Who is responsible for the bad outcomes and the good? Who is to be punished or rewarded? Choose any area of life and this problem is never far from the surface.

Part of the problem is that we lack the all-knowing powers of gods, but another part lies in the simple reality that nature plays an active role in life. A car breaks down. Did it break down because the manufacturer was negligent in its making, because the owner never maintained the car properly, because the owner's teenage son sneaked out of the house four nights a week for wild joyrides, because car parts eventually wear out when used, or because some cars are randomly less well assembled than others? A manuscript is not delivered on time to an editor. Did the failure arise from the author's laziness, or is there truth in the story that his computer crashed and files were lost forever? It took the U.S. military ten years to eliminate Osama Bin Laden. Was this because the military did not try very hard, or because the intelligence they received was unreliable? Whenever there is a problem, there are almost always two potential sources—man and nature—and we often cannot separate and measure their relative contributions.

The problem exists for good outcomes as well. A professor publishes two top articles in a single year and immediately runs to his dean and asks for a raise. Do these two publications reflect the academic's true lifetime productivity, or did he just get lucky or have some leverage with a journal editor? A football player rushes for 1,500 yards in an exceptional season and demands to renegotiate his contract. Is this a permanent change in the player's ability, or was the opposition especially unorganized this season? It is important to know the answers to such questions because a firm that pays out long-term high wages for outcomes that are caused by short-term random good luck will not be in business for long.

As much as this is a problem today, it was an enormous problem 300 years ago and reached into areas of life unimaginable now. Let us go back to Mr. Pepys and read about one of the mundane things that happened to him numerous times: the "loss of labour."

> . . . but missing him I lost my labour. So walked home . . .
> (*The Diary of Samuel Pepys*, 4:102 [April 13, 1663])

> . . . Back to White Hall . . . I by and by found that the Committee of Tangier met at the Duke of Albemarle's, and so I have lost my labour.
> (Ibid., 5:107 [April 1, 1664])

> . . . to the office, where a while, and then by agreement to the Excise Office, where I waited all the morning for the Cofferer and Sir St. Foxe's coming, but they did not, so I and the Commissioners lost their labour and expectation of doing the business we intended.
> (Ibid., 7:134 [May 28, 1666])

> Up, and with Sir W. Pen to White Hall . . . yet the Duke of York is gone-a-hunting. We therefore lost our labours, and so back again . . .
> (Ibid., 7:388 [November 28, 1666])

And on and on it went. Poor Pepys would show up for an appointment to do naval business and the other party would not be there. No doubt such a miss would mean an inconvenience for some other party that Pepys had to deal with. Perhaps one of the other parties might be Pepys's patron. "Why are these contracts not signed?" he might ask. "Well," Pepys may have replied, "the Duke was out 'a-hunting' when I dropped by." What could Sandwich say? The Duke, and others, might just go hunting at the spur of the moment if fowl or fancy suited them. And who would question York, the future king?

But there is more to these episodes than just a series of missed opportunities. Though it was a source of frustration, what the modern reader picks up in the diary reporting is how resigned Pepys was to the matter. Failure to appear was just part of daily life in the seventeenth century, and there was no point getting flustered over it. Weather, sickness, stubborn animals, poor roads, disease, or any number of matters could hinder anyone or anything in the long chain of events that came together in the meeting of two people. Today we get upset when a single meeting is missed, and if it happens a second time, then we find someone else to work with. We know whom to blame. But prior to our modern world of reliable machines and communication, it was difficult to know who was to be held responsible for tardiness: nature or the appointee.

Here is the important economic implication: the inability to identify who or what is to blame leads to an unfortunate type of behavior on the part of those involved. Because nature's role was so large, many meetings could be missed on purpose and blamed on nature. And here we come face to face with the problem for a patron such as Sandwich. He gave Pepys his position with the intention he would act in the earl's interests, but how could he know that the clerk would work toward such a goal when so many other factors out of either's control could get in the way? How many meetings did Pepys miss because *he* was off fishing? Confusion over responsibility for an outcome creates an incentive for what we'll call "bad behavior" on the part of a servant or agent.

The problem is demonstrated in Figure 1.1. Nature contributes to an outcome and so does the servant, and just looking at the outcome is insufficient to determine which contributed what. The dotted line around the two circles represents the idea that a third party looking at the outcome cannot separate the individual contributions. The names given to each source of the outcome are *variability* (for nature) and *alterability* (for the servant). This problem of identification was tremendous during the pre-modern era, especially in areas that now are taken for granted, but the general problem still exists today.

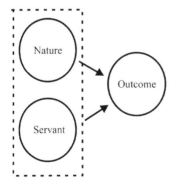

FIGURE 1.1 Variability and alterability

Just about everything we value in life is complex, and influenced by both nature and human intervention. To say that nature plays a role in life is to say that every outcome is *variable* to some extent, and to say that people can influence life is to say that every outcome is *alterable* as well. Consider an Olympic athlete. The Olympics celebrate the top end of the distribution in natural athletic talent. Nature plays an enormous role in who gets to be in the Olympics. People are highly variable and come in all different shapes and sizes, and some end up with bodies that can run, jump, or swim faster than others. For instance, Michael Phelps, the eight-time gold-medal swimmer at the 2008 Beijing Olympics, has a body designed for swimming fast. Compared to an average person of his height, his arms are "too long"; his feet are "too big"; his hands are like paddles. Nature has endowed him with attributes to move quickly in water. Other people swim more like rocks. But nature is not the whole story. Athletes vary in nature, but at the same time they can be altered. Some alterations come through hard work and training, and the Olympics celebrate these alterations. Others come through illegal drug use, and these efforts are considered cheating and are fought against.

It is because talent *both* varies in nature and is alterable by the athlete that a problem exists for the Olympic organization—athletes can cheat and get away with it. If the Olympic organizers knew everything, no athlete could cheat with steroids and walk away with gold medals and endorsements in hand without being discovered. Therefore, cheating would not be possible. But even when the organizers do not know everything, there would be no cheating if the individual contributions of athletic prowess could be easily identified. For example, if athletes varied in nature only, then cheating would be impossible, and of course, there would be no cheating. On the other hand, if every athlete were identical in nature and the effects of honest training were known, then any exceptional performances would be caused only by cheating. Again, detection would be certain, and there would still be no point in cheating.

It is the presence of both variable and alterable outcomes—and the difficulty in distinguishing between the two—that allows for cheating, fraud, embezzlement, theft, shirking, and all the other bad behaviors of life. These conditions create a situation where any outcome is a "noisy signal" of the various inputs, and the individual contributions of nature and people cannot be separated with certainty. With noise, measurement of individual contributions is never perfect, and the measurement itself might have little meaning even when done correctly. That it is so difficult to think of examples of outcomes that do not depend on both nature and human inputs suggests that possibilities for bad behavior are ubiquitous.

INSTITUTIONS AND BEHAVIOR

A basic role of institutions is to control bad behavior by influencing the incentives individuals have to behave in various ways. Writ large, rules of life are chosen so that societies create as much wealth as possible, mindful that every set of rules creates incentives that lead to a certain amount of bad behavior. So it behooves any society to choose its institutions wisely.

So far so good, but now we come to one of the big, mostly unnoticed, punch lines of history: the role of nature and variability was much different in the pre-modern world than it is today. Given that progress has been often little more than the removal of randomness in outcomes, over the past 200 years there has naturally been a reduction in the role of nature. Whenever a new technology or procedure was developed there was an increase in performance and a lowering of average costs, but there was often a shrinkage in the variance of outcomes as well. Life became more predictable, and nature played a smaller role. When nature's ability to generate variability was reduced, then the ability to act badly changed. This had important implications for the *types* of institutions that were created. Institutions that would have been disastrous and unthinkable with high variability became viable under the new state of things. Likewise, institutions designed to handle large roles of nature became too costly in a more predictable world. The end of the eighteenth century saw a radical change in the role nature played in life, and it was this radical change that led to the Institutional Revolution.

The process of institutions responding to changes in variability is ongoing, but as much as we speak of information technology, women's participation in the labor force, and the rise of the service sector, nothing today compares to the introduction of vast numbers of technological improvements that reached critical thresholds for the first time in history during the latter half of the eighteenth century. In the pre-modern era, prior to the Industrial Revolution, almost everything in life involved a large natural component—variance was everywhere, and this led to high variability in the quality of everything produced. It also meant that measurement of an individual's contribution to output was often almost impossible in some fields and nearly meaningless in others.[7]

When nature played a large role, and when one could not separate this role from other inputs, then measurement could not cost-effectively distinguish input contributions and therefore had little meaning. Essentially, the contribution of nature was confused with the contribution of workers in production. Given enough time, learning the particular roles of nature and workers could have taken place, but the huge role of nature meant that learning took too long, and in the meantime a fortune may have been lost. Many of our modern institutions are based on merit and rewarding those who do well. However, such institutions rest on a foundation of measurement, and as a result they were often too costly to implement in the pre-modern era. With the large role of nature, a different solution was required.

This book focuses on the provision of British civil service goods from the fifteenth to the nineteenth century. Today judicial courts, public finance, sheriffs, notaries public, and military services are provided by various levels of government through a professional bureaucracy. In the pre-modern period these were provided either through trusting or venal institutions. These institutions solved the Crown's problem of how to administer the country without having its servants abscond with the wealth of the nation through the bad behaviors that were possible when nature played a large role. Incredibly, merit, at least in the way we currently think of it, was not a primary consideration.

Patronage, in which individuals appoint, promote, and vouch for others they have a personal connection with, was common within the small, personal, and centralized governments of the pre-modern era. At the top of the civil service was the King's Household, which included all the Crown's ministers who served at the pleasure of the monarch. The King's Household was the center of political and social life throughout the pre-modern era, and all major patronage appointments, from a jailer to a bishopric, would be discussed at the king's court.[8] Ministers and members of Parliament would control different parts of the government, depending on their influence. Powerful ministers possessed massive amounts of control. Patronage was passed down level by level: minister to court official, to deputy lieutenant, to sheriff, and to justice of the peace. From these positions, other positions of local government were then handed out to those in favor.[9] The result was a very clannish form of administration, but one where "patrons were careful to select members whose views would not compromise their relations with the government."[10] Under patronage, reputation and social standing were central, and an appointment was made to an office based on the desires of the patron. The appointee was expected to act in the interests of the patron, and the entire system depended on the goodwill of its members and their ability to trust one another.

Although acts of patronage could be made to many members of society, the most important cases were reserved for the nobility. Noble officeholders were often restricted in the ability to sell, bequeath, or otherwise transfer their office. For example, the office might have only a tenure for life, and when the servant died the rights to the office reverted back to the Crown. Many offices (especially the great ones) held a tenure at the pleasure of the Crown—meaning the king had better be pleased with the service provided. Unlike an officeholder who had purchased a minor office, a patronage appointee could often be removed from office without being compensated. The most important state offices and the ones most easily manipulated against the Crown's interests were more likely to be given as patronage and less likely to be treated as pure private property.

The major alternative to patronage was to sell the office outright to a private individual. These were the venal offices, though at that time "venal" did not have the negative connotation it has today. When an office was sold it was generally treated as a form of property, no different from a landholding. The owner could manage the office as he saw fit, sell it, or leave it to an heir.[11] When such an office was held, the owner could be absent and hire deputies to do the work. Most important, an office was a source of wealth, and remuneration was by fees, shares in revenues, gratuities, and perquisites rather than by salaries. As Samuel Pepys noted in May 1665, "Every little fellow looks after his fees, and gets what he can for everything."[12] Other offices collected revenues for the Crown and shared the income. Some offices were simply sinecures, where payments were collected and no service was provided. In these cases, the sale of office effectively acted as a loan to the government, and the payments from the office paid back the loan. In addition to fees, the Crown might pay *gages* or other payments as interest on the capital paid for the office. In the military, commissioned officers were paid a small salary, but were also given shares in the spoils of war. However, often the most important aspect to an office was the set of privileges that came with it. These privileges could have included freedom from certain taxes, access to bribes (which were legal), the ability to enter nobility (ennobling offices), local prestige, and inclusion in the ruling social class. Many of these privileges eventually led to other positions and offices that could generate income. This explains why the financial returns of any given office might be "decidedly modest."[13] The result was that an office was a private interest, and no one prior to the Institutional Revolution would have considered it a public service.[14]

The Crown's choice of offering an office as a form of patronage or as a venal office came down to what made the most wealth for the kingdom. Maximizing the value of the kingdom required the provision of a judicial system, defense, and the revenues to finance both. Since the Crown did not possess any cost advantage in the provision of such goods, it had to exchange with its subjects to engage them in production. In this context, the Crown was analogous to an entrepreneur who enters exchanges with capitalists and workers for the production of goods.[15] The form this exchange took depended on the relative costs and benefits of each method in making the incentives of the servant *compatible* with those of the Crown, given the difficult circumstance of separating variability and alterability. It could hire workers at fixed salaries and monitor their performance (a professional bureaucracy). It could appoint individuals to certain positions in exchange for "loyal" service (patronage). Or, the Crown could sell the franchise rights to individuals for fixed or shared amounts (sale of office). Getting the rules right might have been the most important act of the Crown. Creating proper incentives generated wealth for both the Crown and the subjects. This increased wealth, though it attracted invaders, also allowed the country to outcompete competitors in wars.[16]

The outright sale of a civil office has very strong incentive effects. An individual who earns income from fees, prizes, or spoils of war has a strong incentive to collect and otherwise earn his fees, and to do so in a cost-minimizing fashion. Generally speaking, this is a benefit of sale. Income is higher when the clerk performs well or the army captain wins the battle. Higher incomes, in a competitive market for office sale, means the Crown receives a higher price for the office when it is initially sold. A second, but important, benefit of such a system is that it self-selects quality individuals for the position because those individuals who can extract the most income are those who are willing to pay the most for the office. Individuals who fail to perform lose money and are better off selling their office to the most productive occupier of the post. Hence, the sale of public office has the benefit of eliminating the measurement of qualified people and monitoring the output, since the profit—the difference between revenues and costs—polices behavior indirectly.

Not surprisingly, there were costs to the sale of public offices. Venality could create incentives that were incompatible with the Crown's goal, and could encourage officeholders to engage in activities that enhanced their own wealth at the expense of the Crown. Every office had different opportunities to generate income for the officeholder, and not all of these opportunities were legitimate from the Crown's point of view. However, given the opportunities before him, the officeholder devoted his energies to those activities that worked best for him. His actions produced an outcome, and this outcome may or may not have been compatible with the goals of the Crown. If fees were inflexible or if technology changed over time, then again, the actions of the officeholder could become incompatible with the interests of the Crown. Hence, soldiers might fight too much, bribes might lead to treason, too many guilty verdicts might be found, trials might take too long, and collusion between taxpayers and tax collectors might lead to low revenues. Likewise, the malincentives with purchase might arise with the Crown. When contracts were entered into with a sovereign, the sovereign could use his or her power to renege on deals after nonsalvageable investments were made. The sovereign could also engage in other behaviors (such as starting a war that interrupts shipping) that, after the fact, redistributed wealth to the Crown. Contracting with a sovereign was risky business, and this raised the cost of allocating offices through purchase.

Prior to the nineteenth century, the major alternative to sale was patronage—the selection of an individual who could be trusted to perform his duty. Patronage worked during this time because it required small centralized governments and small aristocratic leadership.[17] When the Crown granted a high office to a noble, it was a source of great wealth, privilege, rights, and other social benefits given in exchange for loyal service on behalf of the patron. What policed the behavior of the officeholder was the threat of expulsion from the aristocracy, loss of the benefits of office, and the loss of other investments if caught or suspected of acting outside the interest of the patron. Looking back from the twenty-first century, it is difficult to appreciate how much aristocratic life depended on this recognition and how serious this threat was. To be accused of malfeasance and cut off from society was a social death sentence. Offices assigned through patronage often did not contain the right of resale. An individual who was found untrustworthy could be punished through ostracism where all social standing was lost, and where the right to mitigate losses through resale did not exist. Hence a servant given a patronage office had a strong incentive to avoid bad behaviors.

Patronage, however, had three major costs to the Crown. First, patronage was not always made on grounds of merit; indeed, merit often played little role in the choice of a servant since loyalty was often more important. Thus an office granted by patronage was more likely to be held by an incompetent person than one granted by purchase or merit, where those who were best suited for the position would have been willing to pay the most for it or were able to prove their capabilities. Second, patronage based on a system of trust required additional institutions for monitoring the trustworthiness of officeholders. As such, individuals in trust positions were required to make special types of investments (explained in Chapter 3) that were used to police political exchanges. These ancillary institutions were sometimes general to society and other times specific to the class, but in all cases they were costly and not required when the office was sold or given on merit. Third, patronage tended to work only when the civil administration was relatively small. As the civil service grows, it becomes logistically impossible to use a system of patronage to any great extent, and just as impossible to police bad behavior through expulsion from the elite ruling group. How small is small is a moot question. Certainly, compared to today, the civil service during the pre-modern period was trivial. In 1727, the English judiciary consisted of only seventeen judges.[18] That seems small enough.

The third alternative for staffing the civil service, and the one that eventually won out, was to produce civil goods in-house through professional bureaucrats. The incentive to use professionals arose from the costs of sale and patronage. The cost, however, is that salaried workers require monitoring. As the ability of the Crown to monitor both the inputs used to provide public service and the output produced improved, and as the profits provided by purchase and patronage began to create wrong incentives, then the desire to move away from a decentralized administration to a professional bureaucracy increased.

The argument for the three different methods of public service provision is presented in Figure 1.2.[19] If there was an effective method to monitor the performance of workers, then the civil service would have been efficiently provided through professionals. Such is the case in our modern world. If such a method was not available, then the question was, did the incentives provided by sale match those of the Crown? If

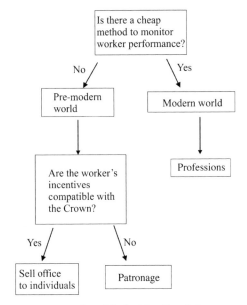

FIGURE I.2 A model of public office choice

they did, the office was offered for sale. If they did not, the office was provided through patronage.[20]

WHY INSTITUTIONS?

This specific argument for why pre-modern institutions took the forms they did is part of a wider body of theory known as new institutional economics. This wider theory began in a 1959 article on the U.S. Federal Communication Commission in which a shy Englishman named Ronald Coase pointed out the irrelevance of institutions within the mainstream economic model. Coase was trying to make a subtle point. He wanted to say that if there was a cave that could be used for a number of things, it would be used in its most valued occupation regardless of who owned the cave. What he actually said was this: "Whether the cave is used for storing bank records, as a natural gas reservoir, or for growing mushrooms depends, not on the law of property, but on whether the bank, the natural gas corporation, or the mushroom concern will pay the most in order to be able to use the cave."[21] It hardly looks like the founding sentence for a Nobel Prize or a subfield of economics, but there it is. The phrase "depends, not on the law of property" points to the core problem with traditional economics when it came to thinking about the law of property or any other type of law, rule, or social norm. In particular, it pointed out that mainstream economics had nothing to say about such things.

Coase would go on to famously elaborate on his cave conjecture, which centered around a concept he called "transaction costs."[22] Transaction costs are essentially the costs of all the bad behaviors mentioned previously. They are the costs involved in running a system of institutions designed to mitigate the bad behaviors. For example, the costs of the Crown's effort to police and monitor a servant, the costs of a servant's effort to cheat the Crown, and any lost wealth that results would be transaction costs. Coase's lasting contribution is the idea that when there are transaction costs—when people engage in bad behavior—then rules do matter and different institutions have different social outcomes. Who owns the cave often determines what it gets used for.

For anyone not trained in mainstream economic thinking, this conclusion is rather obvious. Of course rules matter. But Coase showed that they matter because of transaction costs and that the form of an institution only depends on this one type of cost. The crux of his watershed paper, therefore, was that laws (and other rules or property rights) were consciously designed by economic actors—here the Crown, aristocrats, and servants—to maximize wealth (the monetary value that implicitly or explicitly attaches to everything people value), minus the so-called transaction costs.[23] Understanding the transaction costs of a given situation is necessary and sufficient for understanding the institutional structure of that situation.

Transaction costs are defined as *those costs necessary to establish and maintain any system of rules and rights.*[24] If institutions are bundles of rules, then transaction costs are those costs of establishing and maintaining institutions. They are the costs of mitigating bad behaviors. When the Olympic committee introduces drug testing, all of the costs to administer the tests and the athletes' efforts to avoid getting caught cheating are transaction costs. If a firm hires workers for a given wage and then monitors the workers to make sure they do not shirk, all of the monitoring costs would be transaction costs because they are the costs incurred to maintain the rights laid out in the initial contract. Had the workers been hired on different terms, perhaps a piece-rate contract where they were paid for each unit produced, then a different type and amount of monitoring would have taken place and the transaction costs would have been different. When a lock is placed on a door, the cost of the lock is a transaction cost because it is a cost incurred to maintain the rights to whatever is on the other side of the door. Police expenses are transaction costs, but so are the lost gains from an exchange that never took place because of fear over being robbed. Transaction costs depend on the incentives any system of rules and rights create for both productive and cheating behavior. Thus the transaction costs that arose from providing postal services were different from those that arose from raising taxes.

Individuals come together to cooperatively exchange and produce. They do this because together they can generate much more wealth (broadly defined) than they can on their own. Unfortunately, when people come together they can also behave opportunistically: workers shirk their duties, people write bad checks, spouses commit adultery, agents betray the trust of their principals, neighbors trespass, thieves commit robbery, grocers sell bad produce, one country invades another, and on and on it goes. Many bad things happen in life, and to mitigate these bad behaviors successful societies create institutions that constrain bad private incentives.

And so it was in the pre-modern world, where institutions were complicated systems of rights designed to solve particular problems. Aristocratic rules were there to create trustworthy servants, factory colonies were built to stop large-scale embezzlement, and soldiers were paid by prizes to encourage fighting. In all the different cases the actual transaction costs varied, but their source was in the role of nature (variability), and the institution's purpose was to maximize wealth within the context of a given transaction-cost environment.[25]

Coase's major idea, that *institutions are designed to maximize wealth, net of the costs of establishing and maintaining them* (transaction costs), is the bedrock on which the argument in this book is based, and every specific institution is examined under this lens. The institutions are assumed to be wealth maximizing and chosen subject to the specific transaction costs that arose in their context. When analyzing a specific institution, I will be explicit about the specific transaction-cost problem that was being resolved, and so the term "transaction cost" will seldom be used. Hence the navy rules regulating officers were chosen with the problem of keeping an eye on captains and making sure they had an incentive to fight; factory discipline was imposed in remote factory colonies in an effort to stop the large black-market trade in stolen goods; and dueling was used to screen out ne'er-do-wells pretending to be gentlemen. Providing an incentive to fight, preventing embezzlement, and keeping the wolf out of the sheep pen are all transaction costs. This monolithic and strong theory is objectionable to many because it grinds against just about every social science theory of history.[26] However, the real test is whether or not this hypothesis is able to explain the many odd details of the pre-modern institutions, and here the theory shines.

CONCLUSION

The pre-modern world, in contrast to our own, was a strange place institutionally speaking. We are used to the idea of kings and nobles because they still exist. However, the role of the modern aristocrat is nothing like it was. During the pre-modern era, Britain was ruled by a small handful of people—not for a short time, but for several hundred years. How did they do it? Why did they do it? Why did they behave so differently and in ways that allowed writers like P. G. Wodehouse to exploit them with such comic effect? Likewise, the British navy emerged out of the sixteenth century with an aristocratic officer corps appointed through a complicated patronage, and over the next few hundred years it dominated the seas and was arguably the foundation of the British Empire. Yet things were run differently in the British army where anyone who wanted to be an officer simply could buy his way in. In the pre-modern world, many services now provided by the state were provided privately: the post office, lighthouses, roads, and court services. Among the elite class, dueling was a common occurrence. It was all very strange indeed.

Fortunately, there is a simple key to understanding it all. Following Coase, all institutions depend on transaction costs. Understand these costs, and an understanding of institutional detail practically follows automatically. These costs are the costs of establishing and maintaining rights. They are the costs of institutions, and they depend on the variability of nature. The institutional details observed in the pre-modern era resulted from attempts to mitigate the transaction costs of the time. The reason why the institutions were so different is because the poor people of this period experienced not only large transaction costs, but costs on dimensions that are irrelevant today. In a nutshell, the major problem of the pre-modern world was the enormous role nature played in the ordinary business of life. Keeping time, measuring distances, and relying on a power source were once problems of a first order. Once these problems were solved, new institutions were developed that characterize the modern world. Those who lived in the pre-modern era did what all people do: the best they could with what they had. I hope to convince the reader that there was, indeed, a quiet *other* revolution at the end of the eighteenth century . . . an institutional one.

CHAPTER TWO

Variance Everywhere

The race is not always to the swift, nor the battle to the strong, . . . nor yet favor to men of skill; but time and chance happens to them all.

Ecclesiastes 9:11

It is difficult to grasp how dissimilar the world was prior to the Institutional Revolution because most of the differences manifested in subtle ways. This dissimilarity was most true in the case of the pre-modern era's higher variability. Higher variability meant more randomness brought about by nature. Prior to the nineteenth century, nature played an enormous role in virtually every aspect of life, often at a fundamental level that today we take for granted—like knowing time and distance. Afterwards, nature's role in life was still present, but the ability to identify and mitigate randomness improved significantly. So great was the role of nature in the pre-modern era, and so hard to measure, that most people at the time simply never even tried. Nor did they have to because the ordinary business of life accepted the random changes that arrived daily. The rhythm of daily living followed the seasonal patterns of nature, and so people got up with the rising sun and went to bed with its setting. They made hay when the sun shone and were often idle otherwise. There had long been candles for those who could afford them, but for most people nightfall meant an end to daily activity. Then, slowly and surely, over the course of the Industrial Revolution things began to change. The pace was probably so slow that only the most dramatic changes were noticeable, but eventually the world became more predictable on many dimensions.

Wide variability and inaccurate measurement were everywhere in the pre-modern era. In seafaring, it was difficult to distinguish whether a ship was late because of poor winds or because the captain and crew spent too much time carousing in a foreign port. In manufacture, it was difficult to distinguish the effects of natural power sources from the talents of the workers, resulting in a wide range of output quality.[1] Until the late eighteenth and early nineteenth centuries, the role of nature had been so large in many productive processes that it had been virtually impossible for different workers to produce identical goods in most industries. Variability was the order of the day. This variability had important implications for any master—whether a yarn seller or the monarch—because the inability to distinguish between shirking and sloth, on the one hand, and chance, on the other, meant that transaction costs in the form of measurement costs were pervasive.

It would be convenient for those seeking to understand the past if there was some type of metric called "measurement" or "accuracy" that existed on a government-kept record book. But, of course, such a metric does not exist. Even when records were kept on individual things, certainly no systematic records were kept about variance, except for the odd example (such as time). And if such a thing as the role of nature could be measured by some third party, like a government official or a twenty-first-century academic, then the pre-modern players probably would have easily done the same, and the problem of disentangling nature from human contributions would have disappeared.[2] Having disappeared, the pre-modern institutions would simply have been the ones we have now. Ironically, the inability to measure nature, variance, accuracy, or whatever we wish to call it is *the* fact of life that creates interesting institutional innovations.

All is not lost, however. There are cases where we do know something about variance. In the keeping of time, for example, clock accuracy could be measured, and we know a considerable amount about this. Even more important, we have historical evidence for cases where there was either more or less noise in the environment. In this chapter, I examine four basic examples of how thresholds, or critical moments, in measurement were reached during the years between 1750 and 1850. Technical change had been continuous over time, and methods at improving measurement were no exception. However, during this period one measurement threshold after another was reached, and the culminating result was an ability to sufficiently measure and identify human contributions to output in wide areas of service that had not been previously possible. The chapter starts with the obvious—namely, the changes to the sources of power, which almost define the Industrial Revolution. Next what are perhaps the two most significant innovations are discussed:

solutions for the problem of telling time and for the problem of knowing something as simple as a yard or a bushel. The chapter concludes with the problem of never knowing when a disease will strike. These are just examples to make the point that there were issues of randomness in the pre-modern world that no longer exist. Indeed, all problems dealt with here are seldom considered in our current world, and why should they be? They were solved over 200 years ago.

SOURCES OF POWER

In August 1776, the British army, under the command of William Howe, launched a massive attack against the Continental Army led by George Washington, then holed up in New York. Washington had moved his troops to New York after a series of battles in and around Boston the previous year. He was outnumbered in New York, and would continue his losing streak one battle after another. Cornered by over 30,000 British troops and thirty war ships, defeat looked certain, and the rebellion of the thirteen states looked like it was over. In a last-ditch effort to retreat, Washington crossed the river to New Jersey. Although the British had enormous naval power under the command of Admiral Richard Howe (William's brother) in the area, and although they were aware of Washington's troop movements, there was nothing they could do. The wind was not in their favor, and their ships could not enter the East River and approach the fleeing rebels. Such was the fate of nations in the hands of nature during the pre-modern era.

Admiral Howe's problem was that he did not have a reliable source of power for his ships. Power, prior to the Industrial Revolution, universally came from nature directly. Water turned the wheels of the water mill. Wind drove the sails of ships and windmills. Animals and humans pulled the plow and did the heavy lifting. From a technical point of view, none of these was particularly effective, and when they were replaced with the various machines of the eighteenth and nineteenth centuries, output increased enormously. Of this increase in average productivity, much is known, and rightly so, because this remarkable achievement allowed humanity to escape the Malthusian trap of almost constant per capita income that had lasted for the past 5,000 years. However, by their very design, these early natural sources of power were highly variable. Virtually by definition, natural sources of power contain a significant unpredictable component. The wind does not always blow, nor does the water always flow. Thus, along with the increased output of the industrial power sources came an enormous increase in reliability, replication, and standardization in sources of power. This reduced variance in power had implications for measurement all across the economy.

The waterwheel, which powers a water mill, was known to the Romans. By 1086, William the Conqueror's great survey of wealth in England, the Domesday Book, records that there were just over 5,600 of them in Britain. Water turned the wheel and created energy that could turn a millstone for grinding grain or turn any number of devices for driving other machines. From the Norman conquest forward, a number of improvements were made. Mill owners created dams in order to increase the power of the drive. Waterwheels were lined up, one after another, so that different uses could be made of the diminishing power. Cranks and gears were introduced, which allowed the power to be transferred to a farther distance and different direction. The brest wheel, where the water passes over the top of the wheel, and the turbine were introduced later to increase power. Despite all of the advances, there was no escaping the natural source of power. A water mill's power stems from the volume and speed of the water. Both factors vary by the season and from year to year. Frost, floods, silt, and dry summers change the amount of water and, therefore, the amount of power. Much of the variation is seasonal, but much is random as well. As a result, many mills were not fully employed for the full year, and the power available on a given day in the near future could only be guessed at with error.

In those regions where water power was in short supply, the windmill was a close substitute and operated on the same mechanical principles. The windmill was also used to supplement the water mill in times when water was scarce. More important, wind was used to propel ships, both naval and merchant. By the eighteenth century, a first-rate battleship was a spectacle to behold and a small world unto itself. The British navy, by this time, was perhaps the largest firm in the world, and yet, all of its capabilities were at the mercy of wind and sea. If the wind did not blow in the right direction, an entire fleet could, and did, sit in one spot for weeks at a time. For want of wind, battles might not be fought or escapes not possible. Irregular wind and water conditions made convoys difficult to maintain and piracy more likely. Travel by wind meant that the duration of the trip was unknown. Storm surges and dead seas could tax a ship and its crew beyond the limit, and many ships were lost. Being caught on a lee shore, with the wind driving the ship toward land, could mean disaster for ship and crew.

Animals provided the other major source of power prior to the Industrial Revolution. Horses and mules were mainstays in agriculture until the early twentieth century and were commonly used in industry and for transport, such as hauling carriages across long distances. Other animals were used, and of course human backs were often a major source of power. All of these sources were extremely variable because men and animals vary in size and strength; furthermore, they were complicated by their inherent unwillingness to work.

And so, on the eve of the Industrial Revolution, power was not only limited and low, but intermittent and unreliable. Over the course of the eighteenth and nineteenth centuries, power sources would change dramatically. Starting with Thomas Newcomen's engine in 1712 for pumping water, the steam engine went through a series of innovations that created a powerful, consistent form of energy. The steam engine powered machines for producing fabric, metals, and pottery. It drove ships, locomotives, tractors, rollers, shovels, and pile drivers; it was used in mills, factories, and later, electrical plants; and it allowed production to move away from natural power sources. Steam was the backbone of the Industrial Revolution and led to dozens of other inventions, such as the screw propeller, which allowed for new applications of consistent power. Although it took many years to infiltrate the economy, by the mid-nineteenth century the steam engine was common in many industries.

Steam power introduced an era of *reliable* power. A factory running on steam no longer had to worry about the ebb and flow of a stream; it could produce at the same rate all year long. This meant it could credibly promise a steadier delivery of product to firms down the processing chain, which could then deliver more consistent product and service to customers. Transport by train from Liverpool to Manchester could consistently arrive on time and keep to a schedule, since it no longer relied on horses for the trip. Thus men like Pepys were less likely to "lose their labour." And ships no longer were at the mercy of the wind. Had the War of Independence been eighty years later or had the steam engine been available sooner, George Washington may not have escaped the British in 1776.[3]

The institutional implications of reliable power were far-reaching and went beyond reducing the randomness of life. In addition, reliable power reduced the *seasonal* role that nature played in daily living. Nature is entirely predictable when it comes to summer following spring or the harvest following the sowing. Seasonality restricted the ability to specialize because it was impossible to make a living on a task that only lasted part of the year. When power sources were seasonally idle, most workers went back to their small landholding to scratch out an existence. The concept of 100 percent full employment in a single activity was not a reality for many in the pre-modern era. Seasonality reduced gains from the division of labor and this encouraged small family-operated firms.[4] As a result, seasonality reduced the incentive to improve the standardization of inputs and outputs, and with many uncoordinated family-operated enterprises, the variance in output quality was higher.

Reliable power meant that the effects of seasons changed in a fundamental way. Today, seasonality really only matters for farmers, and most of them have managed to control seasonality by bringing production indoors. The introduction of reliable power started this transition. Reliable power encouraged larger enterprises by allowing for more specialized labor over longer periods of the year; it reduced a major source of variation in inputs and allowed for the standardization of outputs. Many of these outputs, such as tools, instruments, or deliveries, were inputs into other sectors that may not have been directly affected by the reliable power source. And so the influence of consistent power had wide-reaching implications for the level of variance in life.

A BRIEF HISTORY OF TIME[5]

Not knowing the time is a minor inconvenience today. If no one knew the time, however, the effects would be widespread, great, and often subtle. Recall the "lost labour" problem of poor Mr. Pepys as he tried to connect with various interests related to naval affairs. Part of his problem was a lack of access to immediate communication through a telephone, but a more basic problem was coordinating on a specific time. Dates were easy to pick, but how was one to know if they were on time or not? How was one to know if they had missed their appointment and the other party had left? The pre-moderns dealt with the matter as well as they could, but the reality was that not knowing the exact time meant that life had to be arranged differently and inconveniences were inevitable. Central bells were often used, which meant that schedules were necessarily tied to others in the community. Sunrise, sunset, and the crow of the rooster were used, which have obvious drawbacks. But the problem of not knowing the time was not just a matter of inconvenience. Indeed, it was often a matter of life and death.

Such was the case of Clodisley Shovell. While Admiral Sir Clodisley Shovell was leading five ships home from victory over the French near Gibraltar in 1707, he encountered severe fog. Consulting his officers, he determined they were safely in open sea. Several hours later, four of the five ships ran into the Scilly Isles off the tip of England, and 2,000 troops (including the Admiral) were lost. Such a tragic event is almost unheard of today, but in Admiral Shovell's time, it was a plain fact of life at sea. The problem for Admiral Shovell and for any other sailor prior to the nineteenth century was that he could not tell where he was. Since the fifteenth century, men at sea were able to tell, if somewhat crudely, what their latitude was. In the Northern Hemisphere, they could measure the altitude of the North Star. The higher the star was in the sky, the further north the sailor was. In the Southern Hemisphere, latitude could be crudely determined by the position of the sun above the horizon at high noon. Depending on the time of year, the sun moves higher or lower in the sky; so adjustments were required, but a good pilot could be reasonably accurate.

Nothing similar existed for the other important coordinate. Even by the time of Admiral Shovell, there was no accurate method of knowing longitude. The problem of longitude was perhaps the greatest scientific puzzle of the eighteenth century, and a list of great minds including the likes of Sir Isaac Newton, Blaise Pascal, Gottfried Wilhelm Leibniz, and Galileo Galilei worked at solving it. Several countries offered prizes and fame for the solution, and in 1714 the British Parliament offered a king's ransom of £20,000 to anyone who could find a reliable method to determine the position of a ship at sea. As it turned out, the answer to the problem of knowing one's location in the middle of the ocean was simply a matter of knowing what time it was.

The problem of not knowing time provides an excellent example of the problem of variability in the world before the Industrial Revolution—if only because today we measure time so accurately that we have completely abandoned any relationship between nature and time. Prior to clocks, and for most of the world's rural population throughout history, time was defined by nature: the world was the clock and it varied considerably. Life was regulated by daybreak, noon, dusk, and nightfall, and these changed over the course of the year and from location to location. Seasons fell one after another with a regular pattern; even though the formal start date of any season was known, the exact arrival in terms of seasonal weather was never known with certainty. The rooster might crow in the morning, but as every farmer knows, he can be off a great deal. For those more interested in specific times, or at least periods of time, there were sundials, water clocks, fire clocks, and sand clocks. No clock was particularly reliable, and all of them suffered from natural variations in temperature, angles of re-fraction, altitude, sedimentation, clogging, rust, wear, cloud cover, and night. In addition, none of them was portable. The result was that for most of history the concepts of being on time, being paid according to time, and measuring time were of little meaning to most people. There was simply too much variance in the measurement of time for the con-cepts to have a useful meaning in many daily activities.

The earliest clocks were, quite intuitively, based on continuous flows or movements. For example, a sundial tracks the movement of the sun across the sky. Until the fourteenth century, every clock worked on this premise. Then some unknown genius developed a stop-and-go mecha-nism that created the first mechanical clock, and the world of accurate time measurement was born. Although the mechanical clock first ap-peared around 1300, it would take another 500 years before clocks were accurate enough to help the likes of Admiral Shovell, and just as long for timepieces to fall enough in price for average individuals to own one. The mechanical clock would eventually make time measurement independent of nature. That is, all the noise around measuring time would be elimi-nated. By being miniaturized, the clock became the watch and the domain of private keeping; however, that transformation would take—pardon the pun—a long time.

Most of the first clocks were enormous public affairs. Often located in towers of monasteries, town squares, or churches, they could take up to thirty years to complete. They were weight-driven and large; be-cause the components were cut so poorly, they often required weights of a thousand pounds to drive them. These clocks required dozens of skilled workers to complete and continual servicing to keep running; they often needed to be replaced within twenty years and were com-pletely inaccurate by today's standards. Furthermore, most moderns would not recognize them. They usually did not have a dial face with hands; if they did, the markings were more likely to be celestial. The first clocks were little more than automated bells. Still, they had an immediate impact. For example, religious orders could pray at specific intervals and not just at dawn, noon, or dusk. Soon their community would be organized around the bells of time intervals. Bells were used to start work and markets, to summon town members, to indicate curfews, and to announce meetings. Most important, the work day began to be measured in time rather than in natural terms.

From the first mechanical clocks, there was a steady progression to make timepieces smaller and more accurate. One invention after another continued this process, and by the beginning of the pre-modern era, the first watches started to appear. As with most timepieces of the period, they were inaccurate and mostly decorative, but they allowed for the privatization of time and the adaptation of time measurement to individual needs. Throughout the eighteenth century, methods improved with the invention of the pendulum for standing clocks and the balanced spring for portable watches being critical watersheds. For the first time, an accurate time reading could be had if a clock remained perfectly fixed and vertical. Now clocks might lose only five minutes per day rather than thirty or more. Minutes started to have meaning, and minute hands became common. Some timepieces showed second hands, and toward the end of the eighteenth century, the stopwatch appeared.

As is apparent from the case of Admiral Shovell, the great demand for an accurate timepiece came from naval and merchant shipping. Oceanic trade was profitable, but the greatest threat was the problems that arose from not knowing a position in open water. A major hazard was running into solid ground. Because of night, fog, and simple miscalculation, a ship could easily run aground. Given the square rigging of ships, there often was not enough time to correct a course once a ship's watch (again, no pun intended) had discovered an approaching danger. Aside from the tragic crash, ships could often spend extra weeks at sea looking for a destination they had missed. During this time, if a ship had been at sea for several months, scurvy might start to take its toll. If too many men died, there might not be enough left to run the ship and all might perish. Not knowing a location meant it was very difficult to know a ship's speed; although crude methods of dead reckoning were used, miscalculations were inevitable. And so given the high costs and great uncertainty, there was a tremendous demand for solving the problem of longitude.

Many methods were attempted—one of the most serious through lunar observations. Because the moon moves faster through the sky than other celestial bodies, it can be used as the hand of a sky clock. Using the distance of the moon from a given star compared with the same observation from a place with known longitude, one could calculate the longitudinal difference. The problem was that the tables to calculate the sky clock were difficult to make and indeed took decades to complete. More problematic was the difficulty in getting accurate lunar readings on the deck of a moving ship.

The ultimate solution to longitude was found by an unlikely clock maker named John Harrison. Harrison was a self-taught craftsman who was attracted to the problem of longitude by the grand prize offered by Parliament. His genius was in recognizing that the key to longitude was knowing exactly what time it was, and the key to accurate time was solving the problem of friction within the works. Harrison made four frictionless clocks, each with a completely different design from the others. His final effort, H4, was what we now call the marine chronometer. Although the actual design was never used in commercial chronometers, Harrison showed that the solution to the problem was found in a clock.

The point of this story is that until the eighteenth century, even in the greatest laboratories, time could not be measured with much accuracy. At a day-to-day level, most people still relied on nature to give them crude measures of time. By the end of that century and certainly by the middle of the nineteenth century, pocket watches were not only accurate to within minutes each day, but were priced so that an ordinary individual could own one. There was, for all practicality, a collapse to zero in the variance of time measurement between 1750 and 1850. For the first time in history, it actually meant something to tell someone to be at a specific place at a specific time.

The effect of the reduction in the variance of time measurement was felt everywhere. Passenger service on carriages started to put out schedules that linked with other feeder services, resulting in increased trade and integration between towns. Troop movements started to be synchronized by means of plans based on time without the aid of direct sight and flag signals. By the end of the eighteenth century, every officer in the British army would consider a good watch part of his basic equipment. Transport at sea no longer hugged a coast until a given latitude was reached but rather employed the shorter open sea. Naval ships could separate and later rendezvous at a prespecified time and location, even on the other side of the world. Distribution and collection within manufacturing and retail establishments became integrated through large markets based on measured time units. Production could be coordinated in a finely tuned manner. Passengers on coaches worried about being late. And with the introduction of rail travel, this worry accelerated. The ability to be at a specific time and place worked its way down to the common man, who for the first time in history was employed at a job with a specific starting time, worked for a specific length of time, and was paid by the hour. Workers could trust that the unit of time being paid for was true because time could be measured accurately and independently. Ultimately, as train travel drastically reduced the time taken to travel great distances, countries began to impose uniform time across their jurisdictions. In Britain, Greenwich time was adopted across the nation.[6]

WEIGHTS AND MEASURES

In 1792, two French astronomers, Pierre Méchain and Jean Baptiste Delambre, set out from Paris. One went north to Dunkerque and the other went south to Barcelona. What was their task? To precisely measure the arc of the meridian that passed through Paris and thereby, in part, to measure the shape and size of the world. However, the most important part of the mission was determining a new standard of measure by which accurate readings could be taken. Thus the "meter" was defined as one ten-millionth of the distance of the arc from the North Pole to the equator. It was a measure independent of nation, locality, culture, and the human body. It was a truly fixed and definitive standard—a zero-variance measure.

In 1799, the two astronomers finally completed their complicated series of triangulations, and presented the results to the Academy of Sciences in Paris. Their work was hailed as an achievement of the ages. Ironically, a calculating error meant that the meter they established was actually not the fraction they had intended.[7] Although the error remains today, it is irrelevant. A measure is ultimately an arbitrary standard. What matters is the reliability of the standard or its variability. Today, all but three nations use the metric system as the base unit of measure.

England, at the 1066 conquest, had a developed system of weights and measures based on various Roman, Germanic, and Celtic standards. Virtually all units were related in some way to the human body: a stride, the length of a forearm, the amount of grain a slave would consume in a month, and so on. Measurement of everything—distance, speed, and volume—is an everyday part of life, especially in commercial activity. In order to know if an exchange is worth entering into, it is necessary to know what quantity is being exchanged. In order to know if work was completed, the work must be measured. These minimum requirements were hindered by poor standards of measurement. As a result, most monarchs of England spent some time attempting to establish standard weights and measures.

The fundamental problem, of course, is determining on what to base a unit of measure. A stride may be a useful measure of distance for an extremely simple community, but as distance becomes valuable—whose stride is used? In the reign of Edward II (1307–1327), an inch was established as "three barley corns, dry and round, laid end to end." It was hardly a well-defined distance, but as the basis for the foot, yard, rod, and acre, it was an attempt to move away from human-based standards. Like the clock from the thirteenth century on, weights and measures in England were subject to continuous attempts to achieve reliability. And by the standards of other countries, there was considerable success. However, variance in measures was ubiquitous and would take until the early nineteenth century to resolve.

By the time of the Tudors, dozens of royal standards had been established. For example, the king's standard pound was based on 7,680 wheat grains.[8] Despite this, many problems existed. There were ambiguities in definitions, problems with variability in the base measure, and simple issues with copying and maintaining the standards. Essentially the system worked this way: the Crown would produce a standard measure, for example, a bronze bowl to measure bushels or a brass yardstick. Copies of these "standards" would be made and sent to various towns, urban centers, and shires around the kingdom. The standards would be attached to guildhalls or other public buildings for individuals to consult. Copies would be made and these copies "more often than not varied appreciably from their originals."[9] In addition, copies would be made of copies, with further reduced accuracy. Worse, copies were made of wood or metal and would rot, corrode, and simply wear out over time with use. Since they were exposed to the elements, the measures would also change with the climatic conditions of the day. A yard in winter was shorter than a yard in summer.

Despite efforts throughout the pre-modern era, standardization of measures was never accomplished. Improvements continued, but often they introduced more noise as old standards continued in use with the new ones. In remote parts of the kingdom, even older Celtic systems continued, often with the same name. Thus a Scottish mile was different from an Irish mile, which was different from a Welsh mile. By the eighteenth century, there were still ten different systems of weights and measures in use in Britain.[10]

Having consistent weights and measures, like knowing the precise time, allowed for—almost by definition—more accurate and less costly monitoring. The lowered transaction costs of measurement meant that institutions which relied on measurement could be used more effectively. Productivity could be measured in terms of output per unit of time, speeds could be accurately recorded and tracked, commerce could flourish without confusion and error, land and buildings could be surveyed accurately, and fraud could be mitigated.[11] Today, these matters are dealt with easily and to a much tighter standard. Without the ease of measurement, the variability of life would be drastically higher; we would be uncertain about what we were getting and giving in most exchanges.

THE GREATEST KILLER

Queen Elizabeth I was only on the throne for four years when she became ill with smallpox and caused a constitutional crisis. The Protestant queen had no designated heir and the country was in the midst of a religious reformation. Of course, she recovered and went on to rule for many years. When she eventually died the Stuart royal line was established because James VI of Scotland was her closest relative through her grandfather Henry VII. Smallpox would frequently visit the Stuart house and would ultimately put an end to the line. Charles II had smallpox before the Restoration, but survived. In 1660, his Protestant brother, the Duke of Gloucester, died of smallpox. In the same year, his sister Mary died of smallpox, while a second sister survived the infection. After James II abdicated the throne in 1688, his daughter Mary became co-regent with William III of Orange. Mary would die of smallpox in 1694. Her husband, who had lost both parents to smallpox, had survived it as a child. When William died, the crown passed to Anne. Although Queen Anne would have seventeen pregnancies, the one child who survived infancy would die of smallpox at the age of 11, leaving no Stuart to carry on. The two revolutions faced by the Stuarts were nothing compared to the ravages of the smallpox virus.

The impossibility of reliable power, the inability to tell time accurately, and the problem of multiple and varying weights and measures were matters of the physical world, but high variability worked its way even more deeply into the human condition. As the sad Stuart story shows, disease is more than just troublesome for a system of government focused on a monarch and his or her aristocratic servants. Whenever a monarch or other elite was removed from power, the effect rippled down the chain of command. Sometimes the ripple could become a revolution. Disease, of course, struck more than the elite. An Englishman after 1500 was more likely to die in bed than by the sword, and the omnipresent threat of disease meant the variance in age at death was large. Many diseases afflicted the pre-modern world: the plague, the sweating sickness, fevers, leprosy, syphilis, and of course, smallpox. These diseases were always present but would break out in epidemics from time to time to be very disruptive.[12] Towns were closed down, people would leave centers of disease, travel bans would be put in place, quarantines imposed, and daily life within the zone would grind to a trickle. At times even Parliament would be obstructed by poor attendance caused by fear of infection. A simple symbol like a piece of cloth on a door or hung from the mast of a ship would signal others to stay away. Samuel Pepys mentions several times the effects of the Great Plague of London in 1665 and how "sad sight it is to see the streets empty of people, and very few upon the 'Change. Jealous of every door that one sees shut up, lest it should be the plague; and about us two shops in three, if not more, generally shut up."[13]

. By the beginning of the pre-modern era, smallpox had become the number one killer in England, with total deaths surpassing all other forms of pestilence. In London, in 1634 and 1649, more than 1,000 deaths from smallpox were recorded.[14] But the eighteenth century would be even worse. Whereas the London annual death rate from smallpox was estimated at 210 deaths per 100,000 population in the latter half of the seventeenth century, this figure would rise to 300 for the eighteenth century. Over the second half of the eighteenth century, more than 57,000 deaths would be recorded in London alone, just over 11 percent of the population.[15] At its peak, smallpox was killing about 400,000 Europeans every year.[16]

Smallpox was known as the "most terrible of ministers of death" because of the pain, suffering, and disfigurement it caused. Those who survived were often pockmarked for life but could be crippled or blinded as well. Smallpox came in different strains; some, like Elizabeth I's, would cause relatively minor episodes with no long-term effects. Those infected with "black" smallpox, however, would almost always die. Even within the same village or family, the effects could vary widely.[17] The typical mortality rate was usually between 15 and 25 percent, but in some epidemics it could reach as high as 40 percent. In England, about 30 percent of children in the pre-modern era died from smallpox before the age of three.[18]

In the eighteenth century, medical science in England started to advance on smallpox. For centuries, Eastern cultures had practiced inoculation to reduce the effects of the disease. This procedure involved taking samples of the disease—usually ground scabs or pus—from infected blisters on individuals with minor strains of the virus, and then scratching and infecting someone uninfected. The mortality rate from inoculation was between 1 and 3 percent but was considerably lower than a natural infection. Inoculation was introduced in England in the 1720s, much to the chagrin of scientists and preachers alike. The real breakthrough, however, came with Edward Jenner's invention of the cowpox vaccination.

Smallpox is related to a number of similar viruses that affect animals. Cowpox is a minor variant among bovines, and the virus can infect humans. Cowpox has a minor effect on people and often is not even noticed. However, once exposed to cowpox, humans develop an immunity to the smallpox virus as well. Many, including Jenner, had noticed that milkmaids were more resilient to smallpox than others. It was a simple step to begin infecting individuals with the cowpox virus and then to expose them to smallpox itself. Jenner coined the phrase "vaccination" to distinguish the procedure from the earlier inoculation. Although the practice of transmitting animal diseases to humans was also met with great opposition, the proof was in the pudding; the reign of smallpox was over by the end of the eighteenth century. Smallpox would continue to exist well into the twentieth century, but it no longer ruled the roost of infectious diseases in Britain.

Smallpox is just one dramatic example of diseases that played an enormous role in the pre-modern world. Along with smallpox, the plague vanished from Britain by the end of the eighteenth century, although the reason for this is still unclear. During the Napoleonic Wars, lemon juice began to be used as part of the regular diet of sailors, and scurvy, though never as serious as other diseases at sea, was greatly reduced.[19] The virtual elimination of smallpox and the plague did not, of course, eliminate all infectious diseases. Cholera, typhoid, and tuberculosis would strike Britain hard until the end of the nineteenth century. In terms of fatality rates, these other diseases were less deadly, but that is of no matter: reducing the effects of two major diseases reduced the total variance of infectious diseases. Disease created randomness in life. One never knew if travels would bring an interaction with the dreaded virus, nor would the symptoms of an infection be known for weeks. Because the virus took on many forms and because the early symptoms were so similar to other infections, the final outcome from an illness was unknown and varied widely. In short, the random nature of disease in the pre-modern world created variability in life, which could factor itself into just about every area of life, especially in times of outbreak. Ubiquitous disease meant that illness, whether faked or real, could always happen without warning. With vaccinations for smallpox, at least for those who could afford them, this variance in life would be reduced in the nineteenth century.

OTHER INNOVATIONS

Over the broad expanse of time, the eighteenth century was a watershed in terms of innovations that drastically reduced the role of nature in everyday life. Numerous thresholds were met with respect to basic elements of life, thereby making the world consistent enough for meaningful measurement. Progress in technical achievements had always been ongoing, and although every innovator "stood on the shoulders of giants," at some point the innovator on top was able to see over the mountains. That moment, in terms of variability, came between 1750 and 1850. Looking back today, a steam engine is nothing compared to a nuclear power plant, and an atomic clock is an order of magnitude more accurate than a standing pendulum clock. Yet, in terms of breaking with the variability of the past—in terms of making a significant discrete leap—the shift happened with the eighteenth-century innovations.

Four fundamental innovations that radically changed the ability to monitor have been discussed in this chapter, but of course there were many more. Consider, for example, an indirect effect of smallpox epidemics on the variability of life. Since epidemics were so dramatic and so all-consuming, data were kept on mortality rates as early as the mid-seventeenth century. The data were compiled in "bills of mortality" and vital statistics, supposedly for the purpose of warning aristocrats when to leave town. This compilation of mortality data had never existed before, and it allowed early medical scientists to examine it. Thus began the early work on statistics. Statistical methods were developed for measuring mortality rates and for determining whether inoculations were safer than natural infection, and this work was quickly used for estimates of life expectancy and the development of life and health insurance markets. It also spread to other areas of science and commerce, as statistical analysis allowed for the measurement and analysis of distributions of outcomes.

Although eyeglasses had been around since the Middle Ages, supplementary innovations, such as the bifocal lens and the standard frame around the ears, allowed for more robust uses. Glasses also fell in price and became more widely available. Eyeglasses further extended a craftman's working life and created a demand for finer instruments. The wider use of steel and the presses driven by steam allowed for better tools and dies, even for work that was artisan in nature. Thus, even handcrafted items were able to be produced in more standardized bundles. This happened throughout the eighteenth century and early part of the Industrial Revolution, as a steady stream of new tools were developed that allowed standardization where artisan workmanship prevailed. The development of better stamping technology, though not designed for mass production, improved the ability to manufacture uniform goods in engineering, cutlery, and hardware.[20] The invention of special milling machines, turret lathes, and other instruments led to precision in manufacture.[21] As the Industrial Revolution progressed, the creation of steam power, continuous supplies of coal, and new methods of production meant that some industries could free themselves from the rhythm of natural power sources. Increased travel and road safety meant markets became bigger, supplies more regular, and inputs more consistent across long distances. Thus the increased division of labor, the increased use of machines, the use of nonseasonal sources of power, the better roads, and the use of standard inputs all led to a reduction in the role of nature throughout the Industrial Revolution.

At the beginning of the pre-modern era, the introduction of crude smooth bore cannons and muskets revolutionized military tactics and fortifications. With these inventions the inaccuracy of the weapons and the distance they were fired from the enemy made it difficult to tell if the enemy had actually been engaged or not. Rifled barrels on guns arrived in the early part of the nineteenth century and made aiming more than a matter of just pointing a musket in the general direction of the enemy. The improved aiming reduced the role of nature and allowed officers to monitor their infantry more closely.

Lighting to see at night was smoky, expensive, and unreliable before it was discovered in the first half of the eighteenth century that gas derived from coal could be used for lamps. By the end of that century, gas lamps were providing cheap and steady lights for roads, houses, and places of work.[22] Not only were working hours extended, but the variance in lighted hours throughout the year was reduced.

Or consider salt, which had been used for millenia to preserve food. Since salt came from a variety of sources and places, its quality varied considerably, and therefore the quality of food preservation varied a great deal.[23] At the end of the eighteenth century, food canning was developed, and by the 1820s, canned goods were everywhere. Aside from the vast improvement in quality, canning produced preserved foods with much more consistency, again allowing for better monitoring. The improved homogeneity from canning meant that less measurement was necessary to provide quality assurance.

The great and famous innovations of the Industrial Revolution might have been concentrated in a few textile industries, but the effects they had on the role of nature in life were everywhere. Changes in technology were not the only contributors to nature's reduced role in life. Part of the reduction in the role of nature during the period from 1750 to 1850 was the result of improvements in road and water transportation that increased market size and the method of distribution. Better transportation led to more standardized goods, allowing them to be marketed and sold anonymously or by third parties. Early in the eighteenth century, sales by contract were uncommon for many goods, and manufacturers traveled with their artisan wares to sell directly to buyers. By the end of the eighteenth century, a national network of common carriers had developed that allowed producers to sell at a distance by sample and by taking orders.[24]

This increased sale of goods at farther distances required standardization. When goods were sold between a local buyer and seller and when the transaction was made on the spot, variability was less of an issue. However, when hired salesmen use samples to show their customers, a standard product is important since there is no purpose to a sample unless it closely resembles the product being ordered. Thus, the initial and subsequent forces of reduced variability reinforced each other and accelerated the trend.

EXCUSES, EXCUSES

And so we come back to the point of it all: how does this reduction in variability matter for institutions? Recall that high variability has important implications for institutions, those systems of property rights (rules, expectations, and norms) designed to mitigate problems of shirking, embezzlement, and generally acting in one's private interests over social goals. When the world is extremely variable, bad behaviors abound because failure to perform or deliver can always be blamed on nature. Being late has little meaning when there is no reliable clock and you are at the mercy of nature to get you to your destination. Being cuckolded by a wife is possible when paternity was never known with certainty. Not showing up for duty is excusable during an epidemic. A poor bundle of goods can be blamed on the weather, on a rough road, on the horse who stampeded, or on the fact that others on whom one relied died of the pox.

To take a single example, consider a ship due at port on a certain date. Its actual arrival time could be weeks on either side, given the uncertainties of transport by sail. The cargo on the ship could arrive in various states of condition, much of which depended on the length of voyage and the conditions at sea. The natural elements meant that it was extremely difficult to determine how hard the merchant captain and his crew tried to bring the ship in simply by observing the timing of arrival and the condition of the cargo. This variability affected everyone employed with some relationship to the cargo, from the ship's captain and lighthouse operator to the port authority, tax collector, and passengers. Anyone along the path of production bringing the goods to market could blame bad wares on rough seas. When variability in nature cannot be kept out of production nor measured independently, then it is seldom worth the trouble to disentangle the bad actions of nature from the bad behavior of men. And men, when they know they can blame nature, will behave badly. Bad behavior leads others to attempt to stop it, and thus we return to the problem of transaction costs and the institutions used to control them.

The Creation of Free Labor

The institutions of the pre-modern world reflected the large variability of life at the time, even in something so normal and mundane as employment. Consider the following excerpt taken from a sixteenth-century legal scholar on master-servant relations, as regards to a servant's obligations.

> If he be in covenaunt, he may not depart out of his service without his masters licence, and he must give his master warning that he will depart one quarter of a yere before the terme of the yere expireth, or else he shalbe

compelled to serve out an other yere. And if any young man unmaried be without service, he shalbe compelled to get him a master whom he must serve for that yere, or else he shalbe punished with stockes and whipping as an idle vagabond.[25]

Today we have little concept of master and servant relations (outside of certain sexual predilections) and no notion of this relationship in an employment setting. Leaving aside the antiquated language, what strikes us as foreign is how strongly the servant is bound to the master, and the necessity of an unmarried man to become a servant. Today an employer expects an employee to give some notice of leaving, but there is seldom a punishment if this norm is not followed and certainly no forced servitude or whipping!

The historical master-servant relationship goes back a long way. The Statute of Artificers (1558–1560) was a group of laws that essentially updated the fourteenth-century feudal Statute of Labourers; the statutes regulated the working relationship between masters and their servants. In a narrow sense, a servant was a single individual living within the household of a master; the servant provided some service for a fixed length of time, usually a year. In a broad sense, a servant also referred to anyone who provided a service: an apprentice, a casual laborer, or a craftsman. These latter servants were often married, living within their own household, and not subject to the same jurisdiction as household servants. The Statute of Artificers had four basic components: servants could not depart from their agreed employment without the permission of their master; for many individuals some type of service was compulsory; most often service was for a specific length of time, often a year; and wages were regulated. Failure to comply could mean prison, fines, beatings, and a return to fulfill the obligation. Although many aspects of the statute were ineffective and nonbinding, depending on labor market conditions, the general thrust of the laws remained in effect until well into the nineteenth century.

In America today, employers and employees negotiate contracts recognizing their equal legal standing. Workers are unable to sell their freedom by entering into any type of indentured servitude, they are under no compulsion to work for anyone, and they have the right to terminate their employment at will. During the pre-modern era, at least under the law and mostly in practice, the case was the opposite: labor was not "free." Masters had legal remedies for any breach in the relationship with their servants, they could use corporal punishment to correct behavior, and they "owned" certain rights of service while exercising a "kind of jurisdiction" over their servants.[26] In many ways a servant had a legal status similar to other household dependents such as a wife or children and was also entitled to protection and provision from the master. Hence the master-servant relationship was not a matter of slavery, but was a quasi-voluntary arrangement whereby the master held rights of ownership over the flow of service the servant provided. Starting in the eighteenth century, enlightened Western thought began to challenge the consistency between a freeman and a servant, but it was not until the middle of the nineteenth century that the long-standing master-servant relationship evolved into one of employer and employee. Indentured servitude ceased in the 1830s, suffrage was applied to males regardless of property status, and of course, slavery was abolished.

Like the other pre-modern institutions about to be examined, private master-servant labor contracts coincidentally died with the introduction of better measurement. Indeed, the source of these changes was linked to changes in nature and the ability to measure performance as well. One way of understanding the master-servant relationship is to recognize that the servant transferred property rights to the flow of his service in exchange for wages and other supports. The master then directed the servant in his duties, much the way a manager would do so today. Throughout the nineteenth century, this relationship transformed into one where prices and explicit hourly wages did the directing. Employers, wishing certain performance from their employees, began to pay for this behavior explicitly. Laborers made choices based more on wages, and different duties became more bundled with compensation packages. Of course this freedom came at a cost and workers lost many of the protections and rights they had under the old system—as lamented by Marx and Engels in the *Communist Manifesto*. The question is, why would such a change come about?

Wages are payments for a unit of time, usually by the hour or by the day. Paying wages requires a reliable measure of time, and cheap and accurate measurement of time did not sweep into the everyday life of Britons until the nineteenth century. Furthermore, allowing workers to leave part way through an employment means that the degree to which the tasks were completed can be measured. Again, consistent and accurate measures were not the norm until the nineteenth century. Hence the inability to measure labor performance with any type of accuracy greatly discouraged hourly free employment. On the other hand, working until a harvest is in or until a year is up could always be determined with more verifiability. Finally, paying workers for specific tasks meant both parties needed to be able to separate these tasks from others. The inability to do this during the pre-modern era meant that all tasks were essentially bundled together, and as a result, the laborer became a servant under the general and universal supervision of the master. The creation of free labor is just one brief example of how measurement led to a fundamental change in organization, and it is hoped that this example whets the appetite for more.

CONCLUSION

Prior to the middle of the eighteenth century, it simply was not worth the effort, in many cases of life, to distinguish between the role of nature and the role of humans in production. This lack of clarity prevailed in private relations, as in the case of a master and servant, but it was more prevalent in those situations where the state now concerns itself. In areas of public production, government service, and military defense, the state had no meaningful methods of measuring the role of nature. And so it did not. A different approach was used. The Crown took one of two approaches to the handling of nature: it either transferred property rights of ownership over the enterprise to private individuals or it retained ownership and employed only individuals it could trust. In both cases, the resulting institutions were vastly different from the professional bureaucracies that emerged in the nineteenth century, once meaningful and effective measurement was possible.

CHAPTER THREE

The Aristocrats

What is a peer? A useless thing;
A costly toy, to please a king;
  A bauble near a throne;
A lump of animated clay;
A gaudy pageant of a day;
An incubus; a drone!
What is a peer? A nation's curse—
A pauper on the public purse;
  Corruption's own jackal:
A haughty, domineering blade;
A cuckold at a masquerade;
A dandy at a ball.
Ye butterflies, whom kings create;
Ye caterpillars of the state;
  Know that your time is near!
This moral learn from nature's plan,
That in creation God made man;
But never made a peer.

ANONYMOUS

There was once an odd group of individuals.[1] Actually, the individuals were not odd, but their rules of conduct were. The "pre-modern aristocrats" were an extremely small class of peerage and gentry families who ruled Britain, not with an iron fist, but through a social consensus between themselves, the Crown, the merchant class, and the vast numbers of commoners. Aristocrats existed across Europe, and though their immoderation differed in degree, their customs were similar enough that they could recognize each other as institutional cousins.[2] More than almost any other social group before or since, their conduct as a class was governed by a set of unusual, strict social conventions and formal laws. These were not mere guidelines but rather strong social codes: if not followed, they could render a member a social outcast.

The opening poem was written in 1842.[3] Although written at the zenith of aristocratic power, the anonymous writer's poem was prophetic. The end was very near. By 1880, the age of the aristocrats was essentially over, and by 1911, the Parliament Act made the House of Lords second fiddle to the House of Commons, driving the final nail in the coffin. After centuries, the rule of Britain peacefully transferred to commoners with no noble connections. And the same was true in the rest of Europe. Even in France, where a noble-led reform in 1789 got out of control and led to the execution of the monarch, his family, and more than a thousand others in the second estate, the remaining 99 percent of aristocrats struggled through and, by 1825, had restored the monarchy and had returned to power under new terms. Not to belittle the French Revolution, but the French ancien régime essentially lasted until the end of the nineteenth century.[4] The same was true in Germany.

The poem articulates not only the sentiments at the time but also the general perception ever since. Indeed, for the past 200 years, the aristocracy has been frowned upon by academics, social advocates, the poor, and those wealthy merchants who were not included in the ruling class. Such diverse individuals as Thomas Paine, Karl Marx, Henry George, and David Lloyd George were among the many contemporary political figures who saw the aristocrats as evil holders of privilege. George Orwell, writing after the Second World War regarding the British elite, noted that the "bandits" were "simply parasites, less useful to society than his fleas are to a dog." His view was that "for long past there had been in England an entirely functionless class, living on money that were invested they hardly knew where, the 'idle rich'. . . . The existence of these people was by any standard unjustifiable."[5] Among modern economists, aristocrats are described as "averse to work, unwilling to save, ill-disposed to commercial activity, and unable to consider money as something to be profitably invested."[6] Not quite as colorful as Orwell, but they draw similar conclusions all the same.

For many reformers, the pre-modern era before 1800 is referred to as the "old corruption" because a few landed interests controlled the provision of public service through the sale and purchase of ancient private office holdings, the holding of well-paid sinecures that required little effort, patronage, access to the Crown, church estates and bishoprics, rights to parliamentary seats, and hereditary titles. Reformers in the nineteenth century mocked the lavish and ostentatious aristocratic lifestyle, railed against the waste and pomp which seemed to come at the expense of the rest of society, and scoffed at the idea that birth should trump talent. Everything about the organization of pre-modern life seemed to be embodied in the ancient, unscientific, amateurish, and non-modern ways of the aristocrats. So wasteful was the aristocratic life that some historians have claimed they were "prestige maximizers" who were driven by their "uncontrollable urges" into a dissipating lifestyle.[7] Like the fictional Marchmain family of Evelyn Waugh's *Brideshead Revisited*, the aristocrats seem to have idly bided their time on earth, indulging in conspicuous consumption, pursuing pointless interests, and contributing nothing to the broader society.

Of course the aristocrats were guilty as charged. The aristocratic system was laced with intermarriage, nepotism, and private school networks. Many aristocrats simply "hung out" at court with apparently nothing to do but engage in extravagant social living, adultery, and fornication. They shunned commercial investments and they engaged in leisure-laden activities. Although British aristocrats of the time made much of the fact that their elite was open to all, this claim was only true by a technicality. Entry was possible, but the reality was that the social elite was a stable and tight group for almost three centuries. On the surface, there would appear to be few redeeming characteristics among the aristocratic class, especially in the face of the extreme poverty that surrounded them.

So little is thought of aristocrats in today's world that their ultimate fall from power and privilege in the latter nineteenth century is generally considered to have been a move toward a better society. The only apparent mystery is why it took so long. Some would argue that the merchant class reproduced at a more successful rate starting in the late medieval period and that it simply took centuries before their stronger entrepreneurial spirit was able to take over.[8] In a similar vein, other economists argue that artisan parents taught their children that patience and hard work were virtues in contrast to the aristocratic indoctrination of the love of leisure. When the Industrial Revolution arrived, the investments in human capital finally paid off for the artisan class, and the small bourgeoisie was able to grow in wealth and power over the nineteenth century.[9] Still others hold that urbanization and industrialization finally turned the political power tables around in favor of the unenfranchised, and that aristocrats reluctantly handed authority over to avoid a revolution similar to the one across the English Channel.[10]

Yet, could it be that the judgments of aristocratic lassitude are too quick and easy? Given how long they played a central role in the governments, militaries, and economies of European countries, it seems preferable to explain why they were able to survive. For a sense of their importance, let us turn our focus to Britain, the most aristocratic of all countries.[11] As a governing elite, the aristocrats ruled for almost 300 years with the general consent of the people.[12] Prior to 1850, Britain had no public police (and a limited standing army) to enforce the peace, and yet there was no widespread popular revolt against aristocratic rule. Even when Bonnie Prince Charlie led the Jacobite rebellion in 1745, he was unable to muster opposition among commoners against the elite status quo. Aristocrats not only survived Oliver Cromwell's Commonwealth, the Glorious Revolution, demographic failure through high death and low birth rates in the early eighteenth century, various financial upheavals, and anti-aristocratic sentiments on the Continent, they actually prospered until the very end in terms of wealth and power when they voluntarily created new institutions of power and governance.[13] They created a society far from utopian, but their reign coincides with England's transformation from a small fringe country enmeshed with internal struggles to the greatest power on earth. They oversaw the transition to religious tolerance; the creation of a de facto constitution through the English Bill of Rights (1689), the Act of Settlement (1701) and the Parliament Act (1911), the union with Scotland (1706), moderation of royal power and the determination of succession to the throne, victory over France and other European powers, the creation of an empire that never saw the sun set, and the Industrial Revolution. It hardly seems possible that England could have become the United Kingdom, let alone the British Empire, had its ruling elite consumed power for its own sake, been overly engrossed with leisure, avoided hard work, lacked ambition, or dissipated its wealth through 300 years of afternoon tea parties and evening dances.

The puzzle of the aristocracy, however, is deeper still than the role it played in the rise of Britain. Emerging out of the Tudor reign, the premodern aristocracy was quickly established by a set of restrictions, rules, or constraints that defined them. Contrary to popular belief, the aristocrats were not free when it came to landholdings, titles, education, inheritance, lifestyle, marriage, and social behavior. There were both legal and social limits on the choices they could make, and these constraints encouraged aristocrats to avoid business enterprises, engage in conspicuous consumption, and invest in the oddest forms of capital. Furthermore, the constraints they faced were different from the feudal conditions that bound nobles before them and were different from any restrictions placed on modern aristocrats. Indeed, the restrictions are alien to modern eyes, and the outrageous behavior that resulted from them form the basis of modern criticisms of the aristocracy. Yet, the pre-modern aristocracy thrived in this environment, and the more aristocratic they were, the wealthier they became. In fact, the British aristocracy tended to engage in everything aristocratic just a little bit more than their Continental counterparts, and ironically history rewarded them for it.[14]

This oddness is nicely demonstrated in Jane Austen's *Pride and Prejudice*, a fictional love story revolving around the Bennets, a small gentry family of five daughters living in Hertfordshire, and their interactions with Lord Bingley and Mr. Darcy—two wealthy young gentlemen visiting their area. No doubt the eternal theme of love conquering all explains much of its continued popularity, but the quality and detail of Austen's writing are just as endearing. Austen wrote her novel in 1797 (although it was published in 1813) at the height of aristocratic power but also at the edge of the soon coming modern world. Her honest descriptions provide a glimpse of aristocratic life through the eyes of a contemporary. And what do we see? We see a world where there is a strong social pecking order, but where even a marginal gentleman's family such as Mr. Bennet's has a substantial amount of leisure time. In this world marriages are alliances between families; the young aristocrats appear to have no skills other than at dancing, piano, and wit; and others frown over a lack of proficiency in these endeavors. It is a world where there seem to be endless forests to walk in regardless of ownership, and where it is nothing to drop in on the home of a fellow elite and expect a tour even though the gentleman was away. People speak of how much income a fellow makes per year rather than the stock of how much wealth he has. It was a time where homes had names, and individuals had the names of their homes. It was a place where the likes of an evil Mr. Wickham could "talk the talk" in gentry circles and prey on the wealth and daughters of legitimate members. Everything about Elizabeth Bennet's life seems odd to us, but these details were characteristic of all the pre-modern aristocrats.

To understand the world in which Austen's characters dwell, we must define a few terms. The "Aristocracy" describes a wide range of social rankings that in Britain can be placed in two tiers. At the top were the peers. The peerage titles included dukes, marquesses, earls, viscounts, and barons. This group, though extremely wealthy and powerful, was always very small. In 1658, it had only 119 members, and by 1830, it had grown to just 300.[15] Ironically, the largest growth in the peerage came after it lost political power. In 1900, there were 520 peers, and the number grew even higher by the mid-twentieth century when the modern peerage was opened to all social classes, almost as a "lifetime achievement" award. The pre-modern peers were of a different type altogether. Several contemporary and modern attempts have been made to measure the wealth of the peers, with varying degrees of success. As discussed later, by most accounts they became extremely wealthy relative to other members of their society, and the British aristocrats became wealthier than the other European nobles.

The "gentry," a subclass of smaller landholders beneath the peers, formed the second tier of the aristocracy. Within the gentry were further social rankings. At the top were further title holders such as baronettes and knights, who often held the title only for life. Beneath these were "esquires" and finally "gentlemen"; the latter was an informal title during the pre-modern period. The movement down the social ladder corresponded to increased numbers. In the seventeenth century, scholars estimate there were approximately 7,000–9,000 esquires, and perhaps 16,000 gentlemen.[16] All aristocratic families had a coat of arms, and by 1800 there were only 9,458 such families, and by 1900, only 1 in 3,200 people was considered an aristocrat in Britain.[17] Thus the aristocracy was never a significant part of the population in terms of numbers. If we think of the aristocracy as a pyramid, the top was very well defined and tiny, while the bottom was considerably larger, less well defined, and more fluid in terms of movement in and out. The Continental aristocrats were more numerous, with their numbers generally increasing toward the east. In France 1 percent of the population was aristocratic, in Poland almost 8 percent.[18] Unlike in Britain where the lower gentry and younger sons were without title, most nobles on the Continent had titles, younger sons were often co-heirs, and all Continental nobility enjoyed some degree of social status and privilege.[19]

One easily misunderstood characteristic of the English aristocracy was that it was not exclusively defined by a blood line and, in principle, was an "open elite." Ultimately the Crown owned all titles, lands, and privileges and could grant these to any individual. In principle, entry to the peerage by anyone was possible with the Crown's permission, but in practice it was not very open at all; almost all of the new positions were filled by lower-ranked peers. These entrants were mostly in the form of promotion in ranks or the elevation of younger sons and other relatives. Exceptionally few commoners with no aristocratic connections made the social leap to the peerage. Things were different at the bottom of the gentry pool. Wealthy commoners or commoners who had provided some exceptional service to Crown and country, whether economic, military, or otherwise, were able to enter the gentry through the purchase of an estate, which began the process of social recognition. In addition, the gentry was constantly being fed from the top by the younger sons of peers who did not qualify for peerage based on the system of primogeniture. Some of these made it back to the peerage; others remained as gentry or left altogether and became commoners. Thus, to some degree, the aristocracy was fluid in its membership at the bottom.

The British aristocracy was a large and complicated institution whose influence filtered through every aspect of life for several hundred years, and there is no intention here to cover all of it. In this chapter, the focus is on the social rules among the power elite that developed after Henry VIII's confiscation of monastery lands, and which began to break up toward the end of the nineteenth century. The English aristocracy is often thought of as a continuous institution from 1066 AD until the present day. However, very few noble families have titles and genealogies dating back to the 1066 conquest. More important, the institutional constraints varied significantly over time, and it is better to view the aristocracy as having three different institutional eras. These were the feudal lords (1066–c. 1550), the pre-modern aristocrats (c. 1550–c. 1880), and the modern aristocrats (c. 1880–present). Thus, there were two significant breaks in the nature of the aristocracy over time. The early feudal lords had rights grounded in force, and were lordships over the peasants tied to their lands.[20] The modern aristocrats are a remnant social elite who have virtually no political power or privileges above commoners; thus they comprise an aristocracy in name only. The pre-modern aristocrats, however, constitute a puzzling group, and their termination is at the heart of the Institutional Revolution.

THE PRE-MODERN ARISTOCRACY: C. 1550–C. 1880

At the time of William's conquest, England had a well-established Anglo-Saxon nobility. This was replaced and amended by King William, who claimed all English land, with an aristocratic system along

Norman lines. In order to administer the country, he established several powerful "magnates" who ruled large territories under a system of tenancy for life at the king's pleasure, meaning if the king was not pleased, the tenancy—or life—might not be long. These magnates were mostly William's kin who ruled the country through a feudal system grounded in force. They supplied the king with military services, and over time their families often became very powerful. John of Gaunt, 1st Duke of Lancaster (1340–1399), is an exemplar of a feudal magnate. John was the third surviving son of King Edward III (1312–1377), and by the time he was made duke, he owned over thirty castles across England and France. His descendants included the future kings Henry IV, Henry V, and Henry VI. His wealth, household organization, and power were similar to the monarch's, and he played a significant role in the affairs of state when ten-year-old Richard II came to the throne. He was one of the most significant military magnates and like the others, his power and status contrast with the administrative aristocrats who arose in the pre-modern era.

For many reasons, the relationship between nobles and Crown evolved substantially throughout the Middle Ages. The Magna Carta; the formation and evolution of Parliament; the erosion of feudal services, obligations, and benefits; the reduced importance of knights and heavy horse in combat; the War of the Roses (1455–1489); and the general growth of the state all led to a relationship by the turn of the sixteenth century that had changed almost completely. When Henry VIII was crowned in 1509, he was wealthier than William had been in 1066, and his demand for administrative servants was substantially greater. Although he could draw on the small number of large magnates in existence for service, there were approximately only forty in 1509, and so he had to create new positions. Henry VIII's confiscation of monastery land, which accounted for up to 25 percent of England's area, allowed him to create a relatively large number of new estates. These new estates were considerably smaller than those of the magnates, and by the mid-sixteenth century the pre-modern aristocrats began to emerge.[21] As the civil services expanded several times over the sixteenth century, the positions of authority were occupied by these newly created administrative nobles who, although they had the same social status and titles of the feudal lords, were a far cry from warriors.[22]

To contrast the difference between feudal and pre-modern aristocrat, consider two nobles contemporary with Henry VIII: Edward Stafford, 3rd Duke of Buckingham (1478–1521), and Charles Brandon, 1st Duke of Suffolk (1484–1545). Buckingham was a feudal magnate. Like John of Gaunt, he was descended from Edward III, connected to several significant nobles through marriage, and considered the largest private landowner in England.[23] His wealth, power, and Plantagenet lineage gave him some independence from the Crown, and when Buckingham discovered Henry was having an affair with his married sister, the duke unabashedly had her taken to a convent many miles away. Quite reasonably, Henry VIII considered him with suspicion and as a potential rival. By contrast, Suffolk is an example of an early pre-modern aristocrat. He was a lowly esquire with a short pedigree who befriended Henry VIII in their youth. Within five years of their meeting he became a duke. His wealth and influence were minor compared to the Crown's and depended upon Suffolk's good service to his patron.[24]

Unlike earlier lords who lived in castles and whose power was grounded in military force, the distinguishing feature of the new social elite was that its power was based on membership within a group supported by the Crown and by the general population, including wealthy merchants and professionals. The new aristocracy was held together by an implied social contract full of mutual obligations, responsibilities, and expectations; as a result, they lived in a country house and not behind a castle wall. It was this group that remained in power until replaced by bureaucratic and professional commoners beginning in the latter quarter of the nineteenth century. This is not to say that the older feudal lords were exterminated. Many of the great families continued, but the strength of individual magnates decreased relative to the body of pre-modern nobles and gentry who made up the bulk of the aristocracy, and in subsequent generations they would behave in exactly the same fashion as the pre-modern newcomers.

As a result, the new aristocrats were not fundamentally soldiers but rather a group that provided service to the Crown from the highest to the lower offices of the state.[25] Indeed, their purpose for being was to fill the growing number of administrative offices of the state—and eventually there were hundreds of offices. At the highest level these included the great offices of the state: lord high steward, lord high chancellor, lord high treasurer, lord president of the council, lord privy seal, lord great chamberlain, lord high constable, earl marshal, and lord high admiral. Today, these offices still exist, but their powers have changed considerably. Below these great offices, and within the various branches of civil administration, were many other offices. The administration of civil services extended far beyond the executive arm of the Crown, and the pre-modern aristocrats were involved in much of it.[26]

It was a long road to a peerage, and a potential entrant had to invest in certain ways while always under the observation of others in the aristocracy. The starting point in the journey was an investment in land. Land was always the defining attribute of the aristocracy—the test of rank and position.[27] But land was hardly sufficient, and being the first member of a family to purchase a landed estate, by itself, never garnered immediate acceptance into the social elite.[28] Thus the founding member of an aristocratic family seldom made it into the highest levels of society; instead, the newly rich spent time "building a manor house, extending the property, acquiring a coat of arms, inter-marrying with the local elite, and ensuring a proper education for the next generation."[29]

Once a family had obtained an estate, it had to be improved, and these improvements had to be of a specific type. To begin with, a country house, known as a "seat," was to be built. The country seat functioned not only as living quarters, but also as a quasi-public space for other local gentry. Large rooms were built for entertaining and hosting guests for extended stays. Large tracts of land were to be taken out of production and rebuilt as parks and gardens. An interesting feature of the country seat was its isolation—often even isolated from the local village. Many literary writers refer to the boredom of living at the seat, where "the perennial complaint about country houses—apart from the boredom of living in them—was that they cost their owners too much, both to build and thereafter to live in."[30]

In addition to improving the land, the owner's children were to be "properly educated," and they were to marry appropriate members of the elite. Families that continued to marry in the merchant, professional, or lower classes seldom were able to raise their status.[31] This was a major issue in the eighteenth century, and several bills were brought from the Lords to the Commons to prevent "mismatched" love marriages. This culminated with the 1753 Marriage Act, which strengthened the patriarch's power by requiring his permission to marry if the child was under twenty-one, and by requiring the reading of banns (a public church announcement of marriage) for one month within the parish, among other things.[32]

Aside from land, education, and marriage, there was a host of other, less well-defined, terms for entry. For example, many families emerged from the masses through success in some merchant enterprise. It was a standard expectation that the family would give up the occupation that earned the income necessary to purchase an estate if it wished to gain entry to the aristocracy.[33] Similarly, investing in industry or commercial activity was frowned upon and could lead to a movement down in the social ranks.[34] Many have noted that the aristocratic class could easily have financed the great industrial innovations and investments of the Industrial Revolution, but that they did not.[35] Indeed, they did just the opposite and generally avoided industrial investments. This conduct is often taken as evidence that aristocrats had different preferences compared to others, especially the hard-working bourgeois.[36] But this interpretation fails to recognize that abandoning merchant enterprises was an institutional condition for entry into the aristocracy. Any industrialists reluctant to give up an occupation or divest were considered vulgar and not accepted into the aristocratic circle.

Loyal service to the Crown, especially through military service, could speed up the process of entry but did not eliminate the other requirements, and more often than not, aristocratic standing was a prerequisite for service anyway. Most striking of the entry requirements was that there was no hard and fast rule. A family was admitted and considered aristocratic when it was accepted. A good signal was when one was asked to act as justice of the peace, sheriff, or some other position of local authority.

It is of interest that the number of formal privileges that went along with these costly restrictions were few. In earlier times, a noble had rights to crossbows, guns, and hunting, and in the Middle Ages, titles like "lord" and "Mr." had more significance than they did later. By the pre-modern period, a peer could not be arrested for a civil action or imprisoned for debt, was not required to make an oath, could be tried only by other peers and not a jury of commoners, and had the right to decapitation over hanging if convicted of a capital offense. None of these privileges seem significant enough to warrant the heavy costs of entry. Instead of special legal or landowner rights, the pre-modern aristocracy in England was about political power.[37] By far the most important benefit was the right to serve in the King's Household and to be a member of Parliament either through the House of Lords or the House of Commons. Access to these seats of power meant control over lesser offices that were an important source of income and political support through grants of patronage.

Strange as it may seem to us, until William Ewart Gladstone created a civil service based on merit and examinations in 1871, public offices were either sold outright or granted through acts of patronage.[38] It was access to these offices that the aristocrats sought. It was their raison d'être. For example, in the first half of the 1600s, a very minor member of the landed gentry, Winston Churchill, happened to support the losing side of Charles I during the English Revolution. So small was his role that Oliver Cromwell did not physically punish the elder Churchill for his loyalties but rather left the family to scratch out a farming existence on their small landholding. At the time of the Restoration in 1660, and as a reward for his minor loyalty, Winston's teenage son John was allowed to enter the House of York, where he served as a page to the future King James II. John Churchill flourished in this setting, and when James became king, Churchill rose to second in command in the army. John would go on to become one of the greatest military leaders of history and was made the 1st Duke of Marlborough. He was given many offices, including gentleman of the bedchamber and governorship of the Hudson's Bay Company.[39]

An office could easily have an income of £3,000 per year in an age when a commoner probably lived on £10–20 per year. Nor did it stop there, since many of the peers held multiple offices. Of the eighteenth-century peers, forty-nine of them had at least eight offices, and some had over thirty.[40] There was an enormous list of peerage and gentry patronage appointments over the years, each with their respective incomes, though most of these positions have no meaning today, and their titles are foreign. Consider the offices in one branch of the administration—the Exchequer. Within the Exchequer were the clerk of the pipes, the clerk of the pleas, the clerk of the nichils, and the clerk of the estreats, among others. These offices dealt with the record keeping and copies of documents involved in the collection of revenues for the Crown, but they have long been extinct.

It is hard to exaggerate the extent to which, by the end of the premodern era, the aristocracy ruled Britain and held power through its control over these civil offices.[41] Both houses of Parliament were controlled by them until the turn of the twentieth century. The King's Household, which evolved into the executive arm of the government, was the domain of the aristocracy, as were the great offices and tenures of state. The army and navy officers were drawn from the aristocracy, as were the judges, justices of the peace, magistrates, and other local administrators. It is also hard to exaggerate the success of the aristocracy in generating wealth from these offices and from their vast estates. Aristocrats across Europe, and in England in particular, became the wealthiest members of society. And therein lies the puzzle. On the surface, the constraints imposed by themselves and the Crown—the seat, the gardens, the extravagant living—raised the cost of living to great heights, yet the aristocracy generated wealth under these restrictions beyond anyone else, including the bourgeoisie who were not hampered by such obligations. What economic problem were they solving in order to generate this wealth?

A TRUST THEORY OF ARISTOCRACY

The pre-modern aristocracy was an institution—a system of constraints, beliefs, and social norms that was devised to control its members' behavior in order to achieve an objective. These rules were designed by the Crown and the aristocrats themselves to fit the circumstances of a world where measurement of nature's role was difficult and often meaningless. As the late, great twentieth-century aristocrat Winston Churchill noted: "The Crown and the Executive found in this system guarantees of fidelity and good conduct, and no one troubled himself about the obstacles placed in the path of unpropertied ability."[42]

"Fidelity and good conduct"—precisely because it was difficult to account for the role of chance, the importance of character was all the greater. And central to good character was loyalty both to others and to a set of rules. A trusting environment is one of the most important conditions for trade and production to take place. A sufficient level of trust is particularly necessary in the political realm where explicit market prices are often not used, and therefore decision makers cannot be disciplined by directly bearing the financial costs and benefits of their actions. In an age when measuring outputs or inputs provided an unreliable method to determine a servant's effort, other arrangements were necessary. Enter the pre-modern aristocrats. The aristocracy was based on trust, and the system of patronage they employed and the strange entry conditions they required were designed to allow the members to credibly commit to being honest in their dealings with the Crown and each other.[43]

The information problem faced by the Crown prior to the nineteenth century was profound. The final outcome of any service or product prior to c. 1850 was characterized by large variability and difficulties in monitoring. Of course when there were large amounts of variability, then there were always large opportunities for acting against the interests of others. The civil administration—from finance to war—was laced with measurement problems due to the large role of nature in life, and this led to the need for a system of trust. The patronage system generated this trust through a simple idea: "Cheat me and you may gain for a while, but get caught and you'll pay dearly." This idea sought to prevent the temptation of short-term thinking, because it made the costs of cheating and getting caught so much greater than the small gains that occasional, or even frequent, cheating would bring. And of course, the more frequently one cheated, the more likely one was to be caught and punished.[44] It might seem that a potential aristocrat could cheat and then flee the punishment when things turned sour, but the patronage system was cleverly designed so that the severe punishment could not be avoided.

The threat of punishment was effective in binding the interests between the Crown and its servants, most notably the aristocrats. There were at least three, often overlapping, methods by which binding was accomplished within the patronage system. The first method involved the servant converting his ordinary assets, such as gold or land, into something that either could not be liquidated, or done so at great cost. Economists call such investments "sunk costs." A sunk cost, once incurred, cannot be recovered or avoided. Aristocrats converted much of their wealth into forms that were costly to convert back or, more likely, became worthless if they fell out of favor. Investments where a servant converted his physical assets are called "hostage capital" for reasons that will be revealed shortly. The second method, covered in Chapter 4, had the aristocrats invest their time, rather than their physical assets, in activities and skills that were only valued within aristocratic circles. These investments earned a return within the elite world as long as they were recognized by other aristocrats, but if a noble was shunned for some type of malfeasance, then the investment was worthless. Thus, the investment of time was also a sunk cost and is called "hostage social capital."[45] Finally, the third method, discussed in Chapter 5, simply involved the Crown making very large future payments for loyal service, with the threat of being removed from access to this stream of high earnings flowing from the office. Although these three different methods ensured good behavior, they all worked along the same principle: once cast out of the elite, the loss of both past investments in hostage capital and potential future earnings was unavoidable. Individuals would engage in all three methods in different proportions depending on their asset levels, social standing, and occupied office.

The Hostage Capital System

Imagine the situation early in the sixteenth century. Numerous wealthy individuals existed—landowners, merchants, and lawyers—and the Crown was seeking someone trustworthy for a civil office. Perhaps Henry VIII needed trustworthy individuals to lead armed men in confiscating monastery lands and possessions—individuals who would ensure that the king's coffers were lined rather than their own. Perhaps it was an office of much less significance, and the king wished for a trustworthy messenger between himself and the French King. In any case, the servant would have a series of ongoing interactions with the Crown involving the tasks at hand, and the servant always had a wide range of choices in terms of how strongly he could act in his master's or his own interests. The more the servant acted in his own interests in conflict with those of the king, the larger was his private reward if undetected—but the more likely that he would be caught. The king knew the situation, and if he caught an individual in a blatant act of treachery, the punishment was likely to be death. But often matters were less clear because of the darned role nature always played. It was possible that a really bad outcome was not the result of treachery, and even a good outcome might have resulted from nature masking a traitor.[46] For example, in 1534, Henry VIII put one of his chief ministers, Thomas Cromwell, in charge of visiting the monastic properties to conduct an inventory of their assets. Did Cromwell report honestly? As the gatekeeper of one of the largest confiscations in history, even a slight underreporting in his favor would have made Cromwell an exceedingly wealthy man. Such a temptation was known to Henry VIII, and so suspicions were ever present. Something was necessary to increase the confidence of honest reporting. Trust, fidelity, and good conduct were of utmost importance because at the time it was nearly impossible to know for sure if servants had carried out their duties.

The solution found was for servants to invest heavily in hostage capital, and for the Crown and other aristocrats to punish the servants when some threshold bad outcome was observed by removing them from office or court. With no source of income, the servant was left with the unavoidable costs of the hostage capital. Therefore hostage capital acts like a bond. By way of analogy, suppose the servant gives the king his daughter—as a wife, servant, or member of his court. As long as the servant is in good standing with the king, he can see his daughter at court. However, if he falls out of favor for any reason, he is banished from court and never sees his daughter again. Because the giving of the daughter is an act that cannot be reversed (it is sunk), the punishment is automatic with banishment from court. This system worked because honest, talented servants were very likely to get invited back and to continue to interact with other members (including the daughter) and to earn large civil office incomes. Dishonest servants might get away with one big payoff for their bad behavior, but they raised the chance of crossing the bad outcome threshold and getting thrown out of the elite loop. Being expelled from the elite group meant that the hostage capital (the daughter) was then lost. Hostage capital investments could take on many forms, and the goal of the system was to make sure the costs of losing this investment due to bad behavior were greater than any benefits from acting against the interests of the master.

Where a servant had repeated interactions with the aristocratic world, the trust system was characterized by two key features.[47] First, punishments were common, since eventually enough bad outcomes occur that a threshold is crossed. No matter how hard a general tries, he may lose any given battle and will almost certainly lose a battle eventually. Time and chance happens to everyone, and so the battle is not always to the strong. However, in a world where trust is used to ensure good effort, the strong will sometimes be punished when they lose. Second, the punishment happened even if there was no direct evidence of bad behavior. Because the other aristocrats and the Crown could not directly observe whether or not the aristocrat-servant had acted in the patron's interest, they punished for bad outcomes—even though they knew bad outcomes did not necessarily mean bad behavior had occurred. This paradoxical implication of trust constantly reveals itself in pre-modern institutions and stands in stark contrast to most modern institutions. Today, when a project is delayed or over budget, a plane crashes, or a police operation goes wrong, a public inquiry or some other type of investigation takes place to see if a punishment is warranted. This evaluation is possible because we are often able to separate and measure the effects of nature—at least to the point we are confident of the separate roles. In the pre-modern world this evaluation was not possible, and so punishments were tied to outcomes.

For the threat of punishment to be convincing—and thus for patrons to trust their servants—a number of conditions must hold. First, the number of patient members in the elite community must be small because word about an untrustworthy servant must be able to spread throughout the aristocratic circle. Once the word was spread, there would be no social circle from within which the ousted servant could use his hostage capital. If a servant could "cheat and move on," then effectively there was no punishment for cheating, and cheating would take place. Second, members must be patient because the payoff to loyal service included a future stream of high earnings. Since the payoff to acting in one's own self-interest was always immediate, impatient servants might misbehave because they placed too small a value on the future benefits. Finally, the world cannot be completely random; that is, in spite of the variability in life, better performance by a servant must lead to a better chance for a good outcome.

The goal of the patronage system was to work within these conditions to ensure that the net expected long-run payoff for bad behavior—acting in one's own interests other than the patron's—was negative, whereas the payoff for good behavior was positive. For this system to work, investments in hostage capital had to be large to offset the possibility of a large cheating opportunity. And at the same time, the costs of having hostage capital while in good standing needed to be kept low. Thus most sunk investments could actually be used for something as long as the servant remained within the elite circle. The investment became worthless only if the servant was expelled.

But who would be interested in making a hostage capital investment? Theoretically, persons of talent and wealth in the pre-modern era had a few options. They could invest in hostage capital and try their hand at court in the elite market where long-term political trades took place. They could keep their wealth liquid and participate in the bourgeois-merchant market where physical goods and services were produced and traded; even in 1500, there were merchants, artisans, lawyers, and professional people going about the ordinary business of the day. Finally, they could stay on an estate and farm among town and country folk to produce agricultural products.

Joining the political market meant an investment in hostage capital, such as giving a daughter to the King, which announced an intention to the Crown of good performance. It was important that any wealth converted to hostage capital had no use in the bourgeois or farming markets. In the elite market, only a few office positions were available, and they had different values. Some were worth a great deal and others . . . not so much. The more an individual invested (the more daughters he gave to the king), the more likely he would be given a valuable office. That is, if the potential aristocrat invested sufficient assets in hostage capital, everyone realized: "The only way he can make this investment worth the risk is to act in the Crown's interest and participate in the aristocratic market over and over again."

Two lessons may be learned from the hostage capital option. First, in order to enter the elite market, an individual had to have sufficient levels of wealth generated elsewhere to invest in hostage capital—poor people need not apply. Some people had more than enough wealth to join, most did not come close, and some small group just barely made it. The individual who had just enough wealth to convert to the level of hostage capital required for the last position available might be called the "marginal aristocrat" or "gentry." Second, some wealthy individuals would come to the conclusion that it just wasn't worth the risk. Placing one's wealth into hostage capital was not free. The cost of converting wealth into hostage capital was the foregone gains that could be obtained in the bourgeois market. Wealthy individuals in the pre-modern era recognized there was an element of choice over entering the aristocracy, and those individuals with sufficient wealth had to decide whether or not to convert their wealth to hostage capital. The decision to do so depended on the rate of return that could be expected in the two markets, and this rate would vary for different people. If an individual felt the net rate of return to holding offices was greater than the alternative investment, then wealth was invested in hostage capital. If the net returns to hostage capital investment were low for the individual, then no investment was made; the individual stayed in the bourgeois market and remained middle class. Hence even if individuals had enough wealth to invest in hostage capital, they might decide not to do so. This choice is the reason why the bourgeois and the aristocrats always coexisted.

Aristocrats made excellent servants to their patrons because they invested in all manner of sunk capital (not just daughters sent to court!) that was effectively held hostage by the society at large. That is, their investments in hostage capital were equivalent to posting enormous bonds for good performance. These bonds acted as credible signals of their trustworthy intentions because failure to perform could mean the loss of the bond. As long as aristocrats cooperated with the rules laid down by the elite and the Crown, they were allowed to participate in society and government, and thereby to reap the rewards of faithful service.

UNDERSTANDING ARISTOCRATS

Aristocrats, then, were at the core of the patronage-trust system. They were not, as the poem put it, "useless things" nor were they "pauper(s) on the public purse." They were the group of people who invested their time and money in ways that could be held hostage by the Crown to ensure trustworthy performance of duties. Thus the strange behaviors that aristocrats took part in were the manifestations of these investments that played a vital role in the administration of the state. Any attempt to understand aristocratic behavior that does not recognize their role as trustworthy servant and the need to make specific types of investments inevitably concludes that they were wasteful, exploitive, and privileged without justification. On the contrary, establishing a reputation for trust explains how individuals entered and exited the aristocracy, why they voluntarily placed long-term restrictions on their lands, why they were amateurs at everything, why their lifestyles were so extravagant, and of course, why they became so wealthy.

Entry Conditions as Hostage Capital

The characteristics of entry into the aristocracy are easily understood as methods to create hostage capital so that aristocrats could be trustworthy servants. Entry was necessary because the administration of the country was growing and because failure by the existing aristocracy to sufficiently procreate was a stark reality of the pre-modern era.[48] Very precious few families trace their aristocratic lineage back in time uninterrupted, and between 20–40 percent of landowners did not have a surviving son between 1660 and 1800.[49] As a result, new entry into the pre-modern aristocracy was important to continue the growing civil service.

The striking theme among entry conditions was that an entrant had to be patient and had to demonstrate investments in hostage capital through land, education, parties, and the like.[50] While some investments were more observable than others, many took time to observe, and so acceptance took a long time. In addition, in order to achieve repeated cooperation, it was important that the aristocrat be patient and not ignore the future benefits of office. By extending the time necessary to become an aristocrat, the system naturally selected patient people.[51] Critically, it was the founding members of an aristocratic family who had to be patient and forward looking. Reading the accounts of founding aristocrats repeatedly reveals men of ambition, capable of hard work, with a propensity to save and invest, and generally in possession of those traits found in the bourgeoisie of the late nineteenth century.

A well-documented case in point is John Churchill, 1st Duke of Marlborough. We have already met the duke, but here a comment on his parsimony and avarice is in order. His great descendant, the relatively leisure-loving Winston Churchill, wrote: "Every one likes the handsome spender who offers lavish hospitality and eases his path through life by a shower of money. Everyone dislikes the parsimonious man who is gathering rather than dispersing wealth. Censure is particularly turned upon those who are careful about small sums. . . . Judged by this standard, Marlborough lay under reproach."[52] Marlborough was a frugal but ambitious man. When, in 1660, he entered the House of York as a poor page, he possessed a drive for success and a knowledge that without money he could not have the career, wife, or home that he desired. Although it was not uncommon for him to come to the financial assistance of others, like his father, this made his efforts to save all the more important. He did not gamble or carouse, but paid bills on time to avoid interest charges. He kept careful account of household expenses his entire life, had only three coats in 1692 (well into his aristocratic status), and was known to walk in the muck from the palace to his home in order to avoid the charge of a carriage. Winston Churchill found "all this very deplorable, and no doubt the historians are right to mock and sneer at him." But were it not for the aggressive and ambitious behavior of John Churchill, there would never have been a Marlborough. In the end, Marlborough "had acquired a hatred of waste of money in all its forms, and especially of frittering away comparatively small sums. He resembled a certain type of modern millionaires, who accumulate wealth unceasingly, spend hardly anything upon themselves, and use their fortunes for the well-being of their families and the endowment of their children, or apply them to great buildings or public objects."[53] Marlborough hardly fits the description of the incompetent social butterfly that many of his descendents would become. Nor does he fit the description of someone impatient and shortsighted.

In addition to being patient, trustworthy aristocrats had to make specific sunk investments in order to credibly convey to the Crown that they could be trusted. This requirement is clearly demonstrated in their many odd investments that were drastically reduced in value if they were banished from aristocratic circles. First, estates were isolated because urban centers offered a host of alternatives to elite living, which reduced the punishment of social ostracism. Although the elite often maintained a town house, the bulk of their household investment and time was spent at the country seat. The country seat could be a lonely place if one were isolated there with no visitors. Thus aristocrats who were tempted to act against the interests of their patrons or against the social norms of the aristocracy would have to ponder what life would be like on a lonely estate in a remote part of the country. An alternative society might have had its ruling class live in urban centers, but an urban environment reduces the punishment for bad behavior. Indeed, in several locations on the Continent—southern Europe, Prussia, and even France—aristocrats tended to be more urban and either spent more time in the cities or abandoned their estates altogether.[54]

Second, marriage into the aristocracy, even at the lower levels, meant that one's social life was tied to the group. By forcing aristocrats to limit their social contacts, the punishment from being excluded increased. Third, requiring a merchant family to give up its historical source of business removed the obvious exit strategy for cheating. Allowing a family to hang on to a prosperous business meant, again, that punishing bad behavior would be incomplete if the family could remain wealthy through business.[55] Fourth, the informal rules of acceptance made it very hard for strategic pretenders to enter the elite group. A pretender was someone who faked or gave the impression of having made hostage investments, but whose intention was to cheat when allowed in. Cheaters need to know the specific rules, so they can determine if it is worthwhile or not. The ultimate rule of general acceptance meant that a cheater might meet all the explicit terms of entrance and still never be allowed into the ruling class. The rule of general acceptance meant that subjective judgments could be made about an individual's "character" over and above the specific investments. This important feature, a source of ridicule by others, kept the fox out of the henhouse.[56]

In contrast to slow and uncertain entry, exit from the aristocratic group was easy, quick, and usually permanent. A breach of trust, an adulterous affair, or the decline of a duel meant instant and complete exile from the aristocratic class. In addition, often a failure to perform a duty was enough to face removal from office, even if there was no direct evidence of bad behavior on the part of the servant. For example, a naval captain who failed to engage an enemy, regardless of the wind conditions, was likely to lose his command. If the infraction were directly against the king, the punishment might be prison or decapitation, but generally was banishment from court. The family would remain on its estate and live off the rents, but it was socially cut off and removed from office. Although harsh, exit was quick because all that mattered in this system was the knowledge that trust was violated. The purpose of the aristocracy was to provide a pool of trustworthy types. Any discovery that an individual was not trustworthy meant immediate removal from the system. Removal from the system did not usually mean the aristocrat lost his physical assets; it meant he lost his sunk hostage investment.

The Strict Family Settlement

One of the most important forms of hostage capital was land, and its treatment is one of the most interesting and compelling aspects of aristocratic life. The purchase of a landed estate was the initial move toward aristocracy, but it was hardly sufficient because in general land is not a sunk investment given that it can generate income or be sold and so cannot act as hostage capital. In order to play a role in generating trust, some type of restriction on the sale and use of the land must be made. Historically, under the feudal aristocracy, property rights to land were restricted by law. Established in 1285, English property was held entail through primogeniture, which meant that there was a continuing estate passing from one generation to another through the eldest son. Ironically, in 1614, just as the pre-modern aristocrats were emerging, the common law courts of England struck down the ability to place perpetual restrictions, such as entails, on property.

This change in the law posed a problem for the emerging aristocrats. The purpose of restricting property rights to land was to create hostage capital. Land that could be sold and which was unrestricted in its use could not be used as hostage capital. What to do? The ingenious solution was found by the middle of the seventeenth century when landowners began placing a "temporary" conveyance (a legal restriction) on the property called the "strict family settlement." In practice this conveyance amounted to a perpetual restriction.[57]

The strict family settlement was a *voluntary* restrictive contract between the existing owner and future (perhaps unborn) generations to "tie one hand behind their back" and bind the uses of the land. It was a tremendous device created by lawyers at the time acting on behalf of their aristocratic clients. It not only restricted the uses of the lands but provided for other members of the family beyond the eldest son. It is important to note that only those wishing to become aristocrats entered into the strict family settlement. Many large landowners who were not peers but members of the bourgeoisie did not constrain their land because they were not interested in creating hostage capital by reducing the alternative uses of their land. At the same time, on many occasions, when the opportunity presented itself to an aristocrat to leave the settlement, the option was rarely exercised. Indeed, in their data sample, historians Stone and Stone find hardly a single example of abandoning the settlement over 350 years: "The full force of social convention and family custom brought to bear by his kindred, 'friend', trustees, and advisers such as the family clergyman, solicitor, and conveyancer . . . [made it such that] . . . only an unusually independent or unusually irresponsible young man . . . would be able to stand up to such psychological pressures [and leave the strict family settlement]."[58] Such a reluctance to exit the onerous strict family settlement only makes sense if it created some offsetting benefit: namely, the benefit of hostage capital.[59]

The strict family settlement usually contained three key elements. First, the practice of primogeniture was preserved to the extent it was possible, although the identity of the recipient in the family settlement was not as important as the practice of preventing the estate from being split. Often, an estate would pass to others, such as a cousin, nephew, or distant relation, in cases of premature death, lack of an heir, or similar events. Second, younger sons, daughters, and widows were to be cared for through payments from the estate, and these payments could be significant. Finally, the rights of the current property holder were contractually constrained over future generations. The strict family settlement usually covered two generations until the son was 21 or the daughter was married but could cover until the grandson was 21. In practice, it was a complicated document, with multiple conditions, depending on the survival and sex of the future generations. The effect of these restrictions was to prevent the sale of the property, restrict long-term leasing, curb many productive uses of the land (e.g., mining), and increase the cost of mortgaging the land. This legal creation "enabled a landowner to tie the hands of his heir and turn him into a tenant for life."[60]

The strict family settlement dealt with more than just the land. An estate consisted of five elements: the "seat" or home, the landed estates, the furniture and other mobile capital, the family name, and any titles. The major goal of the settlement was to make sure these elements all remained intact and bundled together.[61] Thus, when there were multiple children, the younger sons and daughters were given cash settlements in the form of annuities and dowries. They were not given part of the physical estate (including titles), which was passed on intact to the heir. Many critics of aristocracy focus on this inheritance aspect and note how, even if the original holder had merit, there was no guarantee that his descendants would. However, this misses the point altogether. The primary social value of an aristocrat came from hostage capital, not human capital, and the aristocratic institutions were designed to keep the hostage capital together—more hostage capital meant more trust.

Even more interesting was the desire to maintain the estate even when there was a failure in the male line. The family settlement would contain provisions allowing for a male cousin or other distant kin to inherit. If none were available, then the estate could pass to a daughter, and if she married, the husband would often be required to adopt the family name. In this way, the estate (and everything with it) was passed on to pseudo-kin. Nevertheless, it was very common for a title to go extinct. Between 1660 and 1800 the percentage of families that did not have a surviving son was between 20 and 40 percent.[62] When an aristocratic line went extinct, the estate reverted back to the Crown, and the entire bundle could be reinstated at a later time with the same title to a different family. The average person today, looking at a title such as the Duke of Buckingham, might think the family goes all the way back to the fifteenth century when the title was originally created. But such is not the case. In 1444, Humphrey Stafford, 6th Earl of Stafford, was created 1st Duke of Buckingham, but his line went extinct in 1521 when Henry VIII executed the 3rd Duke of Buckingham. King James I then made George Villiers the 1st Duke of Buckingham in 1623, but the title died with the death of his son in 1687. Queen Anne next made John Sheffield the 1st Duke of Buckingham in 1703, and the title again went extinct with the death of his son in 1735. Finally, Richard Nugent Temple Grenville was made the 1st Duke of Buckingham in 1822. This repeated creation of a title seems odd unless the purpose of the title is understood. At all times the role of an estate was to act as a bond for good performance (regardless if given or purchased), and the goal was to preserve the estate in its entirety so that it could remain an extremely large form of hostage capital. Who actually held the title was of much less social importance.

Adam Smith was greatly opposed to the legal restrictions put in place by the strict family settlement. In *The Wealth of Nations*, he states: "Nothing can be more completely absurd. They are founded upon the most absurd of all suppositions . . . that the property of the present generation should be restrained and regulated according to the fancy of those who died perhaps five hundred years ago."[63] Quite naturally,

Smith saw the settlement as a binding constraint that hindered the incentives of the current landowner without any consequent benefit. He argued that the settlement prevented the land from being put to its best use and discouraged investment: "There still remain in both parts of the United Kingdom some great estates which have continued without interruption in the hands of the same family since the times of feudal anarchy. Compare the present condition of these estates with the possessions of the small proprietors in their neighbourhood, and you will require no other argument to convince you how unfavorable such extensive property is to improvement."[64] What Smith failed to recognize was that the family settlement had a purpose other than agricultural output. Investment in land has the advantage that it is easily observable and valued. The strict family settlement was an ingenious way of placing effective encumbrances on the property, which allowed the land to become hostage capital. Land that was unrestrained could be sold and therefore could not act as a bond for trustworthy performance. As a result, failure to enter into such an agreement negated the ability to enter or remain in the aristocracy.

The strict family settlement included the title, seat, coat of arms, furnishings, and the like because these items were less easily observed and measured when not tied directly to the land. By tying everything together, the aristocracy created an enormous class of hostage capital that others could easily recognize. When others recognized the hostage capital investment, then it became very valuable as an entry condition for political office. Of course, any breach of trust meant that resale was virtually impossible, and most of the investments were lost. In an extreme case of suspected treason, such as that resulting in Henry VIII's execution of the 3rd Duke of Buckingham, the Crown might confiscate everything. The very aspects that Smith complained about were the features that gave the family settlement its value.[65]

Education

The pre-modern aristocracy was a social elite defined by investments in hostage capital, and their education was another important case in point. One of the distinguishing features of the aristocracy was the incentive not just to attend private schools and university but also to attend specific schools and focus on specific types of learning and social behavior.

In particular, the emphasis was on knowledge that was not practical and had few alternative uses. The young gentleman was to learn ancient languages such as Greek and Latin in his study of classic literature and other liberal arts. Time was invested in learning music, dance, taste, and good manners.[66] There was an outright avoidance of any type of training in the trades or skills, and a professional education was tolerated only for younger sons.[67] When John Locke noted: "Latin I look upon as absolutely necessary to a gentleman. . . . Can there be anything more ridiculous, than that a father should waste his own money and his son's time in setting him to learn the Roman language, when at the same time he designs him for a trade" he was recognizing the incongruity of practical lessons with aristocratic ambitions.[68] Indeed, "boys read almost exclusively in Latin authors and when they proceeded to university often did little more than read them again" not because the education system of the time was not working, but because it was designed to work this way.[69]

A proper education also meant that students went to the right schools. In the last half of the eighteenth century, 72 percent of peerage children attended Eton, Westminster, Winchester, or Harrow.[70] Finally, a major part of a gentleman's education came on the "grand tour," where the young man would travel the Continent with a private tutor to "imbibe culture (and perhaps life experience) in foreign climes."[71] In the end, the aristocracy fostered a reputation for amateurism that encouraged pursuits that were unpaid and untrained for. A modern remnant is found in the Olympic Games, which were established on the principle of amateur athletic competition, not because this embodied a truer nature of sport but because the modern Olympics were originally intended as a showcase for aristocrats to demonstrate how much time they had spent perfecting their tennis backhand.[72]

With apologies to modern lovers of Latin, there was a utilitarian economic purpose to an education in a dead language: it was next to useless outside aristocratic social circles. Latin may have been useful in the hands of an academic, a judge, a minister, or even a soldier, but if an aristocrat found himself as a social outcast over some act of untrustworthy behavior, none of these offices would have been open to him. Back on his landed estate among his gardens and large seat, Latin, dance skills, and other social graces would have been of little use. The purpose of attending the same schools was to develop social ties among the aristocracy and to cheaply signal to others that the education was not practical. The switch from private tutors to a few small schools throughout the eighteenth century was to encourage further social connections. Education was a means of developing social ties among the aristocracy. Social connections that lead to productive human capital investment, however, dilute the role of hostage capital. By forcing young aristocrats to invest in learning with little use outside of the elite group, the aristocracy increased the young gentleman's investment in hostage capital. His educational investments would be of little value were he later caught cheating and was expelled from the group.

Extravagant Living and Voluntary Service

> *The man of wealth and pride*
> *Takes up a space that many poor supplied;*
> *Space for his lake, his park's extended bounds,*
> *Space for his horses, equipage, and hounds.*
> *The bore that wraps his limbs in silken sloth*
> *Has robb'd the neighboring fields of half their growth.*

Oliver Goldsmith, "The Deserted Village"

The poet Goldsmith identifies a feature of the pre-modern British aristocrats that set them apart from their fellow Continental nobles, as well as from earlier nobles and the rising bourgeois class—namely, the incredible extravagance that was expected in their lifestyle. Their homes were overbuilt, with large sections that were quasi-public spaces for entertaining the other families in their county. Unlike earlier castles, the country seat had beauty, size, comfort, large glass windows, and private bedrooms, chambers, and corridors. Large sections of their estates, up to 5,000 acres, were devoted to elaborate gardens, lakes, and parks, and taken out of production. They were expected to have parties on a regular basis, and they hosted hunts, dances, and horse races. The aristocracy provided schools and churches for their communities. This type of living was called "port," and an elite was expected to engage in it, for there was "an obligation to spend generously, even lavishly on occasion, as part of one's duty to society, in return for the privileges of wealth and membership of the ruling class."[73] The Continental nobles were more likely to be urbanized, and when in the country were less likely to have an elaborate park.[74]

At the same time, an aristocrat was expected to provide voluntary community service and to engage in charitable activities toward the commoners under his authority. Ironically, even though aristocrats held many offices that paid well, they also served as justices of the peace, sheriffs, deputy lieutenants, lord lieutenant, commissioners for taxes, members of the county bench, members of Parliament, and magistrates in a volunteer capacity. Furthermore, they were actively involved in charity and placed a high value on generosity, considering it a hallmark of their station in life.[75]

By now the role of this type of behavior should be obvious. Expenditures on ostentatious living were visible sunk expenditures that acted as hostage capital. To take another account from the fictional Bennets in *Pride and Prejudice*, when Mr. Darcy's aunt, Lady Catherine, hears a rumor that he has fallen in love with lower-gentry Elizabeth Bennet, she immediately travels to the Bennet home to put a stop to the affair. On arriving, she snubs the Bennets with her first words, tersely noting, "You have a very small park here."[76] In the eyes of an aristocrat such as Lady Catherine, a small park meant only a small amount of trust could be extended, and this trust certainly did not extend to a marriage between her nephew and Miss Bennet.

Volunteer work and charity were other forms of sunk investments. Should an aristocrat ever be found faulty, there would be no recouping the investment in elaborate parties, gifts to the poor, or time spent on the bench. The only way these expenditures could have led to payoffs was for the aristocrat to continue to reside in the elite group, and that meant a continued effort at trustworthy behavior. One problem with using hostage capital to ensure trust was that many might pretend to convert their wealth, when in fact, most of it remained liquid. Thus many of the specific investments were so lavish and public. Conspicuous investments in consumption activities were relatively inefficient investments in hostage capital. However, their observability to others in their community made them worthwhile.

Wealth Levels

Aristocrats earned income from their estates, but given the voluntarily imposed encumbrances placed on these lands, the rate of return would have been lower than land held freely, as Smith noted. Their real source of wealth came from access to the high state offices given through patronage as a reward for trusting behavior. If aristocrats were individuals who became trustworthy servants through the act of creating expensive sunk investments called hostage capital, then two classes of wealthy individuals should have existed during the pre-modern era: aristocrats and a middle class, or bourgeoisie, because some wealthy individuals would have preferred not to enter the service of the Crown. Given the enormous cost, length of time, and uncertainty involved in becoming an aristocrat, the gross rates of return to the aristocracy must have been higher, on average, than those to the bourgeois during the pre-modern era. Thus if the aristocracy were selected and rewarded for its faithful service, then the rewards for such service must have been present and must have been competitive against other occupations. In other words, for the aristocracy to function in the manner described, it must have been profitable. For some individuals, for whom the creation of hostage capital was very costly, however, the extra returns to the aristocratic life would not have been worth the cost, and they would have remained middle class. Indeed, the bourgeois-merchant class grew throughout the pre-modern era and eventually took over. By 1870, there were 4,217 owners of estates 1,000 acres and up. Of these, only 400 were peers. Although the gentry was included in the total number of owners, many commoners were also large landowners.[77]

Unfortunately, systematically comparing wealth and income levels between aristocrats and merchants prior to the nineteenth century is almost impossible. It was not until 1809 that probate records began in a usable form, and although two surveys of estates were made during the nineteenth century, it was not until 1895 that the Inland Revenue began recording estates probated by level of wealth. Indeed, only in the 1858 survey of wealth was occupation listed. Complicating matters, wealth often only included personalty and not realty (that is, not the land), which was tied up in the family settlement. Nevertheless, there is considerable qualified evidence to show that prior to the eighteenth century, being wealthy and being a member of the aristocracy were almost synonymous. That is, the gross rate of return to the aristocracy was greater than to the merchant market for the average wealthy individual.

Estimates of average peer income in the late seventeenth and early eighteenth centuries range from £2,800 per year to £6,030 per year. It is known that several peers at this time had incomes that exceeded £25,000 per year and that, by 1710, incomes greater than £10,000 per year were not uncommon.[78] By 1801, the average peer income was £8,000 per year, whereas the average income for merchants, lawyers, and laborers was £800, £350, and £31, respectively. At a time when a very good doctor or lawyer might make £500 per year, these sums were enormous.[79] Although these numbers are only snapshots of income, they show that the incomes of the aristocracy were enormous compared to all other classes of individuals during the pre-modern era.

In his seminal work on wealth and income among the very rich in nineteenth-century Britain, Rubinstein finds that early in the eighteenth century, this group was dominated by the peers and the gentry, and the proportion of commoners among the very rich started to grow only over the course of the century. In 1873 there were only 77 business incomes in Britain that exceeded £50,000 per year, and of the landed incomes in 1883 greater than £75,000 per year, all 29 were made by peers.[80] Although prior to the nineteenth century a few untitled very wealthy landowners, such as Andrew Montagu, always existed, "by far the single most important element in British wealth structure [was] landed wealth."[81]

One of the more interesting aspects of Rubinstein's work is his analysis of the number of wealthy Britons by profession. Among the category "professions, public administration and defence," a rapid decline occurred in the number of wealthy after 1840. "The decline in this category . . . occurred above all among those who earned their fortunes in the public administration and defence sphere. . . . Why was this? This was the end of 'Old Corruption,' the world of patronage."[82] In other words, Rubinstein is claiming that aristocrats were able to earn large sums in patronage appointments that disappeared when a professional bureaucracy developed. Rubinstein follows with a long list of members of the wealthy elite and the size of the estate they left at death. For example, Charles, 1st Baron of Arden (1756–1840), registrar of the Court of Admiralty, left £700,000; John Scott, 1st Earl of Eldon (1751–1838), lord chancellor, left £707,000; Sir Charles Flower, 1st Baronet (1763–1834), lord mayor of London, left £500,000; and so on. No commoners are included in the list, but each individual listed held some type of office such as principal of the Court of Arches, master of the Prerogative Court, bishop of Winchester, lord steward to His Majesties Household, dean of Windsor, or receiver-general for Lincolnshire. Later, when examining the close relationship to the size of estate in acres and income levels, Rubinstein notes: "As with their wealthier counterparts, there are examples of men with very low landed incomes whose fortunes are inexplicably at variance with their stated incomes. . . . The fortunes . . . can be assigned with some definiteness to 'Old Corruption,' the world of government patronage and place."[83] Again, he follows with a list of titled individuals, such as the

1st Earl of Liverpool, the archbishop of Canterbury, and the baron of the Exchequer.

Prior to the Industrial Revolution, the very wealthy in Britain were almost always members of the aristocracy. During this time and with very few exceptions, only members of the aristocracy were allowed to participate in patronage, and members of this servant class amassed large fortunes. This suggests that the rate of return to the pre-modern aristocratic lifestyle must have been greater than any other option for the average potential aristocrat. What is remarkable is that it took until the twentieth century for the bourgeois-industrial class to take over the positions of the wealthiest individuals—almost 100 years after the Industrial Revolution. Becoming and being a member of the aristocracy was costly, but rewards existed to support those expenses.

Aristocrats on the Continent were similar in form but different by degree and detail from their British counterparts. They were more likely urban, and if not urban, they were more likely feudal. On the Continent, titles were spread out to siblings, nobles were more commercially engaged, their parks were smaller and less elaborate, and they were more likely to be defined by legal status than by social custom. The concept of "lordship" was deeper and survived longer on the Continent.[84] On every dimension, one could argue, they engaged in less hostage capital.[85] It is not surprising then that their wealth levels did not match those in Britain.[86] Of course many fantastically wealthy nobles lived on the Continent, but England had the greatest number of fortunes, both in absolute and relative numbers. "It had a collection of very wealthy nobles equaled nowhere else, and these represented a far higher percentage than any other part of Europe."[87] They owned a larger fraction of the land; the peers alone owned one-quarter and the gentry owned up to one-half.[88] In France, the entire nobility owned only one-quarter. The British aristocrats, by investing heavier in hostage capital, were more successful at engaging in trustworthy behavior. No doubt the state benefited from this "fidelity and good conduct," but the individual aristocrats did not fare too badly either.

The End of the Aristocracy

Dukedoms may be abolished by the year 2000—we pretend to no opinion on that point—perhaps no man save John Stuart Mill could give us even a reasonable prophecy: but of this we feel assured, that if they are not abolished an English Dukedom will in that year be a prize beyond all social compare—a prize such as the

Throne is now—a position of the ultimate goal of all that is great, or ambitious or rich among a race which will by that time be ruling directly or indirectly over half the world.

John L. Sanford and Meredith Townsend,
The Great Governing Families of England

Bold as they were in their prediction in 1865, Sanford and Townsend got it all wrong. At the dawn of the twenty-first century, a dukedom was still a matter of inheritance and elitism, but it had long since diminished as a prize above all others; English dukes no longer rule anyone, let alone half of the world. Yet, at the time of their writing, the future of the aristocracy could hardly have been predicted otherwise. Around the middle of the nineteenth century, the aristocracy was, by most accounts, an elite without comparison. Approximately 7,000 families owned about four-fifths of the land in the British Isles. After three centuries of wealth accumulation, the top 250 pre-modern aristocratic families had estates and treasures virtually without comparison anywhere in the world. Even today, the remnants of their estates are amazing to behold. Their social status was intact and alone. They dominated the church, the judiciary, the army, the law, the civil service, the House of Commons, and of course the House of Lords. By any measure, the aristocracy were an elite in terms of status, power, and wealth . . . just as they had been from about 1550.

Nevertheless, by 1890, the world had changed for aristocrats. Various acts of Parliament had transferred rights from them to commoners and restricted their ability to legally distinguish themselves. The Settled Land Acts (1882–1890) removed the strict family settlement clauses and freed landowners from the restrictions on sale. The County Councils Act of 1888 replaced justices of the peace with elected councillors. The Reform Acts of 1864 and 1867 and the Ballot Act of 1872 allowed Parliament to be dominated by commoners by extending the voting franchise and shifting seats from rural to urban centers. And the Parliament Act of 1911 denied the House of Lords the full right to sanction legislation by taking away its veto powers. These acts, however, reflected a reality that had begun slowly and earlier in the century, when industrialists and the rising middle class began to challenge the status and power base of the aristocracy.[89] Non-nobles began to match aristocratic wealth levels by mid-century and, by 1914, were easily surpassing them. Some industrialists even started to enter into the aristocratic class through the backdoor of purchased titles, estates, and mimicked behavior.

After three centuries of stable dominance, the dramatic decline of the aristocracy in Britain was revolutionary—yet peaceful. Certainly revolts and riots had occurred during the nineteenth century, just as they had in every pre-modern century; by "peaceful" is not meant "harmonious." But Britain did avoid a bloody revolution in the transition from the pre-modern to the modern world, and those who held aristocratic offices were compensated when they gave them up. By the early twentieth century, nearly two-thirds of the aristocratic estates had changed hands after three centuries of monumental legal, social, and political efforts to keep them together.[90] At the midpoint of the nineteenth century, the landed class controlled the voting for parliamentary seats. By 1918, the Fourth Reform Act enacted universal male suffrage, and the landless and working class became the majority of voters. Cannadine places the last nail in the political coffin in 1911: "But it was 1911 that had been the great turning point. At the behest of Lloyd George, the people's trumpet had sounded, and though the blast had been a little uncertain, the citadel of patrician pre-eminence had finally fallen. Symbolically, and substantively, the political power of traditional landed society had been broken for good."[91]

Ironically, the Reform Acts, which brought about this change, were passed by the patrician House of Commons and ratified by the Lords of the upper house. Furthermore, the landed gentry voluntarily sold the vast majority of their estates, creating the largest block of land transfers since the monastic dissolutions that had taken place at the dawning of their reign. In the years surrounding the First World War alone, almost one-third of the land in England was sold by aristocrats.[92] Along with the selling of land came the destruction of the lavish country seats and palatial town homes. The years between 1870 and 1939 saw the destruction of 300 British mansions.[93] That homes were actually torn down or sold to the National Trust is strong evidence of how inefficient they were to live in. The general patronage of the arts ceased, and large collections were broken up. The introduction of open competition into the civil service, ecclesiastical patronage, and the law ended the aristocratic dominance of the professions. The number of titles and honors increased, and recipients were from all classes. It became a common practice for wealthy men to "purchase" titles through strategic donations and to intermarry with aristocrats—even the twentieth century Winston Churchill was the by-product of such a cross-social union. By every account and all margins, the aristocracy left the center of power within a period of seventy years.

The quick decline of the aristocracy is well documented. The question here is: why did the last quarter of the nineteenth century see the breakup of estates, the establishment of bureaucracies in county governments, the removal of patricians from the House of Commons, the development of a professional army, and the dilution of high society? That the aristocrats dismantled this system on their own presents an additional puzzle. There were social forces from commoners and the bourgeoisie, but in the end the aristocrats voluntarily let go. The answer does not lie in falling land values, the introduction of American wheat, Corn Laws, Marxian revolts, or extended voting rights. These were all outcomes of deeper changes. The answer can be found in the underlying fundamental changes to measurement of goods and services brought about by the Industrial Revolution. Approximately between 1750 and 1850, a radical change in the variability of the world took place. Aspects of life became more certain and more meaningful to measure. The increased standardization, brought about by the many innovations of the Industrial Revolution, caused a significant fall in the variance of production outcomes. This fall in variance allowed workers to be monitored directly through observation, measurement of hours, or performance. The effects of measurement filtered through the entire economy—including the civil service. In particular, having pocket watches and using standard units of time allowed for payment to workers in the form of wages, and the effects were felt everywhere.

These effects were felt deeply in the offices of the state. By 1871, the civil service began staffing based on exam performance, professional standards, and input monitoring, which were too costly before the age of detailed measurement. Everything from road and sewer construction to port management was transformed into some type of public service staffed by wage workers. As a result, the role of trust as the foundational building block of public service was eroded. The removal of trust as the basis of appointment meant that the social institution designed to generate that trust was no longer needed. For three centuries political power, social status, and wealth had virtually gone hand in hand because status was a necessary condition for trustworthy political service, which lead to wealth creation. The increased measurement of performance during the nineteenth century put an end to this linkage. Things did not change over night—with institutions they seldom do. However, throughout the course of the nineteenth century, aristocratic offices were replaced or were terminated. By 1911, with the removal of the lord's right to sanction legislation, political power, social status, and wealth were no longer necessarily intertwined.

The best evidence for this claim lies in the peaceful and voluntary nature of the transition—the end of the aristocracy did not mean the end of aristocrats. The aristocratic lifestyle was expensive. The posting of hostage capital was costly and the use of amateur staff meant lost output from reduced specialization. This system worked while trust was so important, but when measurement could substitute for trust, other forms of organization dominated. Hence in the fifty years spanning from 1875 to 1925, aristocrats generally sold out, not because they were on the wrong end of a gun, but because it made them financially better off. There was little point in engaging in such a costly lifestyle when the benefits of hostage capital no longer existed. It is not uncommon to hear tales of aristocratic families still clinging, in their "poverty," to the old ways, like buggy makers who ignored the invention of the automobile. The reality was that most aristocrats moved on.

Cannadine goes through a number of cases where aristocratic incomes were higher after estates were broken up, sold, and the proceeds invested.[94] As an example, consider the Grosvenor family. The family made a significant move into the lower levels of the aristocracy in 1584 when Sir Richard Grosvenor became the 1st Baronet of Eaton. In 1677, Sir Richard's grandson, Thomas, married Mary Davies, who just happened to own 500 acres of land north of the Thames River, just west of London. In 1731, another Richard became the 1st Earl Grosvenor; in 1767, Robert Grosvenor became the 1st Marquess of Westminster; and finally the climb to the top of the peerage was completed in 1874 when Hugh Grosvenor became the 1st Duke of Westminster, just shy of 300 years from the first title. Although the family had started to develop the property in London in the eighteenth century, after the removal of aristocratic privileges and constraints, the family became a major modern international property development company. Their landholdings are spread across the world, and the current Duke of Westminster is one of the wealthiest men in the United Kingdom. Although their early country home at Eaton Hall was one of the largest and most expensive country homes ever built, the building was torn down and replaced by a much smaller home—the Long Room, which can hold only 150 people! The Grosvenors have done all right since they "lost" their pre-modern privileges and obligations.

CONCLUSION

Cannon puts the puzzle together well: "It is not easy to see how the elevation to the peerage of . . . [list of names] . . . contributed to that self sustaining economic growth . . . We are not, after all, dealing with the elevation of captains of industry . . . but with persons who . . . owed their peerages to years of tactful service at court, to sound voting in the House of Commons, or to the possession of borourgh interests."[95] How could this group, known for its extravagant and foolish lifestyle, be a part of the rise of British supremacy in the pre-modern era? The answer is that they provided a very valuable service, and the institutional detail of their group, which looks as complicated as rocket science on the surface, provided the signals of this good service.

As western Europe emerged from the feudal system, the opportunities for wealth creation through trade, exploration, and production grew as well. In order to exploit these opportunities, nations required a strong rule of law and the ability to protect the rights of citizens. In modern times, our ability to monitor service performance allowed for the development of bureaucratic institutions. However, prior to the Industrial Revolution, such measurement was not possible. The solution in Europe was found in granting governing rights to an elite group able to commit to trusting behavior by posting significant levels of hostage capital. This elite group comprised those individuals we have come to call "the aristocracy." The correlation is positive: Britain, by becoming the most aristocratic of all societies, also became the wealthiest and most powerful.

CHAPTER FOUR

A Matter of Honor

In a state of highly polished society, an affront is held to be a serious injury. It must, therefore, be resented, or rather a duel must be fought upon it; as men have agreed to banish from their society one who puts up with an affront without fighting a duel.

SAMUEL JOHNSON, QUOTED IN JAMES BOSWELL, *Life of Johnson*

No pre-modern institution is as bewildering as aristocratic dueling.[1] Consider the famous dueling episode between the Duke of Wellington and the Earl of Winchilsea. In 1829 the duke indirectly offended the staunchly anti-Catholic earl by helping to bring about the passage of the Roman Catholic Relief Bill, which allowed Catholics to sit in Parliament. Later, when the duke became the patron of (Protestant) King's College, London, the earl saw an opportunity to point out what he considered a religious inconsistency, by suggesting in writing that the duke was acting under the "cloak of some outward show of zeal for the Protestant religion" in order that he might bring about the "introduction of Popery into every department of the state."[2] The letter eventually reached the press and the duke sought a public withdrawal and apology for the suggestion that his intentions were anything other than honorable. The earl refused, and so the duke demanded "satisfaction" in the form of a duel. Winchilsea agreed, stating "the satisfaction which your Grace has demanded, it is of course impossible for me to decline." A pistol duel took place the next morning. Both parties missed, and the earl immediately produced a letter of apology.

It is an incredible story. For starters, the ground for the duel was trivial. Why should either man put his life on the line because one suggested Catholic sympathies of the other? After all, the Jacobite rebellion, the last serious Catholic challenge to Protestant dominance in England, had occurred almost 100 years before this incident; there was no serious Catholic threat. The duke's response to settle a "point of honor" with pistols seems to be an overreaction. Given that an offense had been made, could some other resolution not have been found? Perhaps a defamation suit in a court of law? To make matters more curious, the earl's reply of "no choice but to accept" comes across as simply unbelievable. He could have backed down, reasoned with the duke, or issued the earlier requested retraction. The final aspect of this case, which seems entirely inconsistent with the other details, is the immediate production of a prepared apology by the earl after the duel. If he was going to apologize, why not do so before shots were fired? Why not apologize when the duke demanded it to begin with? As incredible and unlikely as these facts appear, they characterized most duels of honor.

The institution of the pre-modern aristocracy was characterized by a system of rules, expectations, social norms, and other constraints on landholdings, social behaviors, education patterns, and specific occupations. These all worked together to produce a regularity of "fidelity and good conduct" in the behaviors of this class. But the capstone feature of aristocratic life was the concept of honor. Honor and nobility went hand in hand and summarized the aristocratic lifestyle and values. It was expected that an aristocrat would be willing to defend his honor to the point of death, even over a minor slight of character. More specifically, death was to occur not in some random fashion but through a duel. The duel, more than any other aristocratic habit, has been mocked to the point of comedy. Everything about it invites ridicule, and it is antithetical to modern secular and historical religious values. Why would this practice have arisen and been maintained by the ruling elite?

Honor to the aristocrats meant that they were seen as honest, fair men of integrity, and men of their word. Having honor meant that they were trustworthy in environments where they were not directly measured. Thus "honor" was a word for another specific type of hostage capital investment made by the wealthy to become aristocrats. Because of the importance of honor, dueling was intimately related to the role of trust and hostage capital.

As previously discussed, aristocrats could be trusted because they stood to lose more by acting in their own private interests than by being trustworthy. For the average well-to-do aristocrat, trust was enforced through physical investments in the family settlement, wasteful parks, homes, and port. However, these forms of investments had several drawbacks. First, lower and younger gentry trying to move up in society generally had little in the way of physical capital to invest in visible forms of hostage capital. Often, when an aristocrat held a patronage office, the threat of losing the high stream of earnings could be enough to encourage good behavior, but a lower aristocrat may not have an office. If trust was only generated from investing a given stock of existing physical capital in sunk assets, then entry into the bottom of the gentry pool would have been almost impossible for many marginally wealthy newcomers because they would have been unable to demonstrate that they were trustworthy. Second, all investments in hostage capital could be "staged" or "faked" to some extent. Perhaps the aristocrat did not completely remove himself from past business and trade, perhaps the strict family settlement was not that strict, or perhaps less was invested than was suggested. Finally, hostage capital can depreciate, and over time it can cease to act as a bond for good performance. Latin and dance skills become forgotten over time if not maintained, parks and houses deteriorate without proper upkeep, and personal relationships lose meaning over time if not nurtured and remembered. As a result, an aristocrat had to reinvest in such capital, and this reinvestment was difficult to observe. The duel of honor was designed to handle the problem of difficult-to-observe hostage capital investments, and it was the ultimate social weapon intended to test the trustworthiness of lower-gentry members trying to move up the social ladder.

In the pre-modern era, aristocrats essentially demanded a complete commitment to the cause of trust. Not only was physical capital to be held hostage, but one's entire life was to be given over to the aristocratic community. One was expected to marry into the elite circle; go to school, parties, and the theater together; and enjoy the London season—the glorious series of debutante balls, charity events, and dinner parties in London that ran from Easter to the start of the red grouse shooting season in summer—with other members of the aristocracy. Nor was merely "showing up" sufficient. Aristocrats were expected to be well invested in quality relations with each other. These social commitments were another form of hostage capital, and they will here be called "hostage social capital" or just "social capital." Aristocrats essentially invested time in their social network. As long as others recognized these investments, they could be members of the administrative elite and earn a profitable income on their investments. If the other members ignored the social investments, they were worth nothing. Although the social investments were not physical, they were still costly and sunk. Like physical capital, social investments acted as a hostage for trustworthy performance. An investment in hostage social capital meant that one's word became a bond and one's reputation was as good as a coin of the realm. In this sense, hostage social capital gives economic meaning to the term "honor."

The problem with social capital—or honor—was that it was not directly observable. If one's reputation for social capital was crucial to one's standing in the community, it was critical for everyone to know whether or not it existed. Enter the duel. The duel was a way to make sure members of the aristocracy had invested in unobservable hostage social capital for the group. Failing to participate in a duel indicated that one was not trustworthy because aristocrats equated unwillingness to uphold one's honor in this way with a lack of social capital. Although dueling was costly, it was productive in this screening way. Dueling helped the aristocratic class filter out low social-capital individuals who were interacting among them—pretenders, much like the fictional wicked Mr. Wickham of Jane Austen's *Pride and Prejudice*. In a world where trust substituted for direct measurement of performance of duty, the duel was designed to keep pretenders out. Perhaps the concept of dueling as a social filter is an outrageous hypothesis, but its ability to explain the details of dueling—that are unexplained by other theories that inevitably portray dueling as inefficient, irrational, and barbaric—provides support for the institutional theory of aristocrats.

DUELING: A BRIEF HISTORY

The "duel of honor" was a pre-modern institutional innovation, and its life cycle spanned the entire pre-modern era. It began around 1500, peaked in the 1600s, and lasted in some places until the First World War. Dueling itself has a long history; around the turn of the first millennium, it took the form of the "judicial duel" or "trial by combat." These duels decided matters of justice with the belief that God would prevail for the righteous. The loser of such a duel, if not killed, would often suffer additional consequences such as the removal of a hand or hanging, depending on the offense. Although the judicial duel lingered on the law books until the nineteenth century, it was not generally practiced by the end of the sixteenth century. The other form of dueling in the Middle Ages was the "duel of chivalry" between knights and other nobles conducted as sport. These duels often took place on horseback, and used lances and spears as weapons. The fading of feudalism marked the end of the chivalrous duel, with the last English example in 1492 and the last French example in 1547. Both of these types of duels were held in public and served an immediate purpose to create judgment or entertainment. The duel of honor, on the other hand, arose with the pre-modern aristocrats, and it lasted until they surrendered their power at the turn of the twentieth century.

The duel of honor had several characteristics. One of the most interesting was the often trivial nature of the causes of the duel. Duels were fought over an insult, a slap to the face, a slur on reputation, "coolness of manner," or—most serious of all—an accusation of lying.[3] Any suggestion that another member of the aristocracy was not telling the truth automatically triggered a duel between the parties. By modern standards, the response to insults appears to be an overreaction. But dueling is stranger still. After a duel, both parties continued to maintain their social standing within the aristocratic community, regardless of the outcome. The winner of a duel remained an aristocrat, but the loser's status remained intact as well. More bizarre, one of the most common outcomes of a duel was a reconciliation between the combatants—just as in the case of Winchilsea and Wellington. Many a case existed where a dying man would claim his "love for his brother" who had just inflicted the fatal wound. On the other hand, failure to accept or carry out a legitimate duel meant a banishment from aristocratic circles.

When dueling first came into fashion it was very lethal, but this lethality fell over time. A duel was lost when one party received an injury of some predetermined level (as in first blood), when a certain number of predetermined actions had taken place (as in the number of shots fired), or when one party was killed. Of course, these outcomes were not necessarily linked to who initiated the duel or committed the offense. Although dueling was generally illegal and the punishments were often severe, duelists were seldom brought to court, rarely convicted and, if convicted, likely pardoned. Among the aristocracy, penalties for dueling usually only occurred if there were evidence the duel was not fair or did not follow a conventional code of conduct.[4] On the contrary, commoners caught dueling would be charged with either murder or attempted murder and would be dealt with harshly and quickly. It is not too surprising that duels were regulated by strict rules. These rules were developed by the aristocrats themselves and were common knowledge among them.

Weapons in the duel of honor were restricted to a subset of lethal weapons. Early duels were fought with a rapier and dagger. The rapier was a heavy, inflexible straight sword used for stabbing; the dagger was used to parry thrusts from the opponent. Soon all defensive weapons such as shields, helmets, and armor were eliminated, and even the dagger was dropped as an allowable weapon. Eventually the rapier was replaced with the lighter, more flexible épée, and duels became much quicker affairs. In various regions, the épée remained the weapon of choice but, in the eighteenth century, the saber was introduced. This was a slashing weapon, and although it could cause much damage, was generally not as lethal as the épée. Finally, dueling with pistols was introduced in the late eighteenth century and replaced most fencing duels.

Duels of honor were a European invention. Starting in Italy, dueling quickly spread to France, what is now Germany, and the rest of Europe and even had a brief history in Canada, Mexico, and the United States. It ended first in the northern European countries by the late eighteenth century, then in England in the first half of the nineteenth century, in the United States by the Civil War, and finally in France and Germany by the First World War. Dueling was the sole domain of the ruling aristocratic class until the late nineteenth century, whereupon upper-middle-class professionals also began to duel.

Given the bizarre nature of dueling, it is not too surprising to find that it has mostly been considered the classic example of irrational male aggression. According to some social historians, males are inherently violent, and dueling is simply its manifestation when society becomes civilized.[5] Dueling is often viewed as a substitute for war, providing a release for aggression: for example, Nye claims that "the duel was still, as it had always been, an occasion to publicly demonstrate the personal courage that testified to the qualities of a man."[6] There were, however, many substitutes for dueling to demonstrate courage, including service in the military.

In contrast, legal scholars have viewed dueling as a social norm substituting for legal proceedings in a court of law. As a result, most conclude it eventually became an inefficient, or even irrational, replacement for traditional courts. When viewed as a court substitute, dueling appears to be a particularly inefficient social norm since the metaphor fits so badly. Lessig, quite dramatically, points out how silly a duel would suffice as a court replacement:

> The duel was like a lawsuit where the judge, after establishing that indeed there was a wrong, flips a coin to decide who, between the plaintiff and the defendant, should be executed for the wrong. . . . No doubt then, the duel often misfired, either because the challenge itself was wrongful and the challenged suffered death, or because the challenge itself was correct

but the challenger suffered death. . . . To us, certain features are clearly ridiculous: the practice is random, it strikes down some of the community's most valuable citizens, and its sanction is not proportional to its harm.[7]

Different legal scholars give different reasons for the rise of dueling as a court substitute: courts were too costly, the offenses were too trivial, courts were simply unwilling to deal with issues of honor, or dueling prevented disputes from becoming feuds between larger groups.[8] Despite these theories, the legal interpretation of dueling is grossly lacking. If dueling were some type of court substitute, then it must always have been an inefficient method of settling disagreements because the state is better at settling disputes and avoiding serial violence than private individuals. It is hard to understand how an inefficient norm such as dueling could survive for so long. More to the point, dueling was restricted to the aristocracy, and yet this group always had access to courts—even special courts for settling matters of honor! If dueling were a court substitute, then the aristocracy should have avoided it and used courts instead. Commoners should have dueled. Neither the social-historical nor legal theories of dueling provide a satisfactory explanation of dueling's existence, and neither theory even tries to explain the institutional details.

On the contrary, dueling is easily understood when placed within the context of the chief economic problem facing the Crown and other aristocrats during the pre-modern period: how could any patron trust his servant? Understanding dueling begins by understanding why aristocrats existed in the first place: they were there to provide trustworthy service to the Crown in an age when measurement of performance was unreliable. Dueling was part of this system, and its puzzling features were not based on culture, gender, or court substitution. Rather, the duel was used to separate individuals into those who had legitimately invested socially into the aristocratic group and those pretenders who had not invested and were out to cheat the others. For the lower gentry, only those who passed the dueling test could be trusted and allowed to enter or to remain in the world of political exchanges among the small ruling class.

PATRONAGE, SOCIAL CAPITAL, AND THE DUELING TEST

Recall that governments during the pre-modern era were staffed by aristocrats, and senior appointments were made primarily on the basis of patronage—no advertising for positions, no examination, no interview, and no requirement for professional qualifications. From today's vantage, it all rings of corruption and nepotism, but it was a method of promotion from within a given class based on hostage capital. For lower aristocrats, those gentry at the bottom of the elite pyramid, investments in hostage social capital allowed them access to these positions of power for which they otherwise lacked the standard physical hostage capital.

The difference between physical hostage capital and social hostage capital was mostly in the latter's reliance on other people. How one was perceived by others was central to one's standing, which was why protocol and manners, along with dress and schools, were so instrumental. Social capital required the cooperation and recognition of others in the group for it to be useful. If others failed to acknowledge one's social capital, it was of no value. As such, it was not transferable to other levels of society and therefore investments in it were sunk. Investments in social capital worked in a similar fashion as sunk physical capital investments (such as parks and seats) to generate trust to facilitate trade. Having invested in social capital, any gentry on the lower rungs found lacking in some way, either through unacceptable behavior or political practices, could be punished with ostracism that destroyed the value of their social capital. Such a punishment was severe because an aristocrat's entire social life, business connections, and persona were based on inclusion within the aristocratic group. To be a social outcast in an aristocratic society rendered all one's stock of social capital worthless. Thus as long as the level of social capital was high enough, members of the lower aristocracy were trustworthy because any gains from cheating were necessarily lower than the lost investment in hostage social capital.

Everyone in pre-modern society was born with a different level of social capital, which was usually observable. Some were born to dukes, others to paupers, and everyone saw the difference. However, anyone could also make costly changes in their social standing. These investments came from attending and participating in the same schools, social events, clubs, and churches. They also came from marriage, business connections, and family history. It is important to note that although the initial level of social capital was observable, the investments were generally unobservable to others. Although attending schools and churches could be seen, the actual social capital created was often difficult to observe because it depended on the quality of the interpersonal associations that took place. The quality of a personal relationship was hard to measure because the association might have been occasional or knowledge of all social interactions a potential aristocrat was involved in may have been difficult to obtain. For example, members of the aristocracy may have known if someone attended a social event, but they could not tell if quality personal connections were made.

Thus, on the one hand, social capital had a strong "hostage" characteristic, making it a valuable tool for generating trust. If the social capital investments had been observable, like sunk investments in a large estate or garden, members of the society could easily have recognized who had made the appropriate investments, and that would have been the end of the story. But, on the other hand, the social capital investments were unobservable, and this made the final level of social capital also unobservable. This led to a serious problem. The inability to know if a lower gentry actually possessed enough social capital unfortunately meant that pretenders could claim they possessed "honor" or hostage social capital. To "pretend," in this context, meant a commoner would seek to enter the aristocracy under the pretense he had the necessary hostage social capital by investing in only outward appearances. This, however, did not make them trustworthy. Indeed, their lack of social capital meant they were untrustworthy. Having untrustworthy types in civil offices meant that the wealth of these offices was lowered to everyone. The pre-modern aristocracy therefore needed some type of institutional tool to determine if an individual claiming to be a gentleman actually possessed the right stuff to be trusted.

The duel of honor provided a solution. It was an acid test to determine social capital because the first and foremost rule of dueling was that a true gentleman always accepted a legitimate duel. Exploiting this rule, the duel was designed to screen for a critical level of social capital among the gentry seeking patronage appointments.[9] An individual who lacked hostage social capital would surmise that the costs of dueling exceeded any benefits and would not duel. Therefore, those individuals who rejected the duel demonstrated that their social capital was too low and they could not be trusted. Alternatively, those individuals who had sufficiently invested in hostage social capital realized that declining a duel meant social banishment and a loss of the hostage social capital. This loss was worse than the prospect of dueling. Frevert puts this nicely: "To be regarded as a coward for avoiding a duel equaled expulsion from society, a social death sentence, to which possible death in a duel was obviously preferable."[10] Thus, those who accepted the duel demonstrated sufficient social capital and were allowed to participate in aristocratic exchanges. In this fashion, the duel was an institutional support for patronage appointments among lower gentry who lacked large amounts of physical wealth but possessed unobservable social capital.

Dueling had two major institutional details, or "parameters," that could be adjusted. The first was the cost of investing in social capital in order to move up the social ladder. It was a matter of aristocratic custom as to what had to be done to be accepted: those born to dukes had to do nothing, whereas those born to small gentleman landholders would be expected to invest great amounts of time in social capital. The decision whether or not to invest depended on how close one was to becoming accepted. Those who were born with slightly too little social capital found it in their interest to invest and join the lower gentry. Others born with much less social capital would find the cost of investing too high and would not invest. This process regarding whether or not to invest ultimately determined the size of the aristocracy.

The second institutional parameter was the chance of dying in the duel. If an individual entered a duel and lived, then he could remain in the aristocratic society and reap the rewards. Of course, if he died, he received nothing . . . at least in the natural world.[11] The chance of dying was determined by the type of weapon, the rules deployed, the skills of the opponent, and luck. Together the cost of social capital and the chance of dying determined the incentives of any individual to enter a duel or not.

In order for the duel to work as an effective screen, these incentives had to be just right. First, the gains from dueling and being trustworthy had to exceed the gains from dueling and cheating. In other words, only those who actually accepted a duel had incentives to be honest and trustworthy. Second, any pretenders had to find the duel unacceptable and therefore had to reject any duel that came their way. Thus those who rejected a duel showed they lacked social capital and therefore did not deserve the trust of others. The conditions for dueling were a balancing act. On the one hand, if the probability of dying in a duel were too low, individuals were likely to pretend they had sufficient social capital. On the other hand, if the probability of death were too high, then it never paid to invest in social capital, and the aristocracy would have been too small. Thus the dueling rules balanced these two forces to determine the optimal lethality of the duel.

It is interesting that, even if the dueling conditions were chosen correctly, commoners might still find it in their interests to duel. For any given commoner might just happen to be a skilled duelist, might want to settle a score with an opponent, might enjoy the act of dueling, or might be staging a duel in order to become a pretend aristocrat. Whatever the reason, a commoner dueling only watered down the duel's role as a screening institution. However, a trivial solution to this problem existed. Because real aristocrats invested in their social capital, there ended up a large social gulf between commoners and aristocrats. This gulf, along with the fact that initial levels of social capital were observable, meant that the problem of commoners dueling was avoided by not allowing those born with low social capital levels to duel in the first place. Everyone knew who the commoners were, and it was easy to identify them when they dueled.

Furthermore, the duel was not designed to assist in policing ordinary business transactions, where trades could be enforced through reputations, contracts, courts, or direct monitoring. Indeed, it was not even meant to be used to police the large and important offices of the state, where sunk physical investments in land and lifestyle were observable and effective. Instead, it was a simple test used to select lower gentry who were investing in unobservable social capital as a means of gaining access to positions of the state during the age of patronage. The duel was designed to be difficult to fake, easy to verify, and unenjoyable in and of itself. Exposure to dueling continued throughout one's life because any given duel could be faked, and the threat of future duels virtually eliminated the incentive to stage a duel.

An interesting implication of the ability to change one's hostage social capital is that, ex post, there were two general types of social capital in society. One type was that of commoners born at a lowly level who did not attend the best schools, learn complicated dance steps, acquire proper manners, or develop the host of other social capital skills held by the aristocracy. The other type was that of the lowly gentry, who at birth might be similar to commoners but who found it in their interests to invest in such talents. After investment, the gentry were much different from their commoner cousins. As a result, a large social gulf between commoners and aristocrats evolved.

DUELING DEMYSTIFIED

Several explanations for dueling have been given, but few of them are consistent with the facts, changes, and quirks of dueling. It is not hard to imagine that aristocrats were servants who could be trusted because of their investments in hostage capital and that the duel was used to filter those who had legitimately made the investment. However, to put this theory to the test, we must ask the question: does this theory explain the details of dueling?

Limits on Participation

Individuals born with observable social capital well above the threshold level necessary to participate within the elite should not be expected to duel, even though some of them dueled on occasion. At the other extreme, because individuals way down the social ladder did not receive sufficient rewards to motivate them to invest, these individuals should be barred from participating. Low social-capital individuals may want to duel for the wrong reasons, but in all cases, allowing these individuals to duel destroyed the purpose of the duel—to sift for trustworthy members of the lower gentry. Low social-capital individuals who dueled imposed social costs with no offsetting social benefits and should have been barred from the practice. Dueling is predicted, therefore, among the members of the lower gentry.

The predicted limits on participation are consistent with the historical facts. Several classes of individuals were not allowed to duel, nor were they allowed to be challenged. Royal family members, for example, were excluded from dueling, and high nobility were often prevented from it. Courts of honor—where a tribunal of noblemen would decide on a grievance of honor—were established for higher nobility to avoid duels, and monarchs often intervened to prevent duels among important and high-ranking nobility.[12] No such actions were taken for lower-level aristocrats.[13] Higher-level aristocrats did not need to prove their honor and trustworthiness, as they had considerable sunk physical investments and observable high birth. Challenges from those beneath them were a social waste. In addition, during times of war and especially during battles, military officers were not allowed to duel. Officers were not allowed to duel with officers of a higher rank. Commercial classes, merchants, bankers, and the like were not allowed to duel. Many of these people were wealthy enough to enter the aristocracy, but they were unwilling to make the necessary investments in hostage capital. This unwillingness meant that they never qualified for patronage and therefore were never allowed to duel.

Another group that was prohibited from dueling were the Jews. King Edward I had expelled the Jews from England in 1290, and they were not allowed to legally return until 1656—in the first half of the pre-modern era. Mistreatment continued and, as a general rule, Jews were excluded from political appointments, though exceptions are found. Given that they were not candidates for patronage, it is consistent that they would be ruled out of duel participation. Finally, another class of individuals who, although not barred from dueling, virtually never dueled: women. Although records of female duels can be found, the numbers were trivial. Their lack of dueling resulted from their lack of participation in civil administration.

All told, most dueling took place among the lower levels of the ruling aristocracy. The duel was designed for individuals such as John Churchill of the late 1600s. Born to a poor squire, he entered the household of the Duke of York as a simple page. Churchill's life was an example of constant investment in social capital through critical personal relationships. Along the way to becoming the Duke of Marlborough, he fought at least two duels to demonstrate this investment. Once a duke, there were no further duels. Which explains why, when, on rare occasions, extremely important individuals found themselves in duels, the social reaction was quite negative. Individuals who were not marginal aristocrats seldom dueled, and were not expected to duel—although some still did. After all, the actual duel was a private, quasi-secret affair (more on this topic later in this chapter), and any two individuals could arrange for a duel, regardless of rank. For example, the infamous Wellington-Winchilsea duel, described at this chapter's opening, was not a duel entered into when the two men were young and members of minor gentry families. Wellington was an old man and had long been a member of the aristocracy. The reaction to the duel among the monarch, government, and other aristocrats was, as it should have been: swift and negative.[14] It made no sense for those who were fully invested in aristocratic institutions to engage in dueling to show their trustworthiness.

The lowest members of European society were prevented from dueling by making dueling illegal for everyone but allowing aristocrats the privilege of dueling without concern over arrest. At first glance, it appears ironic and hypocritical that those making anti-dueling laws were the very individuals most active in dueling. Indeed, many writers on dueling find the practice of dueling among legislators incongruent with laws banning the practice.[15] However, this puzzle disappears when dueling prohibitions are viewed as part of a mechanism to screen for trustworthy lawmakers. Since the aristocrats were the lawmakers, they were also the duelers.

This important point distinguishes legal theories of dueling from the trust hypothesis. Most legal writings on dueling argue the state actually wanted to eliminate dueling through the use of legal sanctions and that the antidueling laws were ultimately successful in changing social norms and eliminating the practice. Several problems with this theory disappear with the trust hypothesis. First, dueling was always illegal, and yet it lasted for centuries. Second, the antidueling laws were enforced and effective—lower-class individuals were barred from dueling. Finally, when dueling ended it was not replaced by law but by a meritocracy. Dueling ended when the aristocratic patronage system ended, not because it was illegal.[16]

The Cause, the Challenge, and the Consequence of Duels

A most puzzling observation about dueling was that the ground for the duel, who was the challenger or challenged, and the outcome were all irrelevant to social standing. It mattered not a whit if the duel resulted from an irreverent glance or a public accusation of lying; if the one slighted or the slighter made the actual challenge; nor if the "victim" of the affront won or lost. All of which is most strange and yet is an implication of the trust theory of dueling. The importance of the duel was its function as a filter, and participants—either as the challenger or the challenged, whether they won or lost—demonstrated they had invested in social capital and could be trusted.[17] They had honor. End of story.

The historical record contains strong evidence in support of this theory. Unlike earlier judicial duels fought over capital crimes, duels of honor were fought over any slight against one's character, family, or reputation. Duels were fought over minor insults, mere suggestions of improper conduct, or some other slight that had no relationship to one's honesty. McAleer, writing on dueling in Germany, noted that virtually all duels were the result of either impoliteness, such as cursing or attribution of shameful qualities, or touching another's person.[18] Within these broad categories, a virtually limitless number of grounds for a duel existed; the historical record shows that duels were fought over trivial slights as well as issues of great slander.

Not only were the dueling grounds irrelevant but who initiated or became the victor was irrelevant in a duel. No social advantage was gained by challenging or by winning: "the restoration of honor did not depend on the outcome of the confrontation. Ideally, a well-fought duel reconciled the two adversaries, reestablished mutual respect, and 'cleansed' the stain caused by the original insult."[19] Indeed, one of the great ironies of dueling—but an implication of its role as a screen for trustworthy people—was the subsequent renewal of friendships among adversaries. Histories of individual duels are replete with such stories. Samuel Pepys's diary contains references to at least thirteen duels. One is a duel between Tom Porter and a Mr. Bellasses. Porter makes a fatal wound and Pepys records the following: "he [Mr. Bellasses] called T. Porter and kissed him and bade him shift for himself: 'For Tom, thou hast hurt me . . . I would not have thee troubled for what thou has done.'" Then Pepys notes "both of them most extraordinary friends."[20]

Social historians have considered trivial grounds for duels as evidence of dueling's irrationality or manifestation of inherent male violence. Kiernan, in one of the most comprehensive studies, states: "The triviality of many disputes, which satire could scarcely exaggerate, and the willingness of so many men, young men in particular, to risk death, maiming, or exile, on the spur of the moment, suggest an infantile mentality, minds incapable of serious thought, and reacting to any stimulus like automata."[21] Similarly, legal theorists often point to the use of deadly force in the face of trivial infractions as evidence of inefficiency. On the contrary, these were the characteristics of an efficient method to sort through trustworthy people.

Making Death Random: The Code Duello

If dueling acted as a filter for hostage social capital where the willingness to participate was what mattered most, then it was critical that the probability of death be beyond the control of the participants. A random outcome was essential for dueling to work, even though this stands in contrast to modern legal views, which see random outcomes of trials as inefficient. When duelists could alter the probability of a fatality, then they invested in skills that altered the probabilities in their favor. Hence a good marksman or a good fencer might find a given duel acceptable simply because he stood a good chance of winning and not because he had made the necessary sunk investment in social capital. Thus, if a participant could swing the odds of victory largely in his favor, then he would accept duels or issue challenges even though an insufficient investment in social capital had been made. From a social point of view, such investments raised the cost of dueling because they led to an "arms race" where all duelists overinvested in talents to increase their odds of winning. In the language of dueling, a "level playing field" was required, meaning the outcome was to be random.

An important method of achieving randomness was through adherence to the dueling rules. Many sets of rules were established, and the first widely popular set was published in Venice in 1550 by Girolamo Muzio. In these early rules, several features were common and long lasting throughout the dueling period: seconds must be present; deadly weapons must be used; generally, the challenged was allowed the choice of weapon and other, but not all, features of the duel that influenced lethality; and the duel was to take place without delay, usually the next morning. The Code Duello was a set of rules drawn up by Irish gentlemen delegates at Clonmel Summer Assizes in 1777. Although the Code Duello was prescribed for use in Ireland, it was generally followed in England, the Continent, and America, with small variations throughout the nineteenth century; in fact, the rules were called "The Twenty-Six Commandments." These rules delineated the rights of the challenged and challenger, grounds for terminating the duel, rules for conducting the duel, and the rights and obligations of the seconds. Many of these rules contributed to taking the probability of death out of the direct hands of the duelists.

For example, pistol duels were conducted with inaccurate weapons, and being hit was largely a matter of chance. This randomness was enhanced by several rules:

RULE 17. The challenged chooses his ground; the challenger chooses his distance; the seconds fix the time and terms of firing.

RULE 18. The seconds load in presence of each other . . .

RULE 20. In all cases a miss-fire is equivalent to a shot, and a snap or non-cock is to be considered as a miss-fire.

RULE 22. Any wound sufficient to agitate the nerves and necessarily make the hand shake, must end the business for that day.[22]

The pistol duel was designed to provide a limited number of attempted shots because better marksmen could better calibrate the weapon and gain an advantage with unlimited shooting. The duel also had a set time for shooting and required the seconds to load. An expert with the pistol would have an advantage in correctly and quickly loading his weapon. Rules 17 and 18 eliminated this advantage. Finally, to the extent a better duelist was less likely to become agitated by a wound, Rule

22 worked against him. Other rules developed to randomize events. For example, not only was rifling the barrel (making a spiral groove in the barrel to increase accuracy) not allowed, but dueling pistols had short barrels (reducing accuracy) and aids in aiming (such as aiming beads and sights) were also discouraged or removed. Dueling locations were chosen to avoid trees and other objects that might assist in aiming. It is worth pointing out that the impediments placed on pistols made them inaccurate, not ineffective. Dueling pistols were well crafted, expensive, and maintained. They were expected to work every time. One might think more accurate weapons, leading to fewer costly duels, might be more efficient. However, accurate weapons open the door for training and marksmanship, which diminish the value of the duel as a screen. Hence more accurate weapons would not have been better, even though they were possible.

A series of rules restricted expert duelists or staged duels. For example, consider the following:

> RULE 6. If A gives B the lie [A accuses B of lying], and B retorts by a blow [B slaps A] . . . no reconciliation can take place till after two discharges each, or a severe hit. . . .

> RULE 7. But no apology can be received, in any case, after the parties have actually taken ground, without exchange of fires.

> RULE 13. No dumb shooting or firing in the air is admissible in any case. . . .[23]

Staged duels reduced the effectiveness of the dueling to faithfully filter out trustworthy gentry. Insults could be traded and a duel agreed to that, in actual fact, was theater rather than real. As Rules 6 and 7 state, however, certain events automatically triggered a duel and, once on a field, shots must be fired. Rule 13 states shots must be fired at the opponent. Any attempt to miss on purpose would be caught by the seconds at the duel, and it was their duty to stop the procedure, reprehend the guilty party, and force a new round. Even if shots were directed at non-fatal parts of the body, in an age lacking antibiotics, any wound could kill. Indeed, most deaths from dueling resulted from infections rather than the wound itself. Thus duelists often stripped to the waist—to prevent soiled cloth from entering a wound. All duels required seconds and usually had a doctor and others in attendance. All of these features lowered the chance of fake duels.

Although it varied from time to time, a general theme in dueling rules was to assign rights in favor of the challenged. For example, consider the following:

RULE 15. Challenges are never to be delivered at night, unless the party to be challenged intend leaving the place of offense; before morning; for it is desirable to avoid all hot-headed proceedings.

RULE 16. The challenged has the right to choose his own weapon, unless the challenger gives his honor he is no swordsman . . .[24]

Rule 16 was not always found in earlier rules, but it took away a major advantage of the challenger and leveled the playing field considerably by giving the challenged the advantage of choosing a weapon he preferred. As Rule 17 stated, other rights regarding the ground and the timing of shots were not held by the challenger. Indeed, because challenges could also be provoked, we should not be surprised that rights were also held by the challenger and the seconds. The general thrust of the dueling rules was to create a balanced set of rights on either side. In German dueling codes, for example, the "insulted" party held a complicated set of rights, depending on the level of insult. McAleer notes these rules were designed to prevent "ruffians with strong arms and practiced eyes to go around intentionally picking fights."[25] Rule 15 essentially protected unassuming victims from accepting duels from strategic challenges in the heat of the moment. A final set of rules pertained to the ending of the duel and essentially amounted to "first blood." Duels, especially toward the end of dueling, were usually not fatal. Aside from efforts to make the duel random, the first-blood rules also reduced the chance of death. The rules on limiting shots have already been mentioned, but similar restrictions held true for swords.

RULE 5. . . . If swords are used the parties engage until one is well blooded, disabled, or disarmed; or until, after receiving a wound, and blood being drawn, the aggressor begs pardon. . . .[26]

In fencing duels, gloves were generally not worn, which meant most first wounds were to the armed hand because it was closest to the opponent's blade. The first-blood rule in fencing duels eliminated any advantage one duelist might have because of physical size or strength. Each duelist used an identical weapon so that the opponent's armed hand was the same sword distance away from the other's. This was not true of the opponents' torsos since individuals with longer reaches had an advantage in attacking the body. Other restrictions on sword duels hindered excellent fencers. If a duelist fell down or lost his weapon, the attack was stopped. The use of the free hand was not allowed, nor was a fencer allowed to switch hands.[27] Nonetheless, it was more difficult to level the playing field in fencing duels than in pistol duels, which explains why dueling evolved into pistol competitions.

The Role of Seconds

One of the most important aspects of dueling was the presence of seconds. These men were chosen by the duelists and played a role from the beginning to the end of a duel. All communication and negotiation was done between the seconds, not the duelists. Weapons were inspected and armed (if pistols) by seconds. Social historians often contend the role of seconds was little more than ceremony allowing the aristocracy to view dueling as less barbaric and above the mere brawl of the common man.[28] To legal scholars, dueling substituted for court actions, and thus the role of the second was to act as a mediator and a judge and to prevent the action from escalating in violence. In this view, the second was to act on the behalf of his friend to achieve the best terms.[29]

However, because dueling was actually part of the aristocratic institutions of trust, seconds played three different roles. First, screening or filtering only trustworthy individuals requires the second to prevent strategic duels and to prevent his friend from becoming the victim of an opportunistic, excellent duelist. Second, the second would have indirectly made collusion among duelists to rig a fake duel more difficult. Simply having more individuals involved in a duel makes collusion more difficult, but because a doctor and other notables generally attended duels, seconds were basically forced to carry out the duel rules that raised the cost of collusion. Third, the second was to ensure the odds of dying were as fair as possible. Weapons were to be inspected, guns were to be loaded, conditions such as the placement of the sun, the firmness of the ground, and the location of trees (for aiming) were to be considered. Such inspection could reveal blatant acts of cheating. An interesting example of cheating is found on the cover of Murray's 1984 catalog of Lt. Col. William Orbelo's collection of American dueling pistols. The cover includes a picture of two .60 caliber flintlock pistols. On the inside jacket it states: "Interestingly, one pistol is smooth-bore and the other rifled. In many early dueling codes rifled barrels were illegal, although some gunmakers produced guns with secret rifling, which was invisible at the muzzle."[30] In other words, these pistols were unfair. No doubt such practices and others were not uncommon, and it was a critical job of the second to minimize this type of cheating.

These roles played by seconds explain one confusing observation of second behavior. Sometimes a second refused duels and other times he insisted they take place. The second's role was not to avoid all duels, only those duels that were not legitimate. The legitimacy of the duel and the behavior of the duelist were extremely important. To misbehave in any way could often be as serious as turning down a duel. Pepys alludes to such a situation in one of his many brief comments on duels of his day: "The world says that Mr. Mountagu did carry himself very poorly in the business and hath lost his honour forever with all people in it."[31] Unfortunately, Pepys does not record what Mr. Mountagu did.

Changes in Lethality across Jurisdictions

That dueling was used to sift for appropriate levels of reputation and trustworthiness—hostage social capital—is demonstrated by comparing aristocratic societies on either side of the Atlantic. Aristocratic societies in Europe had higher costs of acquiring social capital than more egalitarian ones in America. Movement through the aristocratic ranks was difficult and slow. Even for those within the upper class, movement took a long time because the system was designed, in part, to select patient people who would not be attracted to short-run gains at the expense of the larger social interest. In egalitarian societies, social status often only depended on a few dimensions—sometimes just wealth. Hence movement from the middle class to the upper class in Europe was considerably more difficult than in the New World. Given that dueling was characterized by two parameters, the cost of acquiring social capital and lethality, and that these parameters had to be in balance to create proper incentives, when the cost of acquiring social capital was higher, dueling was less lethal. As a result, the trust theory predicts dueling should have been more lethal in America than Europe.

At first glance, dueling's existence in America seems inconsistent with the role it played in screening for honor and reputation because the American Revolution had resulted in a republic lacking a monarch or peerage system. However, until the mid-nineteenth century, the American system of public administration did run on the bases of patronage and trust.[32] As a result, even though no one could be excluded from office by birth, a filter for trust was still needed. Given that the thirteen colonies maintained, at least initially, most British institutions, it is not too surprising that they continued to duel.

The most famous duel in history was the Aaron Burr–Alexander Hamilton duel in 1804.[33] Both participants were members of the American ruling elite of the time—Burr was the vice president under Thomas Jefferson, and Hamilton was a founding father and the first Secretary of the Treasury. Hamilton did not want to fight the duel and wrote a letter during the negotiations outlining his beliefs on the practice. In it he states he opposed dueling because of his religious principles, his concern for his wife and children, his obligations toward his creditors, his lack of ill will toward Colonel Burr, and because he felt he would gain nothing from the fight. Nevertheless, he felt it was unavoidable because to go through with it would give him "the ability to be in future useful, whether in resisting mischief or effecting good, in those crises of our public affairs, which seem likely to happen, would probably be inseparable from a conformity with public prejudice in this particular."[34] In other words, Hamilton felt that dueling was necessary if he were to continue in public service. Although Burr killed Hamilton, he was never convicted or even tried for murder.[35] Indeed, he was allowed to finish his term as vice president, and in 1812 he resumed his New York law practice and continued in that profession for twenty-four years. He was buried in 1836 with full academic and military honors.[36] All aspects of this story are consistent with the interpretation that dueling was a method to sort trustworthy people.[37]

Although no unique American dueling rules arose and American duels were conducted along the same procedures as European duels, there were two essential differences. First, although dueling mostly took place among politicians and lawmakers, duels in the Americas were essentially open to everyone. There were duels among gentlemen and commoners, and between landholders and the landless. In addition to Burr and Hamilton, General Andrew Jackson (the future president) fought in a duel, as did senators and supreme court judges. Abraham Lincoln even met on the field of honor to fight a duel in 1842 with broadswords. His opponent, a small man named James Shields, had second thoughts, and the duel was not carried out.[38] Second, duels in America were more deadly than those in Europe, as Alexis de Tocqueville states:

> In Europe one hardly ever fights a duel except in order to be able to say that one has done so; the offence is generally a sort of moral stain which

one wants to wash away, and which most often is washed away at little expense. In America one only fights to kill; one fights because one sees no hope of getting one's adversary condemned to death. There are few duels, but they almost always end fatally.[39]

The differences between American and European dueling are consistent with the theory of filtering trustworthy aristocrats. Because the United States lacked a well-defined aristocracy, the idea of observing social capital at birth had little meaning. As a result, there were no restrictions on the abilities of anyone to duel. Furthermore, an egalitarian society had more lethal duels. In his discussion of Missouri duels, Steward contrasts the differences in social status between the Old South and Missouri. Whereas the Old South had a formal class structure, Missouri was more egalitarian. It is not surprising that he notes a difference in lethality: "In Dixie many duels were 'bloodless'. . . . While southern duels often left both reputation and body undamaged, Missourians sought satisfaction with blood."[40]

European duels of the nineteenth century had a fatality rate of around 2 percent.[41] In contrast, Schwartz and others claim that the fatality rate in U.S. pistol duels was 1 in 14, or slightly more than 7 percent. In addition, American dueling was more common in the South than in the North, which makes sense given that the social structure of patronage was stronger in the South.

No Patronage, No Dueling: The English Commonwealth

The central importance of dueling in a patronage system is made clear by a natural experiment in history: dueling fell from favor during the brief period of the English Commonwealth. After the second major series of battles in the English Civil War and the execution of Charles I in 1649, Parliament established a form of republic (the English Commonwealth) under the control of Oliver Cromwell that lasted from 1649 to 1660 and the restoration of Charles II. This republican commonwealth administration abandoned much of the historical patronage system, which had strong implications for dueling.

Dueling was very popular before and after the Commonwealth period. Thomas Hoby's translation of the Italian Baldassare Castiglione's *The Book of the Courier* in 1561 was the first English book to mention dueling among aristocrats. Over the next forty years, several treatises on dueling, courtesy guides, and codes of honor were published in England, and a concomitant increase in the amount of dueling took place.

Peltonen reports that "the numbers of duels and challenges mentioned in newsletters and correspondence jumped from five in the 1580s to nearly twenty in the 1590s. The peak was reached in the 1610s with thirty-three recorded duels and challenges, although the number of actual duels and challenges must have been much higher."[42]

In contrast, there was a dearth of dueling in England from 1642 to 1660, the years of the Civil War and the Commonwealth. Baldick notes that "after thriving during the first decades of the seventeenth century, duelling became an extremely rare occurrence in the Civil War. . . . [and] during the Protectorate, . . . After the Restoration, duelling very naturally regained all its previous prestige, and soon ballrooms, coffeehouses and public walks were all scenes of fighting and bloodshed."[43] Kiernan also confirms this decrease in duels: "In England [dueling] fell off after 1642 when the civil wars broke out."[44]

The explanation for this cycle of dueling lies in the role of patronage in the different administrations. During the nonrepublican years, the government of the monarchs ruled much as they had in times past, through the use of patronage. It was the prerogative of the royal court to deliver positions within the administration, military, and general government to whom it pleased and, as discussed earlier, these ministers would then act as patrons to lesser individuals for other positions in the civil service. However, the Civil War and the subsequent Commonwealth government was considerably different, and direct appointment through historical patronage almost disappeared.[45]

It would be an error to suggest that Cromwell, who enjoyed virtually supreme power and had complete control in appointing great officers of state, dispensed with a system of patronage, but just as incorrect to suggest that the system of appointment and promotion remained the same. At a fundamental level, the Civil Wars and the subsequent governments were driven by serious divisions of theology and, at one level, Cromwell chose appointments using a "religious screen."[46] At a personal level Cromwell was concerned with what he termed "the root of the matter," which most historians seem to take as a minimum standard of Puritan belief. Consistent with this was the purging of many administrative positions based on belief. There was the "Plundered Minister's Committee" that was "responsible for purging non-puritan Episcopalian clergymen and imposing tests on all others; these were often replaced by previously 'plundered' puritan ministers."[47] He also introduced the "Ejection Commissioners" to get rid of ministers for "misconduct or non-subscription to the prescribed minimum of Protestant belief."[48]

Cromwell also put an emphasis on merit and ability that was absent in the royal administrations prior to and after the Commonwealth. For example, his Republican Navy, which had officers drawn from the aristocrats before and after the Commonwealth, drew virtually all of its captains from professional seamen, the so-called "tarpaulins."[49] Aylmer puts it this way:

> The Commonwealth was a revolutionary regime. It had come to power through civil war and military force, and its legality was not universally recognised in the country. This put a premium on political or ideological reliability, and meant that loyalty to the government was something which patrons needed to stress, and appointing bodies to satisfy themselves about. *It also led to a formidable battery of tests and oaths.* . . . over and above loyalty and morality, we find emphasis on men's actual fitness for the work in question. It could mean a particular skill in writing, accounting or foreign languages, or a more all-round ability.[50]

Dueling owed its existence to the presence of patronage, its requirement for trust, and the necessity of screening. When Cromwell replaced the pre-modern system of patronage with an appointment system based on theological belief, dueling essentially ceased. At the Restoration in 1660 and the subsequent renewal of patronage, dueling was taken up again.

Dueling's Decline in the Late Nineteenth Century

The final piece of evidence that dueling existed because of patronage in the senior civil service was the decline of dueling throughout the nineteenth century. Dueling was used to screen minor gentry into the aristocracy, and with the fall in power of the latter came the demise of the former. Dueling, of course, had costs: it excluded large numbers of individuals from civil service; it often resulted in death or serious injury to talented people; it created an incentive for individuals to invest in acquiring dueling skills through attending dueling schools and hiring master instructors; and, although measures existed to mitigate it, cheating at duels took place. Hence, when innovations from the Industrial Revolution were able to lower the role of nature in life and allow meaningful measurement to be used, and when patronage was ultimately replaced by a professional bureaucracy based on merit, dueling ceased to be practiced.

For England, the eighteenth century saw tremendous growth in its empire. By the end of this century, the colonies of British North

America and India were not controlled by monopoly companies but rather were being administered by the British civil service. This change was part of an enormous growth in the civil service. Whereas in 1700 members may have numbered 1,000–2,000, by 1914 the British civil service had 167,628 employees, and by 1919 this number had grown to 393,205.[51] Brewer states that in the seventeenth century, "the overall picture is clear: the central administrative apparatus was tiny." He estimates that in 1688 the civil service employment was 2,500 men and that by 1760 it had grown to 16,000.[52] As time went on, these new positions were not filled by patronage but through examinations and interviews with selection boards. France, Germany, and other European countries obtained colonial empires in the nineteenth century with similar civil administrations, again appointed generally outside the realm of patronage. Likewise in the United States, the nineteenth century saw a decline in the role of patronage, culminating in the Pendleton Act of 1883. Johnson and Libecap document how the increase in the sheer size of the civil service over this period prevented the president or members of Congress from controlling and benefiting from their patronage appointments, and note that the federal workforce grew from 26,000 to 51,000 between 1851 and 1871.[53]

But, as discussed in Chapter 2, other changes took place between 1750 and 1850 that also led to the radical reforms in civil administration. The Industrial Revolution, changes in communication technology, tremendous falls in transportation costs and the ability to accurately tell time all led to a significant increase in the size and wealth of the middle class but also led to changes in the ability to measure performance. The increase in wealth outside the aristocratic group increased the gains from trade outside the aristocracy and lowered the attractiveness of hostage social capital within the civil administration as a road to riches. And of course, the ability to measure performance lowered the demand for a trustworthy class and rendered the duel obsolete.

Throughout the nineteenth century, formal patronage was replaced by a professional bureaucracy. As merit replaced patronage, dueling ceased to play a productive role in society. It is not surprising then that the changes in size of governments in England (and elsewhere) coincided with the end of dueling and a general fall in lethal duels. In England, the duel all but ceased to exist by 1850. In France and Germany, the duel remained until World War I, but the probability of death diminished greatly. In Germany, sword duels ceased using the épée and switched to the saber. This weapon was curved to prevent penetration, the tip was often dulled, and the blade rinsed with an antiseptic carbolic acid solution to prevent infection.[54] Deaths were rare.[55] Contrast this with French dueling where "the cream of the French nobility—perhaps 10,000 men—perished in duels in the last decade of the sixteenth and first decade of the seventeenth centuries."[56] Indeed, it has been estimated that over the first half of the seventeenth century, between 300 and 500 noblemen died from duels per year.[57] By the First World War, dueling was little more than fencing with the possibility of scaring due to limited facial protection. McAleer states, "By the end of the nineteenth century, the ritual had become overly refined and excessively formalized, indicating a shrinking, a withdrawal. The self-conscious obsession with technique and protocol was a symptom of decadence."[58] Hughes reports that dueling fatalities also fell in Italy over the last part of the nineteenth century. Of 3,918 duels reported between 1879 and 1899 in Italy, only 20 deaths resulted (Italians in this period also fought with sabers).[59] Dueling had ceased to be used as any form of screen for hostage social capital.

CONCLUSION

Dueling was a highly specialized institution that played a vital role in the lives of aristocrats during the pre-modern era. Viewed from the twenty-first century, it is beyond archaic and makes no sense. In fact, this change in viewpoint no doubt explains why virtually every movie that contains a dueling scene invariably gets it wrong—purposely shooting wide, having commoners duel, allowing defensive weapons, and so on. To portray a duel as it actually would have happened simply would not resonate with a modern viewer. However, seen in the light of the role aristocrats played during this time and the function of hostage capital, dueling takes on a new meaning. Dueling was used to filter out a group of legitimate entrants into the lower ranks of the aristocracy. Dueling was a response to the problem of selecting who would be eligible for positions of power in a world of patronage. When viewed in this way, we see dueling was not a recreational sport, an irrepressible manifestation of masculine aggression, nor a poor substitute for law courts. The purpose of dueling was to screen for individuals who would behave properly in their posts and not threaten the position of their patron.

CHAPTER FIVE

The Royal Navy

"He was an admiral," they told him. "But why execute this admiral?" he enquired. "Because he had not enough dead men to his credit," was the reply; "he joined battle with a French admiral, and it has been established that their ships were not close enough to engage." "But surely," exclaimed Candide, "the French admiral must have been just as far from the English as the English admiral was from the French!" "True enough," was the answer; "but in this country we find it pays to shoot an admiral from time to time to encourage the others."

VOLTAIRE, *Candide*

Voltaire was drawing on recent history when he wrote of Candide's brief adventure in England.[1] Admiral John Byng (1704–1757) was the fourth son of a famous admiral and viscount, and Byng quickly rose in the ranks of the British navy during the first half of the eighteenth century. Meanwhile, in the early years of the Seven Years War (1756–1763), the British island of Minorca just off the Spanish coast in the Mediterranean was under threat of attack from the French. The island was of strategic importance to the British because it was one of their few ports in the area at that time. Admiral Byng was sent with ten ships to defend the fort on the island and relieve the siege pressure. Very quickly the two fleets found each other and briefly engaged; the French used their favorite tactic of blasting up Byng's spars and sails. The state of affairs after the battle are in some dispute. Byng's supporters claim the French crippled the British ships to the point they could not give chase; that the British ships were old and leaking and unable to give chase; and that Byng was seriously undermanned in terms of soldiers and wisely held back. Others suggest that although some British ships were damaged, Byng refused to chase down the French and they unnecessarily escaped with no damage.

What is not in dispute is that Byng decided to return home to England rather than seek local repairs and continue the fight. The latter decision was a grave error on his part. When he arrived home he was court-martialed and convicted under Article 12 of the Articles of War, which states in part that "every person . . . who through cowardice, negligence, or disaffection, shall in time of action withdraw or keep back, or not come into the fight or engagement, or shall not do his utmost to take or destroy every ship which it shall be his duty to engage . . . being convicted thereof by the sentence of a court-martial, shall suffer death." Byng was shot by a firing squad on board the *Monarque* in 1757 for "failing to do his utmost" against the enemy. As an officer of the British navy of the time, Byng was subject to the Articles of War, a brief set of strict rules which, if violated, sentenced the officer to death. By today's standards, they appear barbaric and uncompromising, but as in the words of Voltaire, their purpose may have been to encourage others to fight in an age when measurement of performance at sea was so difficult. Like the duel, the odd institutional rules of the British navy were designed with a purpose in mind: to create a proper set of incentives and induce good conduct.

The British navy shows how the aristocracy was part of an overall system designed to produce trustworthy servants. First, the officers in the navy were dominated by aristocrats. Second, the conditions necessary for a patronage system were present and are well documented. The severe measurement problems during the era are relatively easy to identify in the naval context, the impact of nature's large role on management problems for the Crown are straightforward, and knowledge of the complicated system of patronage used to mitigate these issues is well documented. The term "patronage" sounds bad because it is now associated with mere political corruption. However, the British navy during the age of fighting sail demonstrates how, in practice, it was a complex system devoted toward a clear objective: victory through proper incentives.

The British navy was one of the largest and most significant pre-modern institutions involved in the patronage system. Like dueling, the age of fighting sail (approximately 1580–1827) spans the pre-modern era. Henry VIII, the first pre-modern monarch, inherited fewer than six ships from his father, and only two of any significant size. Nevertheless, he left his successors a substantial navy, and from 1550 on, England was a significant naval power.[2] A detailed look at the navy provides an example of the role of nature in the pre-modern world, the potential for conflict in incentives between patron and servant, the solutions found through the patronage system, and a lesson in how effective these methods were.

By the end of the Napoleonic Wars, the British navy was arguably the largest organization in the world—employing tens of thousands of people. It was, by most accounts, "the largest industrial unit of its day in the western world, and by far the most expensive and demanding of all the administrative responsibilities of the states."[3] It also achieved a degree of success, thereby allowing the claim "Britannia rules the waves." Over the latter half of the pre-modern era (1670–1827), the British navy was successful in fighting the Spanish, Dutch, French, and a host of other smaller European countries. Although Britain lost various individual ships and possessions (including thirteen small colonies in North America), in the larger picture, she dominated the seas. This naval success was a major component of Britain's rise from a fringe country to a world power with major overseas colonies and trade routes.[4]

Historians have marveled and speculated at this streak of victories. A strong case can be made that Britain's enemies were hindered by a series of events that weakened them at sea. Political instability—particularly in France during the Revolutionary wars—weak financial and credit systems, and land battles with other nations are three important factors that affected Continental powers more than they affected Britain. England was blessed with many natural ports and harbors, was an island nation bound to the sea, and held a deep interest in naval defense. Britain often had larger navies than her opponents and may have had access to better manpower.[5] Other theories suggest that psychological expectations of victory on the part of the British were self-fulfilling or that the British preference for eating beef somehow enabled victory.[6]

Of course many of these factors played a significant role in the success of the British navy, and the objective here is not to repeat what is already written. Still these theories seem to fall short in some respects. The standard historical explanation for British superiority at sea—social upheavals on the Continent—seems lacking. First, it mostly applies to France during the Revolutionary wars, but before that period the British dominated throughout the entire eighteenth century and particularly so in the Seven Years War. Second, even during the Revolutionary wars, many of the French admirals were former noble officers of the ancien régime.[7] Third, the British were just as successful against the navies of Spain and Denmark, whose governments were not experiencing upheaval. Fourth, during the age of sail, Britain also experienced domestic revolution and colonial setbacks. Indeed Cromwell purged and replaced many in naval command, and yet improved the navy to the point of terrifying his many foreign enemies.[8] Finally, although constitutional democracy was well under way during the pre-modern era, Britain was also extremely class structured. Hence, it seems unlikely that British naval dominance over the period of fighting sail can only be explained by differences in government structure, poorly trained opponents, or relative levels of technology and manpower, even though the purging of the French officer class after 1790 had its toll.

The British navy was an effective fighting force, not because of its raw physical and human capital (the British were not naturally better sailors), but rather because of the set of rules under which the British fought provided incentives for the naval officers to train their crews and use their ships as an effective fighting force. Although all men at sea had rules to follow, the focus here is on several critical rules for the captains and admirals. On the surface, a navy should hardly have been possible under the circumstances of sail power that created the possibility for enormous shirking. The ship's officers had a great informational advantage over the Admiralty; nature through wind and weather was a major factor in performance; and, as we'll see, the captain's incentives were at odds with the Crown. And yet the British navy prospered under these conditions. At a time when most other countries worried about the technical aspects of fleet maneuvers and ship construction, the British emphasis on incentives compatible with trustworthy officers won the day—often by a tidal wave.

During this time, every navy faced a serious trust problem with the commissioned officers on ship. Ships of war were expensive, powerful, and critical for the protection of overseas trade. Yet they were put in the hands of a captain who was sent out with the most general orders: to blockade a port; patrol for pirates and privateers; escort merchant vessels; and in times of war, engage the enemy. The captain had a large advantage over the Admiralty in London in terms of knowledge of local conditions; in fact, it is hard to imagine a more severe case where a servant would know more than his masters. During the age of sail, communication was intermittent, slow, and limited; the world was still generally unexplored, with shoals, waterways, and trade winds not mapped; flag signals from other ships were often mistaken, misunderstood, or unseen; and even methods for finding positions of longitude were only developed toward the end of the eighteenth century and were not widely adopted until the end of the age of fighting sail.[9] Worse, given that ships were propelled by wind, any disasters, losses in battle, missed opportunities, and other failures of duty could always be blamed on the ill fortunes of nature.

Added to the severe informational advantage was the temptation of a captain or admiral to seek out private wealth and safety rather than engage in more dangerous and less profitable assignments. Speaking of the early part of the pre-modern era, Rodger notes that "there were numerous complaints of frauds and abuses by officers: embezzlement, private trade and smuggling, false mustering [overstating the size of crew] and illicit fees."[10] Captains also had an incentive to use their ships to seek weak, but wealthy, merchant prizes rather than enemy frigates. On the surface, a captain had no obvious incentives to put his ship and his life in harm's way for king and country.

Hence, the Admiralty had no direct means of monitoring captains and admirals; captains and admirals had private incentives to act in ways against the Crown's wishes; and every failure to perform could be blamed on nature. The situation seems hopeless. Yet the British had a large and successful navy, and one where, although captains were occasionally convicted of failure of duty, the overall record of performance was impressive and filled with acts of heroism. How was this accomplished?

The answer: a complex institutional structure provided incentives for everyone to generally work in the Crown's interest. The upper ranks of the British navy, like so many of the state institutions of the time, was based on a system of patronage.[11] An aspect of this patronage involved a clever indirect monitoring system that was only slowly copied by opponents and which worked even for single ships thousands of miles from home. Like all the participants in patronage of the time, the naval officers were dominated by aristocrats. Although some commoners were appointed to the position of captain, "by 1688 almost all the rising generation of English sea officers were gentlemen who had entered as volunteers."[12] Wareham shows that, during the Napoleonic Wars, only 11 percent of frigate captains did not have some connection to aristocratic families.[13] Like other patronage appointments, a successful officer stood to gain immense wealth and prestige, but only if he remained at sea. Failure resulted, at best, in being mothballed at home on half pay with no prospects of the spoils of war, and at worst, in a trip to the firing squad. Some of the institutional rules within this patronage system actually hindered the ability of the navy to do battle. That is, ignoring issues of incentives and considering only the technical aspects of battle, the British should have fought differently. But of course, incentives do matter, and in retrospect, it is clear that during the pre-modern era, when direct measurement was so difficult, attention to incentives was often more important than technology.

The central compensation scheme in the British navy rewarded captains if they were successful and remained at sea. This system revolved around the taking of prizes and spoils of war. All captured ships were property of the Crown and were turned over to the Admiralty when captured. An admiralty prize court would determine the value of the capture, including any cargo and enemy sailors taken, and then pay off the crew based on a well-defined formula. Unlike on land, where prizes were located in specific places, enemy prize vessels floated about. Unlike the army then, the use of prizes in the navy was a two-edged sword—it motivated captains to be active at sea, but encouraged some to occasionally hunt for lucrative prizes instead of pursuing more strategic objectives laid out in their orders. The prize system was an essential part of the incentive structure of all navies and armies of the time, and it lucratively rewarded officers for actual combat. However, payment by prizes in the navy had a drawback; namely, captains preferred the most valuable prizes net of the costs of capture, and these prizes were not always the ones of most military value.

Patronage with prizes was necessary because captain performance could not be measured well enough to make them directly monitored employees paid through wages. Nor could the position of captain be sold off to the highest bidder because the incentives of the captain were often at odds with the Crown. Indeed, the sale of officer positions would have selected the very worst captains because the man willing to pay the most for a ship would certainly not pursue the military objective of the Admiralty. Hence, captains were assigned a ship through patronage, and they were expected to act in the interests of their patron—a senior officer, usually some type of admiral.

In order for this patronage system to work, some form of indirect monitoring was necessary. Thus, in conjunction with the system of prizes, the British navy used the Articles of War, battle formations and fighting instructions, and a unique form of promotion based on patronage to monitor their captains. The entire governance structure encouraged British captains to fight rather than run.[14] The creation of an incentive to fight led to an incentive for officers to train seamen in the skills of battle. Hence when a captain or admiral was commanding a ship that was likely to engage in fighting, that commander had an incentive to drill his crew and devote his energies to winning. He behaved "as though he were the King himself."[15] The linkage between the incentive to fight—and therefore to train in fighting—is supported by the work of Benjamin and Tifrea. They examine the fatality rates of British captains over the pre-modern era and show that British captains learned, faster than their foreign counterparts, how to become effective fighting machines. It was therefore the extra learning that took place on board the ship that made the British Navy so successful.[16]

SUCCESS IN THE SHADOW OF TEMPTATION

What Was the British Record?

Rodger, in his excellent study of the eighteenth century British navy, gives some idea of the difference in effectiveness with respect to the French navy through the differences in casualties of single-ship actions during the Seven Years War, where the ships involved were of approximately equal size. Of the ten encounters, the British had 195 men either killed or wounded, whereas the French had 1,365 men killed or wounded—a remarkable sevenfold difference.[17] In the Battle of Copenhagen 1801, the British had 1,000 killed. The Danes, on the other hand, had their entire fleet destroyed, 2,000 dead, and 3,500 prisoners taken.[18] In fact, over the six major naval battles of the Napoleonic Wars—the Glorious First of June (1794), Cape St. Vincent (1797), Camperdown (1797), the Nile (1798), Trafalgar (1805), and Copenhagen (1807)—the British had just 5,749 killed or wounded compared with 16,313 enemies killed or wounded and 22,657 prisoners of the enemy.[19] Approximately 50,000 men were present at these battles.[20] British casualty rates fell over the course of the pre-modern era and fell relative to their opponents.[21] Indeed, a sailor in the British navy was much more likely to die of disease or accident than from battle. The fact that the British were more successful in the Seven Years War than in the Napoleonic period, in terms of casualties, provides some evidence against the claim that their success resulted only from the French revolutionary purges of the military class after 1789.

Along with a major difference in casualties was a corresponding difference in the number of ships taken or destroyed. Warships were classed in terms of "rates." The largest were the 1st, 2nd, 3rd, and 4th rates—also known as "ships of the line." A 1st-rate ship was the largest, having over 100 guns across three decks and a crew of over 850. A 2nd-rate ship was just slightly smaller. The 74-gun 3rd-rate ship became the most common ship in the British navy. It was powerful enough to be in the line of battle, yet more maneuverable than the larger ships. A 3rd-rate ship might have anywhere between 64 to 84 guns across two decks. These ships were followed by the 5th- and 6th-rate ships. A frigate could be a 5th- or 6th-rate ship. It usually had a single gun deck and carried between 20 and 40 guns and between 150 and 300 men. The size of guns on the ships varied, which makes counting the number slightly misleading. In addition, international standards on rates did not exist, and so comparisons across countries are difficult.[22] The British navy was dominated in the latter part of the age of sail by 3rd-rate ships (having two decks and 60–80 guns) and 5th-rate frigates.

During the Napoleonic Wars (1793–1815), the British lost only 17 frigates to the French, of which they recaptured 9; whereas the French lost a total of 229.[23] Over this same period, 166 British warships of all rates were captured or destroyed by the enemy, of which 5 were ships of the line. In contrast, 1,201 enemy ships were captured or destroyed, of which 159 were ships of the line. Most of these ships (712) were French![24] Again, we see an imbalance—a fivefold difference in total ships and an amazing thirtyfold difference in the largest rates of battleships.

Throughout the eighteenth century, the British navy "was effective enough to win victory after victory,"[25] and by the War of 1812 had developed a reputation of virtual invincibility. C. S. Forester, in his naval history of the 1812 war writes:

> In 1812 the British Navy could look back with complacence over a record of victories frequently gained and easily won. Time and time again it had faced numerical odds and had emerged triumphant. . . . There had been single-ship actions too numerous to count, and in the great majority of these actions British ships had been victorious, and often over ships of greater tonnage, with more guns and larger crews. The British public, and even the navy, could be excused for forming the belief that there was something intrinsically superior in British seamanship and perhaps in British material.[26]

Indeed, by the mid-eighteenth century and certainly by the end of the age of sail, it was expected that a British warship would be victorious in an evenly matched battle. In single-ship confrontations, it was expected that the British ship would win, even if the enemy had 50 percent more crew and firepower.[27]

The fateful meeting between the British *Guerrière* and the USS *Constitution* on August 19, 1812, demonstrates the veracity of this reputation. All U.S. frigates were larger and more powerful than the British frigates. Congress had authorized the building of frigates, and their chief constructor, Joshua Humphreys, saw to it that they were more powerful than any frigate on earth and yet fast enough to avoid ships of the line. The ships were long on keel and wide of beam, carried heavy guns for a frigate, and were constructed with heavy planking. The result was a class of "superfrigates." In effect, the U.S. frigates were the same dimensions as a 74-gun ship but simply lacked the extra deck of guns. The *Guerrière* was smaller, in need of refitting, leaking, and recently hit by lightning, but her captain, James Richard Dacres, engaged the *Constitution* rather than flee, with the inevitable result of defeat. In England, the loss—the first of several ship-to-ship defeats against the Americans and the first loss in nine years—led to massive media attention and a call for heads. In the larger picture, the British navy dominated the War of 1812. The minor losses were inconsequential to the outcome, and Captain Dacres was rewarded for his efforts. Still the loss of the *Guerrière*, two other frigates (the *Macedonian* and the *Java*), five smaller sloops and brigs, and the massive attention they received were the exceptions that proved the rule: Britannia ruled the waves.

Did the British Have a Technical Advantage?

One easy reason for British naval success might simply have been technological. This advantage might have come from better ships, cannons, maps, or other types of ordinance used in fighting. The evidence on this point is weak and mixed; it would appear, if anything, that the British suffered a marginal technical disadvantage. In the early pre-modern era, as nations were experimenting with full rigging, ship design, cannon manufacture and placement, and the host of other logistical matters that came with the beginning of the age of fighting sail, England was comparable to the other major naval nations of the time (France, Spain, Portugal, Sweden, Holland, and Denmark). For example, in the seventeenth century the English were the first to successfully cast effective iron guns.[28] However, at the time copper guns were preferred, and by the time iron guns were perfected and made safer, other nations had the technology. Regarding the quality of ships, it is often acknowledged that after the Seven Years War and throughout the Napoleonic Wars, France had marginally better-built ships. During the age of fighting sail, Britain had no significant naval architect and mostly copied its designs from captured French ships, which were faster, more maneuverable, and better constructed than British ships.[29] However, Rodger disputes this claim. He argues that the British ships were different from other naval ships, not necessarily inferior.[30] He points out that British ship designers simply were not called "architects" and that they actually modified French designs to suit their specific needs.[31] In terms of numbers, the size of the British fleet was also comparable to its enemies— sometimes larger, sometimes smaller.[32]

Although no striking advantage in ships was apparent, the British were often considered to have a faster rate of fire, which is sometimes credited to modest differences in equipment. Unfortunately, no records were kept of how long the British or their enemies took to fire; but Rodger, perhaps the leading expert in this field, states: "With no useful averages of either British or French rates of fire little more can be said than that the French certainly spoke of British gunnery with respect."[33] To the extent that the British had a faster rate of fire, it seems more likely due to differences in discipline aboard the ship rather than differences in technology. The best evidence suggests that differences in construction and other war technology was minimal. Rodger is on the mark when he notes: "If there was a British 'secret weapon' at sea, it was not good gunnery so much as the high state of discipline of which that was a symptom."[34]

Technical and tactical advantage is an unlikely explanation for the British dominance over such a long period. Countries at war quickly adopted the obvious tools and techniques that advanced their relative positions—whether cutting out portholes for guns or using a new gunlock, advances in technology spread quickly. For example, until the sixteenth century, the standard naval tactic consisted of loading a ship with soldiers and boarding an enemy vessel. Large guns, though limited in number, were placed on the upper deck. Once portholes were introduced, many more guns could be loaded onto the ship because the lower center of gravity provided enough stability. Within a very short period of time, all navies had portholes. Likewise, in 1653 the English, while engaging with the Dutch, were the first to adopt the battle tactic of fighting in a line.[35] Before the end of that war, the Dutch had adopted the same tactic.

The Problems of Cowardice and Private Wealth Accumulation

The term "cowardice" is naturally pejorative, but in the pre-modern era it was specifically used to describe the rational failure to fight based

on one's private incentives when they were in conflict with the overall military objectives of the Crown. From the Crown's point of view,
a successful captain had to overcome the temptation to preserve his
own life and to seek private fortune at the expense of the Crown. To do
otherwise was considered cowardice. Although sea battles were rare
and though a captain stood a much higher chance of dying of disease
than in battle, on occasion the enemy had to be engaged and, at that
moment, it was imperative that the captain behave according to naval
objectives.[36] Unlike warships today, however, during the age of sail a
captain was perhaps the most vulnerable person on ship. His position
was on the quarterdeck, a raised deck running from the stern to about
the middle of the ship. From this position, he could see the enemy, the
fleet, most of his ship, and issue the appropriate orders. Unfortunately
for him, the quarterdeck was virtually unprotected from enemy fire—
not only cannon fire, but musket fire from the other ship's decks and
platforms up in the masts. Indeed, Admiral Nelson was killed by a
sniper's bullet shot from the rigging of the French *Redoutable* at Trafalgar. The captain's open position, plus the added peril of being one of
the few uniformed men on deck, made him particularly vulnerable. For
this reason, most tried cases of cowardice dealt not with the crew and
junior officers—who were busy below decks carrying out their orders
in relative safety—but with captains, admirals, and masters. A master
was the senior warrant officer in charge of the safety of the ship and also
took a position on the quarterdeck with the captain.

Examples of cowardice abound in the historical literature.[37] At
Trafalgar, for example, one-third of the French fleet stood aside and
watched the battle. At the Nile the entire French rear division watched
while Nelson's fleet destroyed their comrades, and when they were able,
they escaped.[38] Positive comments about Nelson indicate that he was an
exception in terms of bravery. Earl Howe, inventor of the signal system
of the time, remarked that Nelson's victory at the Nile "stood unparalleled, and singular in this instance, that every captain distinguished
himself."[39] And the victory at Trafalgar "emphasized how half-hearted
had been the urge to victory of all European admirals before Nelson."[40]
It is clear that failures to act in the interests of the Crown were not
uncommon.[41] Rodger's massive and detailed history of the British navy
during the pre-modern era is full of examples of captains standing aside,
ships returning from battle with little ammunition discharged, and
other tales of treachery.[42]

As always, Pepys, in his day-to-day comments during the Anglo-Dutch War of 1666, highlights the problem of cowardice, weather, and poor performance at sea:

> Up, and to church with my wife, and then home, . . . and also comes Captain Guy to dine with me, and he and I much talk together. He cries out of the discipline of the fleete, . . . few of the commanders doing what they should do, . . . He tells me we are to owe the losse of so many ships on the sands, not to any fault of the pilots, but to the weather; but in this I have good authority to fear there was something more. He says the Dutch do fight in very good order, and we in none at all. He says that in the July fight, both the Prince and Holmes had their belly-fulls, and were fain to go aside.[43]

Pepys's skepticism no doubt partly reflected his bad attitude toward aristocratic officers (Holmes in particular), but his words also reflect the difficulty of identifying the cause of the lost battle: full bellies or bad weather.

These types of sentiments are not uncommon in the pre-modern era. Ships were constantly heading to port with minor damage that could have been repaired at sea with no interruption in fighting.[44] And, in given battles, many ships simply hauled off out of range and failed to engage the enemy.[45] The problem of cowardice was common enough that of the 443 captains promoted between 1720 and 1750, 8.5 percent were dismissed or disgraced by court-martial compared to less than 4 percent killed in action.[46] Of course, not all of these court-martials were for cowardice, and the most common termination of a naval career was death by natural causes (18.5 percent).

Even in cases of victory, examples of cowardice exist. In 1782, Admiral Rodney defeated the French at the Battle of the Saints. Although many French ships were disabled, many others disengaged and fled. Rodney could have pursued them for total victory but, when urged on to complete victory, his infamous response was "Come, we have done very handsomely." A similar incident happened several years later when Nelson, under Admiral Hotham in the Mediterranean, made one of two captures in a 1795 battle. Echoing Rodney's sentiment, Hotham said: "We must be contented, we have done very well." Nelson, recognizing the statement for the cowardice it was, later wrote: "Sure I am, had I commanded our Fleet . . . that either the whole French Fleet would have graced my triumph, or I should have been in a confounded scrape."[47]

A second temptation facing a captain was to seek private wealth at the expense of the naval objective.[48] Most naval officers no doubt had a tremendous sense of duty, and were well aware of the prizes, promotions, and job security that could result from a successful military victory. However, in a given moment, with an armed vessel at his disposal, a captain could avoid bloody battles and enrich himself at the same time. The most distracting temptation was prize money from merchant vessels because "remuneration by prize money was not to be scoffed at, but it was a method that often enticed officers from their proper duties and missions."[49]

Generally speaking, prizes came from two sources: enemy merchant vessels and enemy military ships. Sea captains were allowed to take merchant prizes because they disrupted enemy trade; however, they were not to chase merchant prizes at the expense of their stated military missions. The primary objective of the navy was generally not to interrupt foreign trade, which was the task of the Crown's "second navy" called the privateers. Capturing an enemy military ship was also valuable to the captain. The British navy would purchase the ship at market value (as it would with a commercial ship) and would pay head money of £5 for each enemy sailor on board when the battle started. An added advantage of capturing an enemy naval ship was the building of a reputation that would be rewarded with future lucrative ships and stations. It is interesting that the larger ships were not always the most lucrative to be on. Fast and at the fringe of a fleet, frigates offered better opportunities for capturing enemy ships. Different naval stations provided different opportunities as well. Indeed, Nelson was rewarded with a valuable station in the Mediterranean after distinguishing himself at the Glorious First of June naval battle. However, despite these advantages, engaging an enemy naval ship was costly—naval ships fought back. Naval ships were damaged in battle, they carried small amounts of valuable cargo, and as mentioned previously, a captain stood a reasonable chance of being killed during battle.

All of these factors lowered the net value to a captain of engaging an enemy naval ship, which is not to say the net value was negative. An extreme example of a low net value enemy vessel was the case of pirate ships. The value of a pirate ship was generally low: they carried no cargo, and pirates would fight to the death to avoid capture. As a result, captains did not go out of their way to fight pirates. Given the choice, a captain would be tempted rather to go after a merchant ship that did not fight back and might be loaded with a very valuable cargo. The use

TABLE 5.1 Private officer incentives

Vessel	Benefits to Captain	Costs to Captain	Incentives of Captain
Merchant	High	Low	Attack
Naval	High	High	Depends
Pirate	Low	High	Ignore

of prizes was not a mistake; it simply was not always in harmony with naval objectives. The use of prize money was, in itself, a form of compensation that was used to encourage fighting.

The problem with private incentives are shown in Table 5.1. From the captain's private point of view, the best option was to attack a merchant vessel. Lucky was the captain who had a rich enemy merchantman cross his bow. Such a ship provided high benefits to him with low costs. On the other hand, even though the Crown's objective was to attack the enemy's navy, the captain's private incentives were not so clear. True enough, a naval victory meant glory and possible riches, but death lurked closely by as well. Last on a captain's list were pirates. These scoundrels offered a fierce fight with little hope of fame or riches.

Captains had other ways to use their ships for personal gain: they could carry cargo and private goods. With the exception of certain types of gold, this option was usually forbidden. Still captains could be tempted to carry more gold than was justified, divert their course for ports likely to be in need of their transport services, and sneak other goods on board for transport. Such practices of "good voyages" enraged Pepys: "Upon the whole it is plain that this business of money runs through and debauches the whole service of the Navy and is now come to the highest degree of villany and infamy and nobody considers it."[50] Captains could also spend more time in the comfort of port than at sea, and the more comfortable the port, the more time they spent there. Rodger noted that ships in northern waters spent considerably less time at sea than ships in the Mediterranean. He then acknowledges that "a cynic might point to the proximity of England, home and beauty to leeward, and the well-equipped dockyards inviting the minor defect."[51] Foreign ports were also sources of disease, which took the highest toll among sailors of the time. Captains were well aware of these temptations and made pains in their reports to point out that they withstood them. Rodger notes, "Officers might easily find themselves having to choose between private profit and public duty; the very terms with which they congratulated themselves in their reports . . . testify to the suspicion they needed to dispel."[52]

But here we come to an incredible observation: as much as these temptations were present, and as much as cowardice was not unheard of, the actual amount of cowardice and private wealth accumulation was low.[53] We might think that in an age of the cat-o'-nine-tails the British simply beat their sailors into submission and that captains, being no more than glorified sailors, were under similar threats of punishment for dereliction of duty. Not so. Though captains were court-martialed and sailors beaten, motivation was not driven by violence. The navy was disciplined in the sense of good management and organization, not in the sense of being brutal. Although the rules were tough and a few examples were made, the total collection of incentives in the British navy rules were less violent and more subtle, resulting in a limited amount of opportunistic behavior.[54]

So the scene has been set: the environment of a naval ship was full of variability from the point of view of the Admiralty, and a conflict of interest existed between the captain and the Admiralty. Yet in spite of examples of cowardice and cheating, overall the British navy fought well, relative to its opponents, for a long period of time without any distinctive advantage in technology. What were the institutional rules that generated this?

HIGH REWARDS FOR GOOD SERVICE

The cornerstone of the trust system, whether at sea or in the king's court, was its method and amount of remuneration. The goal was to use payments to create incentives that increased the likelihood that the servant—in this case, the captain—acted in the Crown's interests rather than in his own individual interests. Generally high rewards were given for acting in ways that were consistent with the Crown's goals, and large punishments ensued through lost hostage capital when caught or suspected of acting against the interest of the patron. This system of trust founded on rewards and punishment was the organizational backbone of the British navy.

Compensation for captains and admirals was a combination of relatively small salaries and potentially large prizes—not all that different from a salesperson who earns minimum wage with an option of significant income through commissions. Shares in prizes were based on rank: the more senior the officer, the larger his share. An admiral could receive between one-eighth and one-fourth of all prizes taken by his squadron. A captain usually received one-fourth of the prize he captured, the other officers shared one-fourth, and the remaining crew shared the rest. These shares varied over time, and captains within a fleet were known to make alternative sharing arrangements. In addition, ships in sight of a battle also participated in the sharing. Generally, admirals received more than captains, and captains always more than junior officers. Captains could receive 200 times what an ordinary seaman would receive.[55]

The total amount of prize money for a captain and an admiral could be significant, and the capture of a single merchant ship laden with cargo could set up a captain for life. At a time when an admiral of the fleet might earn £3,000 per year in full salary, some admirals amassed £300,000 of prize money over their career—the equivalent to about $42 million in today's currency.[56] Prizes came in several ways. When at war, ships could capture enemy vessels and share the value of the ship and cargo. Although rare, this form of prize money could be enormous. When the British defeated the Spanish in 1762 at Havana, the commanders in chief each received £70,000.[57] In another instance, in 1799 three frigates brought two Spanish ships into Plymouth. According to Howarth, "Each frigate captain got £40,730, lieutenants £5091, warrant officers £2468, midshipmen £791 and seamen and marines £182 4s [shillings]."[58] A seaman's pay at the time was about £14 per year. Indeed, during the Napoleonic Wars, the total prize money taken has been estimated at £30 million.[59]

If the enemy ship was sunk or captured, "head money" was paid based on the number of sailors in the opposing vessel. Ships that captured pirates received the cargo, bounty prices for each pirate, and the ship. Nevertheless, as previously mentioned, given the incentives for pirates to fight, their tendency to minimize the time cargo was kept on ship, and the low quality of their vessels, very few navy ships went out of their way to catch them. Capturing a slave ship could also lead to large rewards. After 1807, the British government paid £60 per male slave freed, and between 1807 and 1822 paid out £318,380 for freed slaves.[60] Howarth notes that "British seamen were as patriotic as anyone else, but what they talked about when they sighted an enemy fleet was not the victory they might win for Britain, it was the prize-money they could hope to win for themselves."[61] However, in order to obtain these prizes, a captain must have command and be at sea.

Which brings us to an interesting fact regarding the labor market for captains. The prizes paid were so large that generally they were higher than those necessary to induce a sufficient supply of naval officers. Those officers who were "lucky" enough to be given a command both made full pay and had essentially won a lottery in expected earnings, and many individuals on shore were willing to take up such a career that had the potential for such wealth. By creating an excessive income package, the navy created a surplus of unemployed captains and admirals who had to live on half pay, and those in command knew full well that the list of qualified replacements who were at home waiting to be given a commission was long. Indeed this unemployment pool acted to discipline those in command of ships because they knew that they could easily be replaced if their service was ever found deficient in some way.

When a captain or an admiral was not at sea earning a salary and a chance at prize money, he was on half pay. As the term indicates, this pay was a form of unemployment insurance. Half pay for a captain was not an income to aspire to, and yet a captain could expect to earn it for part of his career because the navy always had more captains than ships.[62] Henderson states: "There was always a sufficient cadre of commissioned officers to command any probable number of ships."[63] As a result, many captains were on half pay, waiting for a commission. For example, in 1715 the British navy had only 70 ships of war and employed 70 captains and 98 lieutenants. This left 188 captains and 261 lieutenants on half pay.[64] In 1812, ships and vessels in the British Navy numbered 1,017, but commanders, captains and admirals were roughly half again as numerous at 1,531.[65] These two data points may be explained by increases in the service during the Napoleonic Wars and the reduction in ships in 1715. Though the actual numbers varied over the age of sail, the general evidence is that an oversupply of captains was the norm. For reasons that will be explained, this ratio of ships to officers was not true of lieutenants.

One final institutional piece of evidence suggests that naval officers at sea earned high profits to induce good performance: they did not purchase their commissions. The British army, like other European armies, also paid their officers in terms of prizes; however, in these institutions the officers had to purchase the right to the prize income stream from other officers. Better commissions fetched better prizes, and higher-ranked commissions that received the largest share of prizes sold for higher prices than lower-ranked commissions. The price of a commission was not trivial, and during the age of sail, an army colonel might pay £40,000 for the privilege. It is reasonable to assume that the talents of command were somewhat transferable between the army and the navy. If so, then it is likely that the value of naval commissions was comparable to that of an army commission. Yet naval officers, for reasons that will be discussed later, did not purchase their commissions. Some of the high rewards were paid for through waiting on half pay and competing to become a captain, but many captains would have earned exceptional incomes.

Exceedingly high opportunities for income was a form of hostage capital because the future high stream of income was lost if a captain was removed from service. As a result, time spent unemployed on shore was not a social waste but rather a cost of the system. The unemployment pool acted to discipline commanders at sea because any slipup discovered by the Admiralty meant a quick replacement by another commander and a forfeiture of opportunities at a fortune. The historical record indicates that half pay was given to those captains who made slight mistakes, failed to capture an enemy ship, or failed in some other minor duty. Half pay was discontinued if an officer took up some other position outside the navy.[66]

While at sea, a captain made a full wage and had the potential to earn spectacular profits through prizes. It is not surprising then that every captain wanted to be at sea. Although seniority on the captains' list played some role in choosing a captain for command, the British navy was free to choose any captain on its list. Thus a captain suspected of some offense—especially a minor one or one where there was mostly suspicion—could be punished severely by placement on half pay for a long time. Half pay was the equivalent of social banishment of an aristocrat to his landed estate, and the anticipation of life on half pay had strong influence on a captain and induced him to do his duty. The real question is: how did the navy ever know what its commanders were doing in order to enforce this form of compensation, given that the prize system contained disincentives and that nature played such a large role?

INDIRECT MONITORING OF CAPTAINS AND ADMIRALS

During the age of sail the methods available to the Admiralty for monitoring captains were limited, and yet monitoring was critical if compensation containing prizes were used.[67] Sail power meant that ships were literally at the mercy of the winds, and ill winds could easily prevent a ship from entering battle, from arriving on time, or from avoiding a lee shore—where the wind blows from the sea to the shore, hence threatening the ship to run aground. The large role played by nature meant that it was difficult to infer incompetence or cowardice on the part of a captain simply because a negative outcome occurred. Furthermore, in the age of sail communication was primitive at best. Even ship-to-ship communication was limited mostly to flag signals that, depending on distance and weather, were difficult to read and easy to misunderstand. Finally, unlike land battles, where a target was fixed in location, at sea the target was moving—meaning that entire fleets could sweep the ocean for months without intersecting an enemy vessel.

One of the more famous episodes of this sort was Nelson's pursuit of the combined French and Spanish fleet. The combined fleet managed to escape a blockade of the French Mediterranean port of Toulon in March 1805. Nelson, thinking they were headed for Egypt, went east. On realizing his mistake, he crossed the Atlantic, searched the Caribbean, and then crossed back to Europe. He did not engage Admiral Villeneuve's combined fleet at Trafalgar until October—almost eight months of chase. Another famous case was Captain Rodgers' fruitless hunt of British ships in the early years of the War of 1812. The American squadron spent seventy days at sea, from one side of the Atlantic to the other, without running into the British once. Under such circumstances, direct monitoring of captains by the Admiralty was not feasible. The solution was a form of indirect monitoring that included a set of strict rules and a clever placement of "watch dogs" on board the ship.

Fighting Instructions: The Line and the Weather Gage

In 1652, Robert Blake, commander of the English fleet, was defeated by his Dutch archrival Maarten Tromp. Though Blake was outnumbered, he blamed his defeat on the conduct of his captains under fire—and he was probably right. During the early Anglo-Dutch Wars, naval strategy amounted to having fleets simply charge pell-mell into the opposition, choose an opponent of approximately equal size, and begin fighting. This strategy led to two problems: failure to get ships close enough to actually engage the enemy, and sailing in a fashion that got in the way of others and masked their fire against the enemy. As a result of this battle, a set of rules developed which, though modified over time, became the backbone of British naval tradition. These rules were known as the Fighting Instructions, and they remained remarkably unchanged throughout the age of fighting sail.

In general, the fleet was to gain the advantage of the wind (the "weather gage"), then bear down on the enemy at once and impose as much firepower as possible. Ships were to stay out of enemy harbors and not board other ships until commanded. Most of the Fighting Instructions were quite straightforward, but two in particular helped to provide proper incentives to captains and admirals: capturing the weather gage and fighting in a line. To capture the weather gage meant to be upwind of the enemy, and to fight in a line generally meant to fight in some type of linear formation. To form a "line of battle" was a revolutionary change in naval tactics during the seventeenth century, and one that remained in the Fighting Instructions throughout the age of sail.[68] The 1653 instructions state: "All the ships of every squadron shall endeavor to keep in line with the chief. . . . None of the ships of the fleet shall pursue any small number of the enemy's ships till the main body be disabled or run."

The rules for fighting in a line were actually quite complicated and evolved throughout the age of fighting sail; they attempted to take into account the endless conditions of weather and initial positions of the enemy, and they tried to anticipate how they would react to the various attacks. As individual admirals modified the Fighting Instructions, the logistics of the battle line often became more detailed. However, the general idea was always the same: ships formed a line with the admiral somewhere near the center, and would then proceed from the van (front) to pass the enemy line, sometimes blasting away as they went, until the two lines were beside one another. Ships would try to match ships of similar size, then anchor and fight for hours until a victor became apparent, the sides fell away exhausted, or ammunition ran out. During the three Dutch wars, battles would rage on for days, often resulting in a draw.

A puzzling feature of fighting in a line was that both sides must form a line. While one fleet was performing the complicated maneuvers to form the line, the other could simply sail away to avoid the fight or engage in a different tactic. These options led to a curious feature of many early battle line fights: when one fleet had superior numbers its extra ships often sat aside in order to get the other side to fight! Frigates would also stand aside, and it was the custom not to fire on an enemy frigate when engaged with a ship of the line, unless it fired first.

Lining up and fighting one-on-one also provided no particular advantage to either side. Often it was more effective to double up on a ship, or break the line in some way and to "gang up" on enemy ships.

Ultimately, if the fleet downwind in the battle was beginning to lose, all it had to do was set sail and drift away. Hence the act of fighting in a battle line has often been criticized and was often blamed for the large number of indecisive battles.

Many contemporary captains and admirals thought little of battle line tactics. One admiral, Sir John Jervis, remarked, "Lord Hawke, when he ran out of the line [at the Battle of Toulon] and took the *Podeer* sickened me of tactics." In other words, Jervis's sentiments were that formal tactics hindered the ability to fight well.[69] Quite often, the attempt to form a theoretical line at sea proved impossible in practice; thus this strategy has been constantly criticized by military historians over the years. The following provides an example:

> Ships which must be carried by wind and sails, and the sea affording no firm or steadfast footing, cannot be commanded to take their ranks like soldiers in a battle by land. The weather at sea is never certain, the winds variable, ships unequal in sailing; and when they strictly keep their order, commonly they fall foul one of another, and in such cases they are more careful to observe their directions than to offend the enemy, whereby they will be brought into disorder amongst themselves.[70]

Added to this criticism is the appearance that several key victories seemed to result from abandoning the line of formation. In the West Indies on 12 April, 1782, Admiral Rodney intercepted a French fleet. "A shift in the wind suddenly allowed the British to make ground towards the French and, instead of laying along side, Rodney sailed groups of his ships through the French line, encircled groups of theirs and hammered several into defeat."[71] Rodney showed initiative and bravery and, luckily for him, his ships followed. Thus his victory raises the question: if the battle line was difficult to use and ineffective for victory, then why was it standard procedure? From a strict gaming point of view, the battle line was clearly not the best strategy. Although it reduced the chance of masking another ship's fire and brought the full broadside to bear on the enemy, it also restricted movements of ships when other tactics may have worked better. It "exacerbated the already difficult task of commanding a fleet in battle."[72]

The British navy clung to the line formation as a dominant strategy for the simple reason that the line worked: "The English navy performed better and won more battles fighting in a line than it did with group melee tactics."[73] Despite its technical problems, the key to the line was that it gave each captain a clear and simple direction that the admirals could easily monitor. In this regard the battle line was similar to an assembly line that reduces the costs of monitoring workers. When a problem arises on an assembly line it is easy to identify the source. Likewise, the critical feature of the battle line was that it allowed admirals to monitor their captains over the issue of engagement. Whatever form the line took, it was clear when someone was "out of line." The navy, as previously mentioned, struggled with problems of cowardice and failures to engage. The great battles were exceptions in this regard, not the norm. In the early Anglo-Dutch Wars, when individual captains were left to their own discretion in battle, engagement was minimal. The battle line was a simple method by which admirals could identify those ships that broke with the line. Once cowardice could be identified, it could be punished.

One piece of evidence of the line as a monitoring device was the placement of the admirals throughout the fleet. The admiral was always located in the middle of the line, and because the line could be several miles long, a position in the middle provided a better opportunity for viewing the entire line. Still the line would often extend over the horizon, and smoke from battle easily blocked vision; so in addition, vice admirals and rear admirals (and each of these classes had subcategories designated red, white and blue admirals) would be spread out along the line. Because each category of admiral might have more than one member, potentially many of them were available to keep an eye on the line. Keegan recognized that the line could be subject to naval discipline when he stated "Linear organization [fighting in a line] recommended itself because it could be prearranged and then enforced by the code of naval discipline."[74] This enforcement was only possible because the line allowed for some monitoring. Those few admirals who successfully modified the line did so without losing the ability to monitor their fellow ships. For example, Nelson at the Nile simply doubled up the line on either side of the French.

One of the best examples of the line as a device to monitor shirking on the part of captains comes from the Battle of Toulon in 1744. The British had been fighting the Spanish since 1739 and had their fleet blockaded in the French harbor of Toulon, which was a neutral harbor. The Spanish came out and a battle began that ended in a defeat for the British and the greatest number of court-martials for a single battle in British naval history. Ironically, the British commander, Admiral Mathews, is viewed by historians and contemporaries as having made the right decisions. However, he broke with the battle instructions and lost apparently because he was unable to keep his ships engaged. "It would seem that the attack Mathews devised was the best possible under the circumstances, but, being irregular, it had left some of the captains in his own squadron puzzled as to what they should do, *with the result that they did very little.*"[75] Without monitoring, they did very little because the temptation to free ride in battle was too great.

Breaking with the battle instructions was risky, and if it led to defeat, it meant a guilty verdict at a court-martial and the end of one's career; however, the Admiralty was willing to reward initiative at sea that led to victory. Nelson, as a captain, had demonstrated his zeal for total victory, but his first significant victory came in the Battle of Cape St. Vincent (1797). The British fleet met with the Spanish who marginally outnumbered them 19 to 15 in ships but outmatched them 2 to 1 in guns and weight of fire. Despite their advantage, the Spanish attempted a retreat while the British were forming a battle line. Nelson, who was commodore at the time under Admiral Jervis, was third from the end in the rear of the fleet. He saw the retreat and broke with the line to cut off the Spanish escape. Fortunately for him, some other British ships followed and four ships were captured—two by Nelson himself—and the Spanish suffered a major defeat. Both Nelson and Jervis were rewarded for the victory. Hence the rigid use of the line was not for its own sake, but with the intention that it generally enhanced victory. On the surface, it almost appears that Lord Nelson, in each one of his famous battles, went out of his way to avoid fighting in a line. Yet Nelson, like virtually all other British admirals, regularly fought according to battle lines in one form or another.[76]

Although the British used line formation as a method of monitoring, all European navies fought in line formations, so it cannot explain the relative British success. The second critical aspect of the British line tactics, one not generally adopted by others, was to fight with the "weather gage." This term meant to fight upwind of the enemy ship—a tactic that was considered inferior by the military intelligentsia of the time. Throughout the eighteenth century, French strategists discussed the general benefits of fighting leeward of the wind (downwind or without the weather gage). When fighting leeward the ship was tilted, by the wind, away from the enemy and all of the ship's gunports were above the waterline. In contrast, a ship in heavy seas with the windward position was tilted in the opposite direction and might not be able to open its lower gun decks, resulting in drastically reduced firepower. A more important advantage of the leeward position was the opportunity of simply sailing downwind to escape if the battle was going poorly. Likewise, if an individual vessel became severely damaged, it stood a chance of escaping behind its own line. The French proclivity for shooting the masts and rigging of the enemy ships, as opposed to the hull, increased the opportunity of escape, and increased their preference for the leeward position. Given the advantages of not having the weather gage, why were the British so insistent upon having it? The answer is that having the weather gage both increased the incentive to fight and prevented captains from drifting away from battle.

It is important to realize that a square-rigged ship from the age of fighting sail was difficult to maneuver and could sail, at most, only six points into the wind. That is, the ship could not sail well into the wind at all. Not only could it not sail into the wind at any great angle, but the ship would often drift backwards, making no forward progress. Hence when attacking with the weather gage, a square-rigged ship had little choice but to drift upon the enemy. It would have been very difficult for a captain of a British ship in the fleet to casually or inadvertently not engage the enemy once the fleet had formed a line with the weather gage. The same forces applied in ship-to-ship engagements. In these more common battles, a captain downwind could always blame the wind for a failure to engage, whereas a captain whose ship was with the weather gage could not. In the battles of Trafalgar and the Nile, leeward ships among the combined and French fleets failed to engage even though evidence exists that the possibility was open to them. Failure to engage was a major problem, and the requirement to have the weather gage forced the hand of the commanding officers who were tempted by their private interests to save their own skin.

The incentive mechanism of the weather gage was that once engagement was certain, it was in the interests of the British ship to fight most effectively. Just as the weather gage ensured engagement, failure to fight well meant that the ship would eventually drift into the enemy fleet where it would certainly be captured. Thus the real genius behind the British success was the ultimate incentive to train the crew to fight well in battle. Benjamin and Tifrea provide empirical evidence that success was related to the extra experience and training the British had over their enemies. Thus the weather gage was an easily monitored action that encouraged engagement and effective fighting through training.[77]

The Articles of War

The Articles of War were a "haphazard collection of regulations and admonishments largely concerned with court-martial offenses by officers."[78] First passed by Charles II in 1661, they were based on regulations dating back to 1652 after the Dutch had defeated the British navy in several major battles. The articles were modified in 1749 and then again in 1778, and were finally replaced in 1866 with the Naval Discipline Act. These articles were not used, as a general rule, for ordinary seamen but rather were intended for captains and admirals.[79] Indeed, only one article related to ordinary seamen, namely, that they were not to sleep on a watch. As with the Fighting Instructions, many of the Articles of War were straightforward and not relevant to monitoring the private incentives of commanders. An exception was Article 10:

> *Article 10* Every flag officer, captain and commander in the fleet, who, upon signal or order of fight, or sight of any ship or ships which it may be his duty to engage, or who, upon likelihood of engagement, shall not make the necessary preparations for fight, and shall not in his own person, and according to his place, encourage the inferior officers and men to fight courageously, shall suffer death, or such other punishment, as from the nature and degree of the offense a court martial shall deem him to deserve; and if any person in the fleet shall treacherously or cowardly yield or cry for quarter, every person so offending, and being convicted thereof by the sentence of a court martial, shall suffer death.

The sentence of death was a common theme running through the articles and was often written leaving no room for discretion. In 1778, the punishment for Article 10 was amended to allow for something less than death, but the thrust remained the same—the officer had little choice but to engage. The commander that only partially sought engagement did so at his peril. Vice Admiral Sir Robert Clader engaged Villeneuve's combined fleet in July 1805, just months before the latter would meet up with Nelson at Trafalgar. After the initial successful action, Calder, who was outnumbered, in a poor tactical situation with damaged ships, and worried about blockading other French squadrons, decided not to renew the battle. Yet he was still found guilty at a court-martial.[80]

If a British ship came upon an enemy vessel, then it was the captain's duty to engage. Throughout the eighteenth century, it was expected that one should engage a ship even if a considerable difference in size existed. Though no one expected a frigate of 30 guns to engage a ship of the line, ships in the same class were expected to fight, even if they were outgunned by 50 percent. It was under these terms that Captain Dacres of the *Guerrière* engaged the *Constitution*. He had no chance of winning, but he knew that if he avoided the battle for the safe harbor of Halifax, it meant a certain end to his career and a real possibility of death by execution. Whereas if he attacked and lost, his career would still be waiting for him . . . if he survived.

Given the infrequency with which ships might come into contact on the open ocean, the large and unidentifiable role of nature, and the difficulty in monitoring a battle from several thousands of miles away, the rule to always engage effectively ruled out using poor winds, bad eyesight, and other excuses. Had the British allowed engagement to be an option, there would have been fewer battles and relatively fewer victories. Relatively fewer victories would have taken place because forcing engagement encouraged captains to train their crews for battle. The strategy seems to have worked remarkably well over 200 years. In numerous (but not all) battles, the British were constantly outnumbered in ships or guns, and yet they still managed to win most of the time. Article 10 was similar to the preference for the weather gage in the Fighting Instructions and would have provided a similar motivation. Captains, knowing that they would have to engage, would ensure that their crews were properly trained and ready to fight.

The Articles of War were not just an idle threat. As mentioned at the beginning of the chapter, their most famous application came at the beginning of the Seven Years War with the execution of Admiral Byng. Another striking example of the articles in use comes from the battle off Cape Santa Marta (off the coast of Columbia) in 1702. Hattendorf, who edited the court-martial documents, calls this "one of the most notorious cases of cowardice in naval warfare."[81] Here, the British squadron led by Admiral Benbow had superior numbers yet failed to defeat a French squadron because "the English captains ran away from the fight and failed to support their wounded admiral."[82] It is an interesting case for several reasons. First, the winds did not favor the British, their ammunition was low, their ships in disrepair, and most of the captains in agreement that a fight could not be won. In other words, many legitimate excuses for failure existed. Yet the captains were all convicted, and two were executed. Second, testimony was given at the court-martial from many individuals on board other ships, who testified to the fact that the accused captain was either out of line or not close enough for engagement. Third, Crown testimony came from up to twenty-one individuals. It is clear that the line was used as a method of enforcement, the Articles of War were applied with no consideration of circumstance, and lesser officers testified against their captain.

Watchdogs On Board

A critical question remains: although clear rules of conduct existed, how did the Admiralty ever find out that a captain had failed to chase a pirate ship, had not engaged an enemy of equal size, nor pursued merchant ships when assigned to a blockade? The answer lies in the clever form of promotion, based on patronage, that essentially provided an incentive for lesser officers to report honestly on the captain. This process of promotion did not exist in the other navies of the time.[83]

Promotion in the naval officer ranks had what might be called a "discontinuity"; that is, the process had a "stumbling block" or a "bottleneck" built into it. A young teen would enter the service as a midshipman and, after a specified time, could be recommended for the exam to lieutenant. If he passed and was appointed to a ship, he was promoted to lieutenant and, after a period of three to six years, qualified for promotion to post captain. But here it could all stop. Having qualified for captain, someone could remain a lieutenant for his entire career—promotion up the ranks to captain or admiral was not automatic.[84] The chance of being stuck at lieutenant was the discontinuity in the path from midshipman to admiral.

Lieutenant was an important rank. Unlike the officers beneath him, a lieutenant could not be removed or demoted on the sole authority of the captain.[85] Quite often a lieutenant might be made a commander of a small vessel, but this position was terminated with the end of his commission. Out of courtesy, a commander was called a "captain." Still, a true captain was a "post captain," and every lieutenant aspired to this rank. The full process of promotion to captain was complicated. Often admirals of the fleet made promotions at sea, but the Admiralty office in London had veto power. In every case a lieutenant would need some patron to move his case forward. Regardless of who made the actual promotion, it remained true that the entire process of promotion could be stalled and cease at lieutenant. However, once a lieutenant was made a post captain (that is, his rank did not end with his commission), promotion to the top was automatic through attrition. It was only a matter of time before a post captain became an admiral, and if he lived long enough, admiral of the fleet.[86]

For example, one of the most famous ship-to-ship contests of the War of 1812 was between the USS *Chesapeake* and HMS *Shannon*, in which the *Shannon* won a quick but bloody victory. On board was a young 20-year-old second lieutenant named Provo Wallis. This naval contest was to be the first and only one of his life. Five years later he was promoted to post captain. He died at the age of 100 in 1892. At the time of his death, he had held the title of admiral of the fleet for fifteen years.[87]

"Except for the favoured few . . . a large gap [existed] between lieutenant and captain,"[88] and the process of making post captain was the most significant step in an officer's career. The process of promotion to captain in the British navy was complicated indeed, but the most important factor was patronage—a ubiquitous aspect of the navy. An aspiring officer needed to attract and maintain good favor among his superiors, and this necessity was "one of the strongest social forces within the Navy."[89] Rodger emphasizes how patronage gave authority to captains and kept subordinate officers in line. Rodger elsewhere states: "this power of patronage was the key to the eighteenth-century Admiralty's authority, the one element which counterbalanced weakness to command and near inability to punish."[90]

Patronage was key. A patron had a strong interest in the success of his junior appointment. Failure of the servant reflected badly on the patron and reduced the chance of the patron to make further appointments for other young officers. Success meant rewards for the officer and the patron.

Another necessary condition to make post captain, of course, was proper performance of duties as a lieutenant, which included accurate and honest record keeping. Although there were always more captains than ships to sail, the navy did not promote lieutenants merely because they qualified. The navy had in mind some number of captains per ship to maintain, and when this ratio became too low, promotions from lieutenant to captain were more likely to occur. Thus, any vacancies in the captains' list would spur on promotions to that rank. In the normal course of events, attrition in the captains' list would occur through old age, disease, battle, and court-martial. The bottom line for a qualified lieutenant was that an opening in the captain ranks increased the chance of a promotion. Thus the lieutenant had an incentive to report improper activity on board the ship and to testify against his captain at court-martial or when the ship returned to port.

Indeed, it was part of the lieutenant's job to keep a log of the captain's actions. Aside from the Fighting Instructions and the Articles of War, the Admiralty issued general regulations and instructions that held less authority than the first two but were nonetheless important in the duties of officers. Although they were first issued in 1663, the final instructions during the age of sail were issued in 1806. Article VIII for lieutenants states: "It is expected that he do provide himself with the necessary instruments, maps and books of navigation, and *he is to keep a journal* . . . and at the end of the voyage to deliver copies thereof signed by himself in the Admiralty and Navy Offices."[91] Some view the lieutenant's log simply as a matter of training to be a captain, similar to the navigational exercises they performed on board. However, unlike the exercises, upon arriving in dock, the lieutenant was required to deliver his log to the Admiralty—not to the captain. In case of a court-martial, the Admiralty or flag officer of the fleet would interview the lieutenant to see if the captain's log had any discrepancies with his. There would be no point to this interview if the purpose was simply a matter of training.

Further evidence that multiple journal keeping was not intended for training purposes comes from the instructions to others on board to keep journals. Article IX for masters states:

> It is expected, that he do provide himself with the proper instruments, maps, and books of navigation, and keep an exact and perfect Journal, taking care to note therein the coming in and going out of all stores and provisions; and when the ship is ordered to be laid up, he is to deliver a copy of the same into the navy-Office, together with his Log Book, signed by himself.[92]

Because the master could not move to the position of captain, it is reasonable to assume that his journal was used as a cross-reference to the others. Indeed, the journaling also included the captain keeping track of stores. Not only was the captain "to give an account of the expedition, and shall leave a copy of his journal with the secretary of the Admiralty,"[93] he was, according to Part I, Article VIII, to "keep counterbooks of the expence of the ship's stores . . . and at the end of the voyage, he is to deliver the several books, which he has kept of the expence of stores, into the proper offices, signed by himself, the master, and by each officer to his respective counterpart." All of this multiple record keeping was a method for the Admiralty to know what was going on aboard the ship, while raising the cost of collusion among the officers. Victualing was another source of income to captains at the expense of the navy, and in the seventeenth century the British navy put into place a series of checks and balances that remained intact throughout the premodern era. This system of multiple record keeping was again superior to those in foreign navies.[94]

In effect, the lieutenant, among others, was the chief watchdog of the Admiralty. Consistent with this role was that every ship, no matter what its size, had at least one lieutenant on board. A small ship might have only a single lieutenant in charge, but if the same size ship had a captain, then it also had a lieutenant. One might ask who would monitor the lieutenant in cases where he was the commander? It appears, however, that in these cases lieutenants were often put in charge of single task missions (such as returning a prize to port) that would be more difficult to cheat on. Hence they could be monitored by output.

It might appear that this system created an incentive for the lieutenant to lie. Telling tales about a captain might get him removed and open a spot on the captains' list. Aside from deterrents such as penalties for perjury and the formal aspects of a trial with cross-examination, there were three safeguards: the watchful eye of the ship's master, the large numbers of other officers on board, and the role of patronage in promotion.

As previously mentioned, the master was the highest-ranking noncommissioned officer on board and, like the lieutenant, could not be removed by the captain of the ship. In the very early years of the age of sail, the master was in charge of the ship, with captain merely being the leader of a land force on board. Most of the major warrant officers on the ship (such as boatswain or purser) could not be removed by the captain. Because the master was at the top of his career and could not be promoted, he had little to lose in honestly reporting on the captain. The same basic structure exists in modern navies today. The master was responsible for the safety of the ship and also kept a log similar to the lieutenant's. In fact, Article IX for the master was almost identical to Article VIII for the lieutenant, except the master also had to keep an eye on stores. The regulations provide an example of a journal entry and indicate that "remarkable observations" are to be included.[95] If the lieutenant was intending to lie about the actions of the captain, he would have had to collude with the master—a man who had no obvious incentive to act against the captain.

Another factor on ship discouraged the lieutenant from lies or exaggeration: large ships had more than one lieutenant, several midshipmen, and other lesser officers. Although these other officers might have less incentive to report misconduct, they certainly had little incentive to lie and would be called upon at a court-martial. Collusion was difficult at the best of times, and it seems very unlikely that a lieutenant could lie about specific types of conduct (like the capture of a prize) and get away with it. One final safeguard and an important element in promotion was the recommendation from one's captain. A lieutenant who lied but failed to have his captain removed would have little chance at promotion on any ship in the navy.

The infamous voyage of HMS *Bounty* in 1789 shows some of the dynamics of command and control through subordinate supervision. William Bligh was actually a lieutenant in command of the ship, and until he promoted Fletcher Christian to acting lieutenant, his second in command was the master John Fryer. In addition to keeping logs, various clerical duties on board required multiple signatures. On at least three occasions, disputes arose between Fryer and Bligh over missing stores. On one particular instance, Fryer refused to sign. Bligh called all hands on deck, read the Articles of War, and then commanded Fryer to sign. Hough states: "Fryer takes the pen, and in a voice so loud that none will miss his words, he says 'I sign in obedience to your orders, but this may be canceled hereafter.' And he does so. According to Morrison [a member of the crew] this was only one of several rows between commander and master before they reached Tahiti."[96] According to Hough, Bligh was constantly worried about Fryer's log and how it would be interpreted by the Admiralty, even over matters as trifling as some missing cheese.

SOME EVIDENCE

It is time to put the British navy into the context of the larger argument. The pre-modern world was laced with variability that was difficult to disentangle from human efforts in many areas of production. This variability allowed individuals in positions of opportunity to further their own interests at the expense of the Crown or some other patron. One solution to this problem was for the patron to use only individuals he trusted, and he trusted only those who stood to lose more from being caught behaving opportunistically than they might gain from being dishonest. These individuals were mostly aristocrats who occupied the institutions of the Crown. The British navy was but one example. We see within the institution of the navy all of the key sources of problems in the pre-modern era. Nature played a large role in naval outcomes; the Crown had no means of directly monitoring commanders; and commanders had the means and incentives to act in ways incompatible with Crown goals. The solution was to allow aristocrats command positions and to offer them extreme rewards for good service. The navy used large potential prizes as a reward for good service; failure to perform meant a life on half pay back at the seat, with no opportunity for future prizes (and likely little chance for other offices on shore). Given that officers began their careers as young midshipmen, it was possible for the lowest members of the gentry and even commoners to enter the officer class. However, the officer class was dominated by aristocrats.

The navy also shows how detailed and complex the patronage system could be, and how many of the institutional details of the pre-modern navy can be seen as methods to indirectly monitor the actions of commanders. These institutional details were not without other merits: the battle line increased firepower; the weather gage could have aided in control over the timing of battle.[97] However, looking at the entire institutional system within the context of the general practice of patronage, it seems reasonable to conclude that the navy rules were designed to keep officer incentives compatible with the Crown. This argument not only explains the details of the navy experience, but it also explains why privateers were organized differently, why the army did not use patronage, why the men of the lower deck were paid differently, why the complicated system ended with the introduction of steam power, and why the French and others won so few battles against the British.

Privateers

It is interesting to contrast the differences in the organization of the navy with those of the "private navy" known as the privateers. Privateers were not pirates. They were sailors on private ships, licensed by the king to capture enemy merchant vessels and goods in time of war. Privateers were always an important part of naval warfare during the age of sail. In fact, during the Elizabethan era, twice as many private ships were involved in the war against Spain as ships owned by the Crown.[98] However, when used as naval vessels private ships proved most ineffective. Not only did the captain-owner not want to risk his own life; he seldom wanted to risk the loss of his ship.[99] As a result, over the course of the pre-modern era, the privateers came to be used only to attack enemy merchant vessels.

Despite the nautical similarities between the British navy and the privateers, the institutional rules for privateers were quite different. Most notable, although privateers were paid strictly through a share of the prize that they captured, much as in the navy, the Crown never directly or indirectly monitored the ship's owner. Nor did the Crown impose any of the naval rules of promotion or engagement on the privateers. The owner of the vessel would be paid a share of the prize, whereas the crew may be paid by wages, shares, or some mixture. The actual details of payment could be quite complicated.

The difference in institutional rules stemmed from the different objectives of the navy and the privateers. After the Anglo-Dutch Wars, privateers were not expected to fight enemy war ships, blockade harbors, or be involved in other forms of combat.[100] The sole purpose of the privateer was to hinder enemy trade. In this case, payment by prizes perfectly aligned the incentives of the sailors with the objectives of the Crown and thus eliminated the need to monitor performance. These compatible incentives resulted from the fact that merchant ships were generally the most valuable, net of the cost of capture.

Andrews, referring to the British privateers in the war with Spain, circa 1600, notes that colonies with poor defenses were exposed to "continual harassment by the Elizabethan privateers, who preferred to seek their prizes in these less dangerous backwaters."[101] In other words, privateers could select prizes that put up little resistance. The Crown knew that privateers would attack merchant ships. Hence monitoring privateers was unnecessary, and the discipline and hierarchy of the navy was absent. In fact, privateers were known for their lack of discipline when compared to the navy.[102] For the navy, prizes were used to create incentive pay, but the easiest prizes were not always in a given captain's best interest to capture. The navy's use of payment by prizes created incompatible incentives. Thus, the navy had to engage in other subtle forms of indirect monitoring to ensure fighting.

Salaries on the Lower Deck

Was the system of patronage and trust used throughout the aristocratic system and in the Royal Navy, in particular, the result of a failure on the part of the Crown or the Admiralty to recognize that salaries with direct monitoring could be paid? It was certainly not. When measurement was possible, the Royal Navy used salaries and promotions based on performance. This method of payment was the case with those men on the lower decks of the ship: the warrant officers, petty officers, and seamen.[103]

Warrant officers were historically the oldest positions on the ship; they included the master, boatswain, purser, carpenter, surgeon, and others. These men, along with petty officers, generally managed various groups on board the ship. Most men on board were seaman who were ranked from untrained landmen, ordinary seamen, and able seamen. Of course, above all of these men were the commissioned officers of the quarterdeck: admirals, captains, lieutenants, and midshipmen.

While the Admiralty found it impossible to directly monitor the captain at sea, on board the ship it was feasible to measure the performance of the men on the lower deck. Their performance was measured and rewarded through promotions to ranks with higher pay. It was, in the words of Benjamin and Thornberg, "a meritocracy of the first order."[104] They argue that seaman performance was relatively easy to measure, and as a result promotion was based on their absolute skills. "A sailor who demonstrated sufficient skills and a proper attitude could expect to move up from landmen to ordinary seaman to able seaman."[105] When measurement was easy, even in the pre-modern world, wages and direct monitoring were used.

Methods were slightly different when it came to the warrant and petty officers. The work of these men involved the management of teams of seamen on board. When production takes place in teams in an environment where nature plays a significant role in outcomes, it is notoriously difficult to measure individual performance. However, the relative performance across teams was fairly easy to measure, and payment to these officers was based on this measure. In modern corporations, rewards based on relative performance are quite common; they are often called "tournaments" because the winning team receives a large reward relative to the other losing teams—as in a sporting event. Benjamin and Thornberg examine the pattern of wages for the various warrant officers and conclude that they reflect a tournament wage profile. Those with the best relative performance were promoted with significant increases in pay. In particular, they find that the smaller the chance of promotion, or the greater the effort level of the higher position, the larger was the change in wages—wage movements consistent with a tournament. Where measurement was possible, even if only in a relative sense, the British navy was able to use an institutional structure that corresponds to modern corporate governance.

Thus on board a single ship, three distinctly different systems of incentives were present to induce the appropriate behavior to make an effective fighting machine. At the lowest level, direct monitoring of seamen meant that the bulk of their income came from a flat wage structure. When monitoring was possible, but incomplete at the individual level, performance was measured and rewarded at the team level through tournaments. These two methods we recognize as modern forms of organization. Indeed, Benjamin and Thornberg claim the navy motivated the lower deck "much as the most successful business firms of today motivate their employees."[106] On the quarterdeck it was a different story. Among the commissioned officers, measurement was not feasible, and the system of patronage led to the complicated system of promotion so alien to modern times.

The Introduction of Steam and Chronometers

The most critical factor allowing for incentive problems in the age of sail was the wind. The large role played by the wind made it virtually impossible to monitor captains based on output. The ending of the pre-modern era was driven by the many innovations of the Industrial Revolution, and the institutional apparatus of the British navy was no exception. The age of sail for the navy ended in the first half of the nineteenth century with the introduction of steam. The first steamships used large paddles on the sides of the vessels. Because they reduced the sailing and fighting qualities of the ships, paddle propulsion was more popular among merchant vessels than naval ones. However, with the introduction of screw propulsion, which improved sailing and still allowed for a full broadside of guns, the navy completely committed to steam power by the mid-nineteenth century. The removal of the most significant role of nature (the wind) from battle, made shirking on the part of captains much more difficult, if not impossible. The early part of the nineteenth century also saw the common use of the marine chronometer in naval ships. This device allowed ships to have an accurate knowledge of position and created a revolution in accurate mapmaking. Together, steam and the chronometer allowed for direct monitoring.

As argued, the institutional details of the navy were designed to encourage trustworthy officers, so most of the rules used to monitor captains should have ended with the introduction of steam and the chronometer. Obviously, requirements to enter into battle with the weather gage became obsolete and disappeared. But, less obviously, the Articles of War disappeared as well. The introduction of steam and a good clock allowed for cheap, direct monitoring of captains in most circumstances; therefore, it is not surprising that direct monitoring replaced indirect and reduced penalties replaced the more severe penalties of death. According to Rodger, the new Naval Act of 1866

> represented the final stage in the process by which centralised, legalistic naval administration had come to regulate in detail the internal affairs of the Queen's ships, and the daily lives of her officers and men. . . . Treachery and cowardice were not serious problems in the nineteenth century Navy. . . . Once it had been all the authorities could hope for, and more than they could achieve, to keep admirals and captains to their duty, now they could regulate in detail men's responsibilities.[107]

Changes in naval organization did not end with discipline. In the areas of recruitment, promotion, retirement, and general control of officers, the Admiralty eventually replaced the system of individual captain autonomy. Whereas in the age of sail the Admiralty often had only veto power on promotions, by the second half of the nineteenth century it had complete control. Lieutenants once acted as the watchdog of the navy, and the system of discontinuous promotion provided the incentive for a lieutenant to do this job. But with the advent of steam and the chronometer came the phasing out of this practice in the 1860s.[108] The purpose of having captains play a major role in promotion was to hinder the incentive of the lieutenant to lie about a captain's performance. With steam this role was not required, and the Admiralty took over the process of promotion. In fact, of all the organizational rules discussed (wages based on prizes, the weather gage, promotion, etc.), the only one to survive the introduction of steam was the line of battle. Although this tactic changed dramatically, it was retained in order to utilize maximum firepower against the enemy.

The French

Perhaps the best evidence that incentives and rules matter for performance comes from comparing the rules of the British navy with those of the French navy. Like every other navy, the French navy certainly had a problem with cowardice and shirking of duty. As mentioned previously, there was evidence of cowardice in the Battle of Trafalgar when "the van of the combined fleet [the French and Spanish], under Dumanoir, held its course for another hour after Nelson's breaking of the line, turning back only after the worst had been done."[109] Like the British, the French paid their officers wages supplemented with prize money. However, the prize system did not reward captains and admirals as well under the French system.[110] Nor did the French have a similar method of record keeping, exams on board, and promotion. Further, the incentives and French tactics were different, which led to different methods of fighting. The French were more wedded to a formal line of fighting than the British, but they also insisted on taking the leeward position. Admiral Tourville issued a set of Fighting Instructions in 1689 that became the French standard: "Tourville did for the French navy, and ultimately for all navies, what *marechal* Jean Martinet did for the army. His contribution to the science of naval tactics lay chiefly in drilling his very large fleet into a disciplined and controlled force which could deploy from a relatively sophisticated order of sailing to other sailing formations, or into the line of battle."[111]

In 1727 Paul Hoste, professor of mathematics at the Royal Seminary in Toulon, published the first major work on naval tactics, and it dominated French thinking for much of the remaining part of the century.[112] Tunstall and Tracy summarize his work:

> Hoste's whole system of sailing and battle formations was based on his five *ordres de marche*. These retained their primacy in the French service throughout the age of sail. The basis of these orders of sailing was that each provided a means of forming a close-hauled line of battle, which Hoste strongly favored. . . . The strongly defensive tone of Hoste's work is obvious. Much attention was given to avoiding an engagement. . . . Above all, his defensive cast of mind is revealed by the continuous acceptance of the leeward station as a basis for tactical demonstration.[113]

In general the French system of fighting was considered more scientific and rational than that of the British.[114] It was logical to hold the leeward position for all of the advantages it conferred. It was a defensive position, and the French tactics were generally defensive: "French fleets never attacked, as indeed they had never attempted to do since 1704. Their tactics when opposed by fleets of equal strength were mainly defensive."[115] Indeed, in stark contrast to the British, the French Fighting Instructions contained a section called "To Avoid an Engagement."[116] This section was combined with other rules, such as the following, that created a heavy price for a ship's captain if he lost a battle: "The National Convention had decreed that the captain and officers of any ship which hauled down her colours to the enemy, however numerous, 'unless the French ship should be so shattered as to be in danger of sinking' should be liable to the death penalty."[117]

The British navy never punished its captains for losing if they had done their duty. Indeed the British navy rules encouraged fighting even in instances where defeat was likely. However, the French rules were more rigid and provided an incentive *not* to engage unless they thought they could win. Whereas the British fighting instructions "taken as a whole, . . . tended to concentrate more power in the hands of the admiral, while giving him wider tactical initiative,"[118] the French instructions stressed defensive tactics and an avoidance of the large mistake. Defensiveness and caution played out in other features of the French navy. French ships were generally better and faster, and the French navy was known for its rigid and difficult fleet maneuvers. The French would have trained more at sailing than at fighting, with the result that they lost most battles when they could not sail away. The French tactic of shooting up the spars and sails of the enemy and then fleeing away is certainly consistent with this overall philosophy. It is unfortunate for the French that their rational approach failed to properly consider the effects of their tactics on incentives; as a result, they were unsuccessful against the British.

It is interesting to speculate on why the French did not copy the British rules exactly. A continental power such as France no doubt faced different constraints than its island neighbor when it came to directing efforts on land and at sea. For Britain, its navy was its chief form of defense, whereas for France the navy was primarily used to keep in touch with overseas possessions and to protect merchant trade—neither of which were as vital to France as they were to Britain. Historically, countries that relied heavily on trade by sea have also been naval powers, and the first true navies were developed by the Italian states of Venice and Genoa.[119] But institutional rules, unlike military technology or operations tactics, are more difficult to observe and often have built-in inertia. The French designed rules and built ships that gave them the advantage in flight and in defense. In retrospect, by 1815, with the loss of hundreds of ships and many colonies, their strategy had clearly failed, but it seems reasonable to assume it was based on a calculated risk. In fact, the great fleet battles of the Napoleonic Wars only took place because the British were generally able to trap the French against a lee shore and cut off their escape. It also seems reasonable to suggest that in light of France's strong beliefs and investment in theoretical naval tactics and relative less vulnerability to sea power, there would be reluctance to change policy, especially given the noisy information they would have received over any battle. That is, the information they received at any particular time over the century was inadequate to change their behavior. Throughout the eighteenth century, only 53 fleet battles took place; most were indecisive, some the British lost, and all had enough variability that the truth was no doubt a casualty as well. The strong French beliefs and noisy information would have contributed to the long period of unchanged tactics.

CONCLUSION

The age of fighting sail spans the entire pre-modern era and provides an excellent example of how an institutional governance structure was designed to generate performance even though direct monitoring was virtually impossible. It shows the necessity of patronage when sale of office and bureaucracy were not options. It shows how important nature was, and how technical changes reduced this role. Most importantly, it shows how getting the institutional details correct, relative to rival nations, had a large impact on outcomes.

Though the British Admiralty had limited information regarding the actions of their commanders, they had confidence that dereliction of duty would be minimal. It is interesting that British success did not depend on superior technology, geography, or luck. The long string of successes depended on a scheme of indirect monitoring that was "inefficient" from a sheer technical point of view but proved efficient in controlling the problem of cowardice among its commanding officers. The organizational rules surrounding these officers were designed to encourage engagement, and with engagement likely, officers had an incentive to drill their crews to fight. It turned out that the way to systematically win naval battles was the same way to get to Carnegie Hall: practice, practice, practice.

By paying their officers through prizes, the British navy encouraged them to want to be at sea. Once at sea, the officers were under the Fighting Instructions that essentially forced them to engage the enemy, and to do so in a way that allowed others on board to monitor their actions. Knowing they would engage the enemy provided captains with an incentive to practice and train for battle. At the time, scholars and tacticians shunned fighting in a line with the weather gage for their obvious shortcomings; however, the success of these methods stemmed from the ability they provided to monitor performance and from the incentives they provided to fight—and therefore to train. Once back at port, the navy could count on an accurate reporting of events, given their system of discontinuous promotions and patronage. This system of rules was absent from the privateers and army, where the incentives of those fighting were more compatible with the Crown's interests. It was also missing for the men of the lower deck who could be observed by the commanders of the ship. Furthermore, the rules were discarded with the introduction of steam and the marine chronometer, which allowed for direct monitoring of captains. Finally, the rules were different from, and sometimes the opposite of, those of their enemies—especially the French.

CHAPTER SIX

Purchasing Army Commissions

Every step in the commissioned ranks of the Army, whether gained by seniority or good service, had to be purchased. A captaincy, a majority, a colonelcy, the command of a regiment, of a troop of Life Guards; . . . all passed to new recipients of the royal favour at a market price which varied with supply and demand like the membership of the New York Stock Exchange.

WINSTON CHURCHILL, *Marlborough*

The purchase of command positions within an army surely strikes the modern reader as most odd, and quite possibly, perverse. Even the strongest advocate of free enterprise would likely hesitate to advocate applying market principles to the distinctive circumstances of the military. And yet, during the pre-modern period, the sale of commissions from one officer to another was the dominant method for staffing armies. Perhaps just as surprising, the use of private offices, sale, and market-like mechanisms for the provision of public services was quite common; postal and court services, lighthouses, and roads are a few examples.

That the Crown was aware that different circumstances required distinct sets of incentives is apparent in the contrast between the navy, where positions of command were distributed through patronage, and the army, where the primary mechanism was sale. Because of the difficulties in monitoring naval officers, and because officers often had private incentives opposite their patron's, trust was of utmost importance. However, in the army many situations presented the opposite case; that is, the officers' private interests were compatible with or matched the interests of the Crown. It was still the case that the Crown could not directly monitor the performance of army captains and so could not hire them as employees. However, in these cases, the ranks could be sold directly and become private property. As private owners paid by the profits left over at the end of the day, the officers policed themselves.[1]

The British army, provides an excellent example of how market incentives could be exploited to overcome the problem of monitoring the Crown's servants. The army paid its officers in a manner similar to the navy, namely, with small salaries plus the chance of large prizes, honors, and fame. However, because the army operated on land, less variability in fighting conditions existed compared to that of the navy. The reduced role of weather, wind, and other natural factors in land battles allowed for a completely different form of organization: the purchase of commissions and the exploitation of private market incentives. The army officer had a strong profit incentive to monitor his own behavior, which relieved the Crown from this burden. Still the use of purchased commissions remains puzzling to modern thinking.

Consider the extraordinary case of the 1st Duke of Wellington, Arthur Wellesley. His military exploits in the war against Napoleon are well known, not the least of which is his victory at Waterloo. What is perhaps less well known is that Wellington (or at least his family) purchased his first commission as ensign in 1787, and after purchasing seven further commissions and having seen no military action, nor having received any military training, had reached the rank of colonel and was in charge of his own regiment by 1794. His first military engagements (and defeats) in the low countries of the Rhine delta were just short of disastrous, and from a twenty-first-century perspective they could hardly have been otherwise. Indeed, even with his subsequent victories, the practice of using purchase over merit and formal training for military leaders might seem folly both on the part of Wellington and the British army. Yet Wellington was hardly alone because the purchase system, crudely founded in medieval times and continued until 1871 in Britain, was the central means by which Britain (and indeed Europe) staffed their army officer corps.

As with many of the pre-modern institutions, most historians appear to have a dim view of the purchase system. Cooper is typical in stating: "It was a system which hardly admitted of any defense, so illogical was it and so much harm had it done to the Army."[2] Contemporary critics of the system were also common, an early criticism made in the 1641 House of Commons, stated that "the buying and selling . . . of the commands of forts, castles and places of trust, are causes of the evils of the kingdom."[3] Strong words, but the purchase system often took the bullet for army problems that had nothing to do with the purchase of command.

Indeed, it is common in the historical record to find the purchase system blamed for the excesses, foibles and disasters of military history; seldom is it given any credit for victories.

Yet this conclusion is probably false, resulting from a myopic view of the role the purchase system played. The purchase system was an integral part of all successful armies for great lengths of time. The purchase system was also used for many other offices of the state. It must have had some redeeming quality. Indeed, as with other pre-modern institutions, the purchase system was an incentive scheme, an imperfect but effective solution to a difficult monitoring problem. Understanding the purchase system requires understanding the incentives of individual officers, the constraints faced by the Crown in staffing its military, and the role nature played in battles. To consider it only in isolation or to compare it to a modern army organization naturally leads to the conclusion that it was illogical and an impediment to success.

Like many of the pre-modern institutions, the purchase system in the military survived a long time under the most competitive of environments. When successful, innovations in all aspects of the military, from weapons and tactics to fortifications and organization, were quickly adopted by other states. The spread of military technology was especially true during the pre-modern era. For example, the adoption of bastion fortifications, musketeers, archers, and volley-line tactics during the sixteenth century has been called the "military revolution"—a moniker coined by historian Michael Roberts in 1955—because most countries switched so quickly.[4] Although the actual spread was never as complete and as thorough as the term implies and although the relative impacts of changes in tactics, fortifications, firearms, and battle lines are subjects of debate among many historians, it is clear that any major power had to keep up with the latest effective technology.[5] In such an institutionally competitive environment, it would be unlikely for the purchase system to survive for several hundred years if it failed to assist the army in its function. Therefore it makes sense to inquire into the merits of the purchase system—from the points of view both of the soldier and of the Crown—all the more so, given that staffing an army with officers having no military experience is incongruous with common sense.[6]

The modern perception of the purchase system as irrational no doubt begins with this basic stumbling block: individuals (mostly from the aristocracy) paid money to be an officer. It seems illogical for someone with no formal training in war to actually pay to lead a company. Furthermore, these men not only paid to be officers but paid handsomely even though by all accounts the official wages of these positions were low. The market to which the twentieth-century Churchill referred in his biography of his pre-modern ancestor was quite distinct from official policy, given that the Crown established official prices for every rank. However, the prices individuals were willing to pay were often higher. For example, in 1832, Lord Brudenell bought a lieutenant colonelcy for between £35,000 and £40,000—well above the regulated list price of £6,175.[7] Although it was illegal to trade at nonregulated prices, the practice of trading was common, and the transacted prices seldom were close to the regulated ones. The transaction was between the two officers, so in this case, the officer selling the colonelcy would have received the £35,000–40,000. Based strictly on the wages earned in the various ranks, sale prices were often four to five times higher than the present value of the stream of future wages; that is, the value of the commission did not reflect the value of the expected wages. Based solely on wages, the investment was a poor one. But wages were only one part of compensation, and a small one at that. The real potential return on investment came from prize money in victory.[8]

In addition to the purchase of their commissions, higher-ranked officers incurred other expenses. Although the Crown subsidized them, colonels were required to pay for regiment expenses. These included the costs of recruitment, uniforms, wages, equipment, and any welfare paid to the wounded or widows.[9] Wages for commissioned officers remained at the same level over the last 200 years of the system.[10] All told, the system appears to be a bad deal for officers.

Yet no serious and persistent grumblings or revolts took place among the commissioned officers about the purchase system. Indeed Harries-Jenkins notes that "surprisingly, while this lower rate [of pay] was a frequent source of complaint, it was never a major controversial issue."[11] In fact, for most of the purchase system's history, the major opposition for terminating the purchase of commissions came from the officers. Their lack of concern for reform might only have reflected their vested interests. After all, they had purchased their commissions, and an uncompensated elimination of their right to resale would have made them worse off. However, discussions regarding the termination of the system always included compensation for investments and, when the system was finally ended, those who had paid for their commissions were compensated at the black-market prices.[12] Hence the officers' opposition to alterations in the purchase system probably did not reflect concerns over losing their monetary investments.

That the purchase system lasted for centuries without major opposition from the Crown or officers suggests that there was likely more to the system of purchase than meets the eye. Scratch a little beneath the first layer, and it turns out the purchase of commissions was part of a rational scheme designed to best staff the army. It becomes clear that the method of compensation consisted of more than straight wages: prizes were an important part of compensation. An army is more than just a group of men: it needs good soldiers with an incentive to fight. In light of the natural variability of the pre-modern world, the purchase system survived for so long because it solved two problems in raising an army: first, selecting quality officers, and second, providing them with incentives to fight that were compatible with the incentives of the Crown. The purchase system, generally speaking, provided an adequate solution to both of these problems. It encouraged officers to self-select according to ability and provided them with incentives to fight that matched reasonably well the overall objective of battle. The purchase system solved these problems in an age when the Crown could not solve them directly.

As with the other organizational victims of the Institutional Revolution, the end of the purchase system came with the end of other pre-modern institutions. In England, the military purchase system ended in 1871, along with the fall of the aristocracy, dueling, and the rise of modern institutions. On the Continent, the system ended around the time of the Napoleonic Wars.

THE ARMY PURCHASE SYSTEM

The practice of purchasing a position in an army dates back to the thirteenth century, came into its own in the seventeenth and eighteenth centuries, and died out during the nineteenth century. Throughout this time, the purchase system evolved, but by the beginning of the pre-modern era it had essentially stabilized into the institution that would last until the late nineteenth century. All countries in Europe used a purchase system for their armies throughout the pre-modern era.

The English purchase system had its beginnings when Henry II (1133–1189) relieved the landed class of a medieval tradition introduced by William the Conqueror that required landowners to supply the king with knights for forty days of the year. Instead, Henry II taxed the lords and used the funds to hire mercenary companies—many of whom were not nationals. During this early period, the entire company was made up of mercenaries who, among themselves, would sell and trade positions within the military "firm." In part, the modern commercial connotation of the word "company" reflects the commercial nature of these early armies.

In addition to nominal pay from the Crown, the companies received a fraction of the plunder of war, including any ransom from captured prisoners and payments from landowners for protecting private property during battle.[13] Shares in these companies were determined by the capital investment of its members, which included horses, equipment, and possibly cash, and these shares were tradable.[14]

The purchase of shares by active officers was the institutional forerunner of the formal purchase of commissions, which fully developed in the seventeenth century. This organizational innovation was soon copied by the other European powers of the time, and it was spurred on by medieval innovations in weapons. The pike and longbow effectively eliminated knights from battle and increased the value of foot soldiers. Although foot soldiers were cheap relative to knights, an army required a large number of them. Technological advances continued throughout the pre-modern era, but the watershed came at the beginning, with small and large artillery. Very quickly pikes, lances, crossbows, and halberds were replaced by large numbers of archers, musketeers, and artillery. Ultimately, the musket and artillery came to be the foremost weapons of pre-modern armies.[15] Throughout this transition, the size of armies continued to grow.

Although the early companies were composed mostly of foreign mercenaries, over time they became dominated by nationals. By the time of the Tudors and the beginning of the pre-modern era, the Crown was granting commissions almost exclusively to landed subjects who then raised a company in service only to the English monarch. By the seventeenth and eighteenth centuries, the officers were all (with a few exceptions) nationals who bought their commissions from other officers, whereas the regular troops remained a mixture of nationals and hired foreign mercenaries right up until the Crimean War.

Until the late 1600s, England never had a standing army. In times of war, the Crown would raise an army in the fashion just mentioned, and it would be disbanded in peacetime. After the Restoration in 1660 and the Glorious Revolution in 1688, great debate occurred over the necessity of a standing army. However, perpetual problems with France, other Continental powers, and colonial struggles resulted in a de facto standing army, to which the practice of purchasing commissions carried through.

Under the institution of purchased commissions, the Crown and the Parliament did not have total control over the staffing decisions of the army because the commission was controlled in large part by the officer who had the right to resell it to the highest bidder. This right of resale led to several conflicts between the Crown and the army and to attempts by the government to regulate resale, establish list prices, and exert pressure on and veto certain transactions. For the most part, these efforts were fairly ineffective. Black-market prices continued to exist, and apparently the Crown did not make any stronger effort to prevent it. When the time came to abolish purchase in 1871, the Crown compensated the officers for the actual prices they had paid, not the formal list prices. The Royal Commission looking into the matter concluded that the centuries old "tacit acquiescence in the practice" amounted to "a virtual recognition of it by civil and military departments and authorities."[16] The governments of the day were more successful at regulating minimum ages for purchase, minimum times between ranks, and conditions for transfer.

At the turn of the eighteenth century, it was possible to purchase a first commission above the lowest ranks, but by the end of that century, it was almost always the case that an officer would enter the army at the rank of ensign—the minimum age of entry being 16. Once in the army, promotion could take place with the purchase of a commission immediately above the current one; that is, by the end of the eighteenth century, one could not "skip" ranks. It seems peculiar that an individual who was willing to pay the most was not always the one who ended up with the commission. A general pecking order based on regiment and seniority prevailed over who was able to bid but allowed for a plethora of exceptions and ad hoc cases where merit and experience determined who was able to purchase. In such cases, senior officers, war ministers, and even the king might influence who was eligible to purchase. As Houlding notes: "The value of experience and merit, was a much more important aspect of the promotion system than is usually credited."[17]

Nonpurchased commissions, that is, cases in which an officer was promoted on a nonfinancial basis, did exist but generally could not be sold. Such appointments caused unrest among the other officers, and as Wellington claimed: "Nothing is more difficult than to promote an officer, excepting on a very long standing, to a troop or company without purchase."[18] Most of these commissions took place in the heat of battle. When an officer was killed, a junior officer would be promoted on the spot to replace him. However, most commissions, about two-thirds of them at any given time from 1700 to 1871, were purchased. Harries-

Jenkins claims that, prior to 1838, approximately three-quarters of promotions were filled by purchase.[19] The rest were obtained by a host of other methods, including rewards for exceptional service in battle.[20] All purchases were subject to the approval of the Crown, and the monarch reportedly paid close attention to the granting of commissions, especially at the higher ranks. When one officer "sold-out," retired, or transferred to another unit, he created a chain reaction through a series of vacancies. No one could move up in rank without selling his current position, and one sale led to another.[21]

The purchase system had several interesting features. First, once an officer was promoted past the rank of lieutenant-colonel, the commission could not be sold; the commission effectively became a sunk cost, or a form of hostage capital. As a result, once an officer reached the rank of lieutenant-colonel, he had to make a choice whether to commit to the army or sell out. When an officer of lower rank retired, he could sell out or move to the half-pay list. In this latter case, he received half pay for life but remained on the active list and could still be promoted based on seniority. On the other hand, a lieutenant-colonel would eventually lose the ability to sell his commission if he went on half pay. Second, as in the navy, although all officers received prize money, most of it went to the higher-ranking officers. Finally, payment by prizes was only used when attacking, and looting was not considered a form of prize money.

WHY A PURCHASE SYSTEM?

One traditional argument for the existence of the purchase system was that it kept the army in the hands of the aristocracy, who had a stake in the survival of the constitution. Wellington states:

> It brings into the service men of fortune and education—men who have some connection with the interests and fortune of the country besides the commissions which they hold from his Majesty. It is this circumstance which exempts the British Army from the character of being a "mercenary" army, and has rendered its employment for nearly a century and a half, not only consistent with the constitutional privileges of the country, but safe and beneficial.[22]

Ironically, Wellington was not a man of great fortune or education. He was the third of five surviving sons of a Protestant Ascendancy family in Ireland. He showed little by way of talent or ambition as a youth, and when he first asked permission to marry the daughter of the Earl of Longford in 1793, he was turned down because his prospects looked so poor. His family's limited resources were mostly directed at his older brother, and Wellington dropped out of school for both financial and academic reasons.

As were the holders of almost all civil offices of the day, the officers of the army were almost exclusively from the aristocracy, but the purchase system was not the cause per se. Purchase was a common method of dealing with many public services, and many nonmilitary offices went to individuals who were not members of the aristocracy. In contrast, the Navy and other high offices of state were also dominated by members of the aristocracy, and yet these positions were grounded in patronage, not purchase. Thus, purchase was neither necessary nor sufficient for the dominance of a certain class within a profession. In fact, the purchase system often allowed men from families of industrial wealth, who were not part of the landed class, to enter.

Another common theory for the purchase of commissions was the opposite of Wellington's: that it allowed wealthy, nonlanded individuals access to membership in the aristocracy. This theory fails as well. The ultimate source of acceptance into the aristocracy was a demonstration that an investment had been made in some type of hostage capital. Because a purchased commission could be sold, it was not a sunk investment, thereby excluding it as a form of hostage capital. Thus it was not an asset that could assure the Crown of trustworthy performance—an ever-present objective of the aristocracy.[23] For the wealthy, nonaristocrat, a purchased commission might have been used as a signal of intent to gain cultural acceptance and respectability, but it was never the case that honor was up for sale—especially during the pre-modern era. Other theories of purchase exist.[24] All of the theories, like Wellington's, fail to see the bigger picture within which purchase was placed.

The key element of any purchase system was the willingness to pay for a commission based on expected future returns of prize and glory. Because commissions fetched a positive price, these returns also had to be positive. Officers expected to earn a living off the prizes of battle and hoped for a fortune. Officers were not interested in mere personal fulfillment from joining the army, and they certainly would have been unwilling to pay for a commission if it yielded a loss. A willingness to pay for a commission, however, depends on an ability to pay. Wealthy members of the aristocracy may have had the ability to pay for the commission, but they were not alone in their willingness to pay. Marginal gentry without the immediate capital, but who expected to receive large rewards in the future, would have been willing to borrow on those future returns in order to pay for the commission. The ability to borrow depended on capital market conditions, and many officers borrowed money from family members or individual investors in order to purchase a commission. For example, Wellington borrowed money from his family, while Marlborough had the help of his father, the Duke of York, and especially, the financial assistance of the Duchess of Cleveland, the mistress of the king and also Marlborough's lover.[25] Access to such family and friends, then, no doubt contributed to the large fraction of the landed class in the officer corps.

Self-Selection

A major problem in raising an effective army was to find high-quality officers. An army full of men willing to fight but whose soldiers were totally inept at fighting was a losing army just the same. Prior to the nineteenth century, it was generally thought that a great officer was born, not made. This belief implicitly reflected the fact that the inputs for a good officer were unobservable; in other words, a reliable way to separate out luck from legitimate effort in battle did not exist. What makes a great military leader? One who could motivate troops, ensure they were fed, take some risks but not others, and make the right decisions in the heat of battle? The relationship between traits, behavior, and outcomes had a considerable element of randomness—as in the answer to this question: "what makes a great entrepreneur?" It is reminiscent of the story in which Abraham Lincoln was told that General Grant was a drunkard. "Well," responded Lincoln, "find out what brand of whiskey Grant drinks, because I want to send a barrel of it to each one of my generals."[26] Furthermore, during the pre-modern era, direct supervision of officers in battle was difficult because officers essentially made their decisions in isolated situations where communication and coordination were difficult and where, as always during this time, nature played an extremely large role. This variability increased during the pre-modern era. Early firearms were unreliable and inaccurate, gunpowder smoke reduced visibility greatly, and horses and weather contributed to the variability. In addition, easily observable signals correlated with ability generally did not exist. Although the first military academy opened on the Continent in 1616, none existed in Britain until the end of the era, nor were there obvious skills that could be taught and measured that would have allowed for direct monitoring.

Under these conditions, military officers could best be paid by receiving a share of the profits from battle. The purchase of commissions acted in the same manner as the purchase of any business, with soldier entrepreneurs self-selecting what type of fighting they were best suited for. Those who were correct in their personal assessments were rewarded by large prizes and continued to purchase higher positions, which in turn led to larger shares of prize money. Those who were incorrect were likely to exit the industry . . . permanently and horizontally. The key to the success of such a market structure to the officer corps would be the process of self-selection. Only those who truly thought they could command successfully, that is, those who were keen and ambitious, would advance in the ranks.[27]

Incentives to Fight

Having high-quality officers, however, was only half the battle. Officers required the proper incentives to perform. These included not only the incentives to fight but also to fight in the interests of the entire army. Due to the extreme situations and opportunities for being killed, incentive problems abounded in armies at war. The private desire to preserve one's life, regardless of the effect this desire might have on the overall mission, is a problem of the first order that all armies must overcome. These problems were no doubt extremely prevalent in army regiments where one's life was on the line.

Several studies in the economics of modern warfare corroborate the existence of this problem. Brennan and Tullock examine the private incentives of soldiers under attack and conclude that armies are partly designed to mitigate the incentive of individual soldiers to save their own lives at the risk of losing the battle.[28] For example, it is well known among military historians that many soldiers in Second World War battles failed to fire their weapons in combat; indeed, reports show that at most only 25 percent of weapons were fired in any given World War II battle.[29] Many historians interpret these actions as reflecting a reluctance for taking another life.[30] Another explanation is that firing a weapon draws attention to one's position and intentions, thereby increasing the chance of returned fire. Regardless of the cause, in modern warfare the best strategy is to sit quietly in a protected spot and wait.[31] Warfare in the trenches of the First World War was similar.[32] Soldiers who faced the same opposition week after week began to cooperate and either ceased firing or missed on purpose. The army's solution in the trenches was to rotate its troops. Concepts of morale and loyalty and of positive and negative rewards were intended to overcome a soldier's private incentive to save himself at the expense of his company.

Failure to engage the enemy in the interests of the Crown was a problem in pre-modern times as well. Even during battles where soldiers formed tight formations for musket fire, the number and rate of deaths were too low when compared to what they should have been if the weapons were all fired at an average rate directly at the enemy.[33] According to Field, this problem was made worse with the introduction of muskets. Prior to muskets and the widespread use of archers, combat was more likely hand-to-hand from start to finish. Contact is at least observable to the commander on the ground. However, it is more difficult to observe where a musket ball goes, and even if it does go wide, such was the nature of smooth barrels. As a result, soldiers would often aim high because "the musket made a lot more noise, and was thus much better suited to posturing."[34] In modern armies loyalty, national pride, and monitoring are used to overcome these incentives. Modern armies also have more reliable and accurate weapons that lend themselves to monitoring. During the pre-modern era, these tools were mostly absent from the battlefield, and so payment through wages would not have been effective. Instead, payments through prizes were used in an attempt to offset the private incentive to avoid engaging the enemy. Such payments were far from perfect, but at the time it was the best that could be achieved.

The key aspect of the purchase system—namely, that officers were ultimately rewarded through profits—was the important mechanism for establishing incentives to fight. Officers received minimal levels of pay for supplies, but their incomes could only grow through actual battle. Profits mostly arose from the prizes of battle, but also came directly from the Crown for victory. In paying officers this way, the Crown encouraged them to engage the enemy. The common theme in the historical record is that the hope of reward was a major motivator of the officer corps. Soldiering provided an occupation, a possibility of adventure, and a chance of demonstrating one's true character, but everyone's underlying drive was the chance to earn prize money in one form or another. Every commission was an opportunity for capital gain.[35]

Matching Individual and Army Incentives

The purchase system that evolved out of the late medieval period was a pre-modern solution to the problem of raising an effective army. The payment of prize money to officers was useful in attracting quality men and provided a strong incentive to fight. Such an incentive could still have hindered the army had the private incentives it provided jeopardized the object of the mission. As with the case of the Navy, paying by prize was a two-edged sword and could encourage too much or inappropriate fighting. Premature or excessive looting that prevented the army from victory had to be discouraged.[36] If looting or extortion, in themselves, affected the overall agenda of the army, then the purchase system would not have survived. "Too much" fighting also might have hindered success if regiments had strategic value in containing or defending an enemy rather than attacking.

The purchase system was obviously part of the incentive structure of the individual officer, and it did its job most of the time. Its Achilles' heel was that under some circumstances the incentives of the individual officers to fight did not match those of the army. When the incentives reasonably matched those of the Crown, all was well, but when they did not, the system failed. In 1766 Lord Barrington, secretary of war in the mid-eighteenth century, was concerned enough about various sales of commissions within certain regiments that he wrote a letter to the judge advocate general in which he stated the essential problem of compatible incentives:

> That colonels of regiments should not attend to . . . [general army matters] . . . is not matter either of wonder or blame; their care is extended no further than to their own corps, and while they command it; but the officer of the Crown, who is entrusted with the important charge of the whole army, a body whose probable duration infinitely exceeds the short space allotted to individuals, cannot be too vigilant, least confined temporary convenience or compassion should produce general permanent mischief or distress.[37]

In other words, Lord Barrington was saying that a colonel often acts in ways that only benefit the returns to his own corps and that are not always in the general interests of the army.

The major difference between the army and navy was in the role nature played with the strategic targets. At sea, during the age of sail, it was difficult to directly monitor in any modern way to prevent a captain from exploiting the prize system to his own advantage. The temptation to capture a merchant ship, combined with the moving enemy target, the difficulty in establishing position, and the role of the wind meant that the Crown could not trust a captain who purchased his commission. The captain who was willing to pay the most would necessarily be the one least trustworthy because maximizing the revenue stream would mean going after lucrative and safe merchant ships rather than enemy naval vessels. With the army, a few things were different. The target was fixed, travel over land was more predictable than at sea, and armies were less likely to get lost. Officers in the army had fewer natural excuses to use compared with their counterparts at sea, and certainly towns did not up and move overnight. The result was that opportunistic fighting could be discerned and punished, and therefore prizes and purchase could function together without loses to the Crown.

Thus the system of purchasing a military commission was used to self-select officers into the military, given the general difficulty in observing military talent and the lack of alternative screens of quality. Additionally, the purchase system, by the use of payment through prize money, provided an incentive to engage the right enemy in the right battle. It encouraged both the officers and the soldiers to engage the enemy, though providing this incentive may have helped avoid some battles as well. Knowing that individual opponents had a private incentive to fight, some towns may have offered tribute in order to avoid invasion. Indeed, this practice was very common; for example, Napoleon took most of northern Italy in this way. Still, this form of payment, by encouraging the ever-present incentive to engage, could lead to "too much fighting" when the overall objective of the army might have required a more defensive position. This problem was a cost of the system; in order for purchase to function properly, both the individual soldier's and the commander's incentives to fight must have matched those of the Crown.

EVIDENCE FOR THE PURCHASE HYPOTHESIS

The Payment of Prize Money

It is unfortunate that no systematic historical study on the actual returns to soldiering has yet been undertaken. However, ample indirect and anecdotal evidence supports the theory that officers across Europe were paid out of the spoils of war. Napoleon, in his early successes in northern Italy, extracted £80,000 and "twenty fine paintings" from the Grand Duke of Parma and later extorted £800,000 from the city of Milan.[38] No details are provided as to how this money was divided, but given the French reputation for living off the land of their victims, these were probably not isolated cases. In the 1826 British attack on the forti-fied city of Burtpore, 100 miles south of Delhi in India, "the survivors divided £480,000 among themselves in prize money. Combermere's [the commander] share was £60,000."[39] Finally, Redlich notes: "Much more important as a source of income to common soldiers was booty, legitimate and illegitimate alike. . . . Some soldiers accumulated small fortunes from loot, as much as 8,000 to 20,000 talers [a silver coin equivalent to a dollar]. . . . Provided that the troop was at full strength, out of every 1,000 talers available, the commanding general would re-ceive 100 and each common soldier, 5 talers."[40] During Cromwell's 1650 Scottish campaign, he accumulated prizes from war that filled sixty of his ships.[41] The Scots still speak ill of Cromwell.

Further evidence that officers received payment in terms of prizes is that the price of a commission reflected the expected future incomes of the commission. For example, if an officer expected to move quickly up the chain of command in a given regiment, he was willing to pay more for a commission in that regiment. Hence troops returning from overseas charged higher prices for their commissions because the sick and wounded in the regiment would soon retire; whereas troops heading to poor locations, such as the West Indies, had the price of their com-missions fall. Because the West Indies were notorious for disease, the price fall reflected the reduced chance of survival. Poor management of a regiment was also reflected in the price of commissions. In addition, these fluctuating prices provided opportunities for capital losses.[42]

Not only were officers paid by some form of prize money, but for the true winners, such as Wellington or Marlborough, the rewards were enormous. Wellington would end up one of the wealthiest soldiers of all time, but even after his early years in India he had saved £42,000 and was able to return to England and convince his love's family that his marriage prospects were not so bad after all. The case of John Churchill, 1st Duke of Marlborough, is an interesting one. Recall that he was born to the minor gentry and had to work his way up the ranks in the army through a series of purchases. During the War of the Spanish Succession (1701–1714), he achieved a series of stunning victories at Blenheim (1704), Ramillies (1706), Oudenarde (1708), and Malplaquet (1709). Queen Anne and Parliament decided to reward him with a palace. Blenheim Palace would take almost twenty years to complete, would occupy seven acres, and cost close to £250,000 (the equivalent to about $60 million today). However, nothing in the life of Churchill was ever simple. Po-litical troubles meant that he spent £60,000 of his own fortune to get the project started, and the family had to finish the house on their own. The point being that, in addition to the furnishings, paintings, and other artifacts he had collected over his years in battle, Churchill had amassed a fortune in prizes and was able to supplement the gifts from the Crown and complete one of the great architectural treasures of England.

Redlich, in one of the few historical attempts to estimate the wealth of various military entrepreneurs, argues that the sixteenth-century German commander Georg von Frundsberg's estate, made up of gifts, prizes, contributions, and salary was "equivalent to about one and a half million pre-World War II dollars."[43] Redlich provides estimates of three other German military enterpriser's wealth from the same century, concluding that they all died wealthy. For the purpose of the argument here, it is only necessary to show the possibility of generating large sums of income from military leadership that more than offset any initial purchase price of the commission. Ample evidence supports this theory. These large plunders were not that common, and Parker cites a seventeenth-century commentator who claimed that only 2 percent of soldiers could expect a fortune.[44] But a 2 percent chance of a fortune was likely to be enough to encourage many—given the realistic alternatives of the pre-modern world—in the same way that impossible odds and enormous winnings encourage so many moderns to part with their money at the local lottery outlet.

The Purchase System Rules

By the time Britain had a standing army, the purchase system was well defined. It had evolved into a well-developed set of rules with an economic logic to promote the dual feature of purchase: namely, to self-select qualified officers and to provide incentives to fight. Self-selection simply meant that those individuals most confident that they would be successful in command and battle would be the most likely to purchase command. However, it was critical that these individuals be qualified as well as confident. Self-selection was not without its problems, and the internal rules of the purchase system helped to correct these.

For example, people are often overconfident. Individuals and their families may have had a biased or utterly mistaken view on the necessary talents for military success, thereby making mistakes in measuring one's own ability inevitable. Furthermore, cases of adverse self-selection may arise, where individuals with particular looting talents join the army, but their skills do not increase the chance of victory. Attempts to safeguard against this problem explains why purchase was made initially at the lowest rank, why minimum years of service were required for different ranks, and why minimum ages at which to join the service were prerequisites. It also explains why officers above lieutenant-colonel were prevented from selling their commission. This rule forced colonels to make a final and complete decision to throw their wealth and welfare into the army. Only those that truly believed they had the opportunity to succeed in battle would carry on. Eliminating the ability to sell created a hostage-capital investment for the senior officer, and this investment of course made him a more trustworthy officer, in the same way hostage-capital investments made aristocrats more trustworthy. Lower-ranked officers make smaller mistakes than higher ones, and thus impose fewer costs on the rest of the army while they discover whether or not they have talents for fighting.[45]

Another problem with individuals self-selecting into the army was that they might take extreme risks for quick riches. To counteract this possibility, the purchase system distributed prize money based on rank, with the higher ranks receiving a disproportionate share. This method of payment avoided large payouts for good luck to new junior officers. Survival and success to the upper ranks was more likely to be based on the key human capital that makes a good officer. Were payments more equally distributed, individuals would join the lower ranks, not because they thought they might be successful officers, but because the expected payoff was simply high enough for them to risk their lives in a single battle.

In order for the purchase system to self-select good officers, it had to offer an opportunity to make a profit, which explains why officers purchased their commissions from other officers and not directly from the Crown. Because the value of commissions in an entire regiment partially depended on how well the regiment was run and on the chance of survival, allowing officers to earn a capital gain on their commission encouraged the unit to be more successful. Had the Crown retained ownership over the commission, this incentive would have been absent. It might appear that the Crown suffered, in terms of its own revenue, in giving up ownership, but it was likely to have been revenue neutral. Had the Crown retained the purchase price, then salaries or prize shares would have increased to compensate. Prices and rates of return were determined by market forces, but the form these payments took were determined by the incentives they created.

Self-selection was not the only purpose of the purchase system; it was also designed to produce effective fighting. Hence the use of prize money as a reward was only made when the army was attacking. When the army held a defensive position, such as with forts, payment was made in a lump sum to the officer in command. This officer was required to manage the fort and was allowed to keep the residual as income. This rule held for governing colonies and the day-to-day management of the regiment. In addition to this rule, there were strong restrictions on looting that attempted to match the incentives of the individual soldier with those of the Crown. Throughout the history of purchase, restrictions on looting were in place; as battles became more coordinated affairs, the restrictions increased until payment by looting was finally replaced by prize money determined by a prize court. Looting could be dangerous, distracting, and could cause riots and counterattacks that might lead to the ultimate loss of battle.[46]

The Ordinance Corps, Marines, and Mercenaries

The British army had all different types of soldiers and details, and they were not all treated the same when it came to the purchase of commissions. When the duties of a particular type of soldier were compatible with the purchase system, it was readily used. When, for whatever reason, the purchase system caused problems or when direct monitoring of a particular type of soldier was possible, then the purchase system was not used. Hence the purchase system was common in the infantry, cavalry, and guards regiments, but not in one group in the British army: the ordinance corps (made up of the engineers and the artillery). The ordinance corps provides a nice example of how technological change allowed for easier monitoring.

Prior to the Industrial Revolution, the ordinance corps was not a separate unit but a minor component of the army often plagued with contributions by nature.[47] With the development of rifled barrels, better carriages for transport, explosives, and other physics applications came the ability to develop these weapons and monitor their performance. The result was a branch of the army that took on a professional bureaucratic form—even while other branches were organized along pre-modern lines.

The ordinance corps was paid by salaries, not by prizes. This method of payment reflects the relative low costs of monitoring ordinance performance compared to monitoring the average soldier and the army's ability to monitor training within this branch. Relative to the infantry, where no formal training was required for service, the ordinance corps required intensive training. Students unable to complete this training were unable to enter this branch of the army. Training was not sufficient for a good officer, but it was necessary. Hence, the existence of a decent screening device provided a substitute for the use of self-selection based on willingness to purchase a commission.

One of the advantages of the purchase system was the incentives it provided to fight and perform duties in situations where it was difficult to monitor efforts. These incentive were less of an issue in ordinance where output was potentially easier to measure; hence this branch was paid by wages. The installation of a bridge, the accuracy of large cannon fire, and so forth were at least theoretically observable and much more so than the performance of an officer in the heat of battle.

In addition to the ordinance corps, the marines provide another interesting example to test the argument. Generally speaking, the differences in the methods of staffing the army and navy—purchase versus patronage—are explained by the fundamental fact that payment by prizes in the army created no major incompatible incentive problem between the officer in charge and the Crown, whereas it did in the navy. This difference resulted from the fixed targets on land and the limited role wind played in the army. Hence the navy needed to indirectly monitor captains and admirals to prevent cowardice through the patronage system. The navy never could have used a purchase system because those naval captains willing to pay the most for a commission would have been the ones most likely to act against the interests of the Crown.

But consider the role of the marines. The Royal Marines, who were essentially army soldiers at sea, did not purchase their commissions. Because they were at sea, they suffered from the same influence of nature that the naval officers did, and so they were appointed by patronage and not purchase.[48] A marine who purchased his commission would have had incentives opposed to the Crown and would have been able to blame nature for outcomes that the Crown was not pleased with. The marines provide a nice example that demonstrates that purchase was related to monitoring and not to the army per se.

One final category of soldiers were the mercenaries. The use of foreign soldiers within an army was yet another common pre-modern institution. When George Washington crossed the Delaware River on Christmas 1776, the British troops he surprised on the other side were speaking German, not English. Almost one-third of the British troops during the American Revolutionary War were Hessians. Organized use of foreign mercenaries began with the Swiss tactical infantries in the late 1400s. As with all successful military innovations, the Swiss practice of using foreign soldiers was quickly copied by other countries. From 1500 to 1700, all of the European countries used foreigners in their armies. For example, in 1743, Prussia's army was 66 percent foreign born.[49] Often armies would use mercenaries from different countries, and it was not uncommon to have half a dozen languages spoken on one side of a battle.[50] Throughout the eighteenth century, the use of foreigners began to diminish, and Britain's efforts to raise 16,500 Germans, Italians, and Swiss for the Crimean War was the last time a major country tried to hire a foreign army. By the nineteenth century, most countries had regulations prohibiting foreign military service.

It is interesting but not coincident that the rise and fall of the use of foreign soldiers parallels the rise and fall of the purchase system—and for the same reasons. Foreign soldiers, practically by definition, are less patriotic and less willing to sacrifice themselves in limb and body than their national counterparts. However, when purchase was used to staff the army, and direct prizes were the method of payment, the incentives of the foreign soldier were still reasonably in line with those of the host monarch. As war became more complex, as battles became larger, as measurement of soldier performance became possible, and as regiments and armies began to require coordination from a battlefield general, the incentives generated by payment through spoils of war become less aligned with those of the Crown. Under the changing circumstances, foreign soldiers could no longer be trusted to act in the national interest. National soldiers became more reliable than foreigners, and the latter faded out of the military landscape.

The Fall of the Purchase System

In the pre-modern era nature's variability played a significant role in the fortunes of war, and it was difficult to separate this influence from that of skill. The purchase system was the best response to this problem, but of course it was not perfect. As the role played by nature changed and as variability decreased, the ability to directly monitor and distinguish the role of skill increased. Eventually, the purchase system was replaced by a professional army paid through wages. Purchase ended in England in 1871, and on the Continent about 70 to 100 years earlier.

Changes in the role nature played in warfare account both for the elimination of the purchase system and for England's lagging behind its continental peers. The beginning of the pre-modern era in the early part of the sixteenth century had seen a revolution in military technology that had increased the "white noise," thereby making the measurement of soldier inputs more difficult; the end of the pre-modern era was marked by a series of innovations that tended to remove this noise, thereby allowing for the introduction of direct measurement and monitoring. The innovations of the Industrial Revolution had an enormous impact on the technology of war and the methods of fighting. In particular, it changed the ability of commanders to monitor the performance of individual soldiers and therefore the ability of the Crown to monitor its officers. When monitoring, albeit imperfect, became feasible, the private market forces of purchased commissions gave way to bureaucratic professional modern armies—with flatter pay scales.

The key to the purchase system was that rewards could be based on conquest, permitting minimal direct monitoring of the regiment. However, a key to its success was relatively small battles. In the early years of medieval fighting and even until as late as the end of the eighteenth century, battles were small and rewards amounted to what could be looted and carried away. Throughout this time, soldiers fought in a line, a column, or a square, and the outcome usually hinged on individual soldier or officer performance.[51] Prior to the late eighteenth century, battle size was often constrained by several factors. First, movement was limited. Before the widespread use of rail, troops had to march, and on a good day, only twenty-five kilometers could be managed. Transportation not only affected the speed of troops, but also the speed of orders. Until the introduction of telegraphs, orders were transported by horse. Both of these features constrained battlefields to be small.

In these isolated battles, the Crown wished for a victory; the colonel wished for the opportunity to sack. The two incentives matched and minimal monitoring was necessary. Because each soldier received a share of the plunder, a soldier's pay also depended on profits and the need to monitor them was reduced. As battles became larger and more coordinated among the soldiers and regiments, simple looting was replaced by more organized distribution of the spoils; ultimately, the rewards came from the Crown and penalties were imposed for looting. As battles became even larger events, the private incentives to maximize individual wealth started to impede the success of the war. Hence one of the chief advantages of the purchase system became a major drawback. As in the navy, the incentives of the prize reward system started to become incompatible with the incentives of the Crown as the nature and size of battles changed.

Increased battle size was not the only factor that determined the institutional design of the army: tactics and fighting technology also played a role. Changes in tactics and war technology in the early nineteenth century began to demand certain amounts of formal training. The new training schools provided a substitute for the self-selection mechanism provided by purchase. Changes in recruitment and the ability to reduce desertion also began to take place toward the end of the eighteenth century. Veteran mercenaries were not the only soldiers in the pre-modern armies. As battle size grew, low-quality recruits and conscripts were brought in. Often convicts were used to fill the battle line. Desertion rates were high and "variation in troop strength . . . made it almost impossible for generals and governments to be sure of the exact size of their armed forces at any given time."[52] The introduction of prisons, transport, and increased training both lowered desertion and helped to monitor officer performance.

Further innovations in the sixteenth century introduced firearms and altered fortifications, and the evolution of firearms played a role in the termination of the purchase system. For example, the use of the musket spans the pre-modern era. The musket was notoriously inaccurate and to be effective in battle required coordinated shooting. This type of shooting usually required forming a line three men deep. The line, however, turned out to be very difficult to manage and quite dangerous to move. "A brigade of four battalions at full strength would occupy almost 800 meters when deployed three deep."[53] Indeed, one of the major French innovations was a foot drill that allowed troops to quickly move from a column formation (used to advance) to a line formation (used to fire). This innovation not only allowed for quicker movements of troops but also for larger numbers of troops. One of the major advantages Napoleon had over his opponents, it "enabled the Republic's generals, and especially Napoleon Bonaparte, to run rings round their opponents, who clung to the staid maneuvering of earlier years."[54] The introduction of the breech-loading rifle drastically altered the way armies fought by changing the ability to monitor performance and therefore changing the way soldiers were paid. The rifle increased both the range and accuracy of shooting. Furthermore, the breech-loading process allowed soldiers the advantage of lying on the ground while shooting because the gun was no longer loaded from the end of the barrel. Whereas armies in the eighteenth century fought in the wide open where cumbersome lines could be maneuvered, the nineteenth century saw fighting move to the woods and towns where soldiers could conceal themselves.

Finally, the new methods of measurement, including the development of the watch, accurate maps, the rifle, and the telegraph, eventually allowed for coordinated battles in which officers could be held accountable for their actions. Showing up at the wrong spot at the wrong time or missing the target could less easily be blamed on nature. All of these events culminated in the demise of the purchase system that was replaced by a professionally trained and paid army. These modern armies were more bureaucratic and had direct monitoring. Of course these changes were gradual and took place over one hundred years across Europe. The purchase system hung on in situations where the small-scale and remote battle was common.

The leaders in almost all military advances during the nineteenth century were the Prussians. They were the first to develop and exploit breech-loading weapons, steel guns, machine guns, and advanced military training. A flurry of formal military schools were established at the turn of the nineteenth century (Sandhurst in Britain, 1802; St. Cyr in France, 1808; and Berlin in Prussia, 1810). As these developments took place, the purchase system began to be abolished, and officers were paid straight wages. The ability to monitor officers directly had economies of scale because once the monitoring systems were in place, it cost little to monitor additional officers. The result was that armies became larger. Universal mass conscription was instituted, but it was not compatible with the purchase system because it reduced the value of prize-money payment to a trivial share for each individual soldier. Conscription, as we think about it in modern times, begins in 1793 in France and shortly after in Prussia. If armies had drafted their officers as they did their enlisted men, the draft would have been completely inconsistent with purchase, and the two systems could not have existed simultaneously. However, it was only in the twentieth century that officers began to be drafted; the early uses of conscription were strictly for regular troops paid with wages. Drafting large armies, however, does lower the share of prize money, which in turn hurts the incentives of the purchase system. Hence the simultaneous birth of conscription and the death of purchase is consistent with the purchase system being used to replace direct monitoring. Furthermore, the Prussian army was directed by a general staff that coordinated operations across the entire state and ensured that troops were directed under a single plan.

Included in these organizational innovations was the introduction of a new rank, the field marshall, whose job it was to coordinate the series of battles. This type of coordination was completely different from the relatively independent regiments of 100 years earlier. The swift Prussian defeats of Austria in 1866 and France in 1870 caught the attention of the whole world as other armies scrambled to catch up by imitating their organization.

The 300 years between 1500 and 1800 are bookended by two military revolutions. Within these years battles grew larger, but the infantry dominated army tactics and organization, leading to relative stability in the organization of armies.[55] After 1790, however, the impact of changing technology, which had reduced the noise around measuring soldier performance, had large effects on organization. All of these innovations— the movement of troops by train, communications by telegraph and the subsequent coordination of larger armies, the introduction of rifles, and the switch from open field to covered fighting—reduced the role of nature and reduced the advantage of rewarding officers exclusively in terms of individual or regimental performance. First, advances in these technologies often separated individual effort and remuneration, which eroded the incentive to fight under the purchase system. Second, and perhaps more important, the incentives of a large coordinated army no longer necessarily matched the incentives of a colonel or his soldiers. A central headquarters may wish for a city to be held or avoided, or may wish for a strategic placement of troops to counter the enemies opportunities—all of which may lower the opportunities of soldiers paid in terms of prizes.

The military advances reduced the usefulness of profits as a method of compensation. Once this method of payment was eliminated, purchase could not survive because no one would pay to be a soldier simply to receive a soldier's salary. At the same time, these advances provided new opportunities to directly monitor officers and they substituted for the process of self-selection provided by the purchase system. Furthermore, innovations in timekeeping meant that monitoring could be more effective during battle. Taken together, they spelled the end of the system of purchase.

England vs. the Continent

Purchase ended on the Continent before it ended in England. For example, the Prussian army was overhauled from 1806 to 1808 in the midst of the Napoleonic Wars. Subsequently, officers were to be selected based on training and education. Further, "when the new supply administration was put into effect on August 1, 1808, the captains' personal profit derived from the management of the company and squadron 'housekeeping' came to an end. No longer were captains permitted to sell small stores to their men."[56]

In France, the purchase system had evolved, as in England, out of the mercenary companies; but officially only colonels and captains could purchase their commissions. Any other promotions or appointments required the colonel's permission, which was usually acquired at a price, so in practice the army was staffed similarly to Britain's.[57] French efforts to abolish purchase were initiated from 1775 to 1777, and the system formally ended in 1790. In both the Prussian and French cases, the system ended considerably earlier than in Britain, where the army played a secondary role to the navy in defense of the islands.

When technical advances in the methods or tools of war reduced the role of nature, a concomitant change in the organization occurred, as discussed in the last section. However, after the introduction of the longbow in the twelfth century, virtually all advances in land warfare took place on the Continent before occurring in England. In England and the British Isles, the "transformation in fortification and siegecraft was incomplete, gradual, and relatively tardy."[58] In addition, although rail was developed in Britain, the tracks were laid for commercial purposes. In Prussia, the tracks were laid for strategic reasons.[59] These railways were designed to move troops quickly to the front. Developments in weapons and tactics were also more advanced on the Continent than in England, as has been mentioned, in regards to rifles, troop maneuvers, and telecommunications. Quite naturally, the island nation was more innovative with its navy than its army relative to the Continental powers. After 1815, England fought little on the Continent and mostly in small, colonial affairs. Fighting in Africa, India, and the other colonies resembled the conditions of pre-modern battles. This contributed to the lag in technical advances, which led to the lag in disposing of the purchase system.

CONCLUSION

On the surface, the purchase of officer commissions was a puzzling phenomenon. But scratch the surface and the puzzle becomes even greater, given the large sums paid to be an officer. The resolution of this puzzle is that purchase was used to solve two problems: to select officers of high quality and to provide proper incentives in battle. The first goal was achieved via the self-selection aspect of purchase. Those willing to pay large sums believed they could be successful. The second goal was achieved because the purchase system created incentives by offering a fraction of the spoils of war as payment. In both cases, we see a very specific example of a class of pre-modern institutions. In this era, monitoring was difficult, but when the incentives of an office owner matched those of the Crown, the solution was to sell the office to the servant. In this particular example, the office in question just happened to be that of an officer in the army.

This incentive system explains not only the existence of purchase, but its decline as well. From the introduction of the pikemen to the introduction of the rifle, few military advances took place that reduced the variability of nature. The relative increase in the value of infantry and the larger scale of fighting led to the conditions that supported the purchase system. The introduction of strategic rail, telegraphs, and the rifle radically altered the role nature played in the battlefield. Large, coordinated battles were no longer consistent with officers receiving residual claims and thus purchase ended. The dependence of purchase on a noisy environment consistent with its lagged existence in Britain over Europe; with the rise and fall of mercenary troops; with the internal rules of the system; and with the absence of purchase in the Navy or Ordinance corps.

CHAPTER SEVEN

Lighthouses, Private Roads, and the Treasury

June 18, 1660: Back again to the Admiralty and so to my Lord's lodgings, where he told me that he did look after the place of the Clerk of the Acts for me. . . . June 22: In the afternoon, one Mr. Watts came to me, a merchant, to offer me £500 if I would desist from the Clerk of the Acts place. . . . July 30: . . . the sword-bearer of London (Mr. Man) came to ask for us: with whom we sat late, discoursing about the worth of my office of Clerk of the Acts, which he hath a mind to buy and I asked four years' purchase. . . . August 6: This night Mr. Man offered me £1000 for my office of Clerk of the Acts, which made my mouth water; but yet I dare not take it till I speak with my Lord to have his consent.

SAMUEL PEPYS, *The Diary of Samuel Pepys*

In his short entries, Pepys reveals some hallmark characteristics of patronage and venality. Quickly he received multiple offers for his clerk's office and had the opportunity to turn it into a tidy sum of £500–1,000 in a matter of days. Though we know nothing of the talents of Mr. Watts and Mr. Man, no doubt they held the same professional qualifications as Pepys. Still, given that it was a patronage appointment, Pepys was reluctant to sell unless his patron, the Lord Sandwich, consented. Pepys was always keen to avoid alienating his support and worked in the interest of his patrons.

Whether or not the 1st Earl of Sandwich discouraged the sale of Pepys' office, we do not know; fortunately for the British navy, Pepys remained in the office of clerk of the acts (the Navy Board's secretary) for thirteen years and gained an everlasting reputation as an able administrator.[1] He also gained a considerable fortune far in excess of the annual salary of £350 he received as clerk, in the form of fees, prizes, bribes, and access to other offices and commissions. Indeed, Pepys's diary contains dozens of references to bribes unabashedly received, everything from silver plate and diamonds to oysters and beef tongue. In dozens of other entries he expresses his desire for more. From his entries, it is clear that bribes and gifts were the social norm of the time—simply one means by which payments were made to the owner of an office. Pepys's matter-of-fact tone in recording the financial transactions of what we now call public service underscores the everyday character of these offices during the pre-modern era. The purchases in the army may receive the most historical attention, but they were everywhere.

The role of purchase and patronage was ubiquitous in the pre-modern era, and reading through Pepys's entries during the middle of the seventeenth century provides a glimpse at how common they were. One also discovers that these positions were not blindly given, but some consideration was often given to ability. In Pepys's case, he was very much aware that his important administrative post was given to him as a young man, not based on merit or training but upon loyalty to a peer during the restoration of Charles II. At the same time, Pepys was well aware that his continued political favor depended on his competence. He recognized later in his diaries "how little merit does prevail in the world, but only favour—and that for myself, chance without merit brought me in, and that diligence only keeps me so."[2]

The ubiquity of venal office holdings as one solution to the problem of measurement in the provision of what we now call public services is illustrated by the examination of three additional venal offices: lighthouses, roads, and tax farms. On the surface, each case appears to be a poor candidate for private provision. A light keeper provides light for paying customers, but those who do not pay also see the same light. The ability to free ride on light service reduces the incentive of ships to pay for light and hinders the ability of the light keeper to recoup his investment. Such an enterprise sounds like a poor business opportunity. A road or bridge builder faces the same "public good" problem. Although a road keeper might be able to exclude the use of a bridge, roads can generally be used by anyone with access. In addition, both lighthouses and roads involve large initial fixed costs to construct but low marginal costs to operate. Consumers know this and may only offer low payment for the service, again leading to losses for the private provider. In short, these are classic examples of areas where an assumed gap exists between private incentives to provide a service and collective, or public, benefits from the service to be provided. The modern iconic "solution" in such cases is for the public, via the government, to provide the services. Despite this modern bias, lighthouses and roads were successfully provided through quasi-private institutions for centuries. The third example, tax farming, strikes moderns as the most alien. Taxes are notoriously difficult to collect because the taxpayer is so unwilling to cooperate. Today collection seems possible because of the state's strong threat of force, fines, and incarceration; yet until the middle of the seventeenth century, many taxes were collected by private individuals and consortiums. As always, the rise and fall of these private provisions depended on the role of nature. When the Crown was unable to directly monitor, and when profit incentives aligned with the Crown, then private offices functioned sufficiently. Once nature was reduced through steam, chronometers, highway science, and bookkeeping, modern institutions arrived.

THE LIGHTHOUSE

I walked in the garden with little Captain Murford, where he and I had some discourse concerning the Light-House again, and I think I shall appear in the business, he promising me that if I can bring it about, it will be worth 100 per annum.

Samuel Pepys, *The Diary of Samuel Pepys*, February 27, 1661

Starting in the mid-nineteenth century—toward the end of the Institutional Revolution—economists began writing about lighthouses as an example of the "proper office of government." John S. Mill and others claimed that lighthouses suffered from the problem of providing a service without a means to collect payment. Unlike the owner of a toll road, who could refuse passage for a nonpayer, the owner of a lighthouse could not prevent a ship at sea from using the light without charge. Lighthouses could not be profitable, and therefore no one would build them. Yet lighthouses were necessary, and so the state must provide them. This argument was picked up in the twentieth century by others who noted the additional problem that the light was also produced at zero additional cost. That is, once the lighthouse was built, it cost almost nothing to shine the light. Socially speaking then, the light should be free. Thus, even if a lighthouse could be privately provided, it should not because the private light provider would provide too little light. A private light keeper worries about profits, which means that charges for service must cover the total cost of the lighthouse. From a social point of view, however, an additional unit of light should be provided as long as anyone wants it because the cost of an additional unit is basically zero. The private and social interests diverge.

Even though the role of lighthouses has faded and almost disappeared in the age of satellites and global positioning systems, they often continue to be used as the "poster child" for government provision of goods and services. Ironically, despite the claims of various economists stating, one way or another, that private provision of light simply could not exist, a brief history of lighthouses in England and Wales reveals (surprise!) a story laced with private light provision.[3] It is true that they were not purely private institutions but were rather like most other offices of the time: quasi-private affairs in which the Crown was involved to some extent. Like the purchase system in the army in which the Crown regulated prices, approved sales, and generally had an interest in outcomes, pre-modern governments also took an interest in lighthouses and their dues, operation, and construction. Private interests in public offices during the pre-modern era were never ones of unrestricted free markets. Lighthouse owners kept the income over expenses, but they operated in the shadow of the Crown.

Private lighthouse provision was not unique. Had Mill and others used a different example of an office proper for government provision, such as sewers, they would have discovered similar private interests at work. As with all other examples of goods that we moderns think of as "public," they were provided through institutions we now think of as odd and inappropriate. Samuel Pepys, a member of the guild Trinity House, which was heavily involved in the provision of lighthouses, had numerous diary entries on the subject. In most, as with many of his entries, his mouth waters with the thought of fortunes to be made through light provision. At the same time, he was often torn, given his view that lighthouses should be used to generate incomes for families who had lost loved ones at sea. Nothing was ever simple with pre-modern institutions.

A Short History[4]

Lighthouses have been in place since antiquity, but during the Middle Ages both the demand and supply for them seems to have been small. Although the first English grant from the Crown for the building of a lighthouse was in 1261 in Winchelsea, very few lights of any kind were built until the beginning of the pre-modern era in the sixteenth century. These early lighthouses were often provided by ecclesiastical authorities, and often were run as charities financed through volunteer contributions or indulgences. None were large, complicated, or financially supported through endowments.

It is interesting that the problem of collecting dues does not appear to have been that critical. Private citizens or groups would petition the Crown for a letters patent for the right to collect dues; the ship paid these dues for the incoming lights upon arrival in harbor and also paid for the outgoing lights when leaving. These lights would not only direct the ship to harbor but would warn of dangerous shores and shoals. The force of the Crown stood behind the collector, meaning that any ship that refused to pay had the Crown to deal with. Collectors could also refuse port service if the ship's captain refused to cooperate. The authority and backing of the Crown over mandatory fees was important; in cases where lighthouse fees were voluntary, the lighthouse usually failed.

At some, now unknown, point during the Middle Ages, a seaman's guild called Trinity House was formed. It started as a guild of mariners with the purpose to look after aged seamen, widows, and orphans. Henry VIII granted them a charter in 1536 to operate their first lighthouse. For reasons further unknown, the members of Trinity House took this charter to mean they had a monopoly over the provision of light, and they restricted the number of lighthouses and failed to build additional ones until 1609. By the seventeenth century, the Stuart court challenged their monopoly interpretation and lost, but eventually found loopholes through which private patents could be given to others.

During the seventeenth and eighteenth centuries, most of the lighthouses were operated by private individuals, town councils, shipowners, or other groups. They operated either through leases from Trinity House or through perpetual (ongoing) patents from the Crown. Payments were based on tonnage, and the record suggests that ships would often attempt to avoid payment but that lighthouse operators used great ingenuity and influence to collect.[5] As might be expected, shipowners complained about the high dues as "oppressive and injurious" and even claimed that they were a "restraint to trade" because they increased the cost of trade. In 1836 an act was passed that abolished private lighthouses. The leases and perpetuities were purchased by Trinity House. The rights to produce light were sold at significant values. In 1846, for example, Trinity House acquired the rights to one house for £309,531. It is clear that the private houses were able to capture enough trade to be profitable. Today Trinity House continues to manage lighthouses but since the turn of the twentieth century without handling funds.

Why Private Lighthouses?

Sea travel prior to the nineteenth century was extremely dangerous for two major reasons. First, ships were propelled by wind, which could easily force a ship onto rocks or a lee shore. Second, it was virtually impossible to know longitude with any accuracy. The result was a simple method of sailing. Ships would stay within sight of land, hugging the shore, until they reached a given latitude. They would then sail along this latitude until they reached land. It was dangerous, and many ships were lost simply because they were further west or east of where they thought they were. Often, fog or darkness prevented ships from knowing their position relative to shore. Many shipowners would not let their ships sail at night or in fog. This restriction would reduce the chance of running aground but came at the cost of a longer voyage.

The extreme danger that led ships to stay within sight of shore allowed for the feasibility of private lighthouses in the pre-modern era. The grounds for some type of public provision were that a private lighthouse would be unable to collect dues and that the marginal cost of service was zero. Both of these problems were mitigated when all ships were close to shore. Ships required the lighthouse service and generally required all of the lighthouses along their route. Sooner or later, they would put into port and pay for all of the light service they had received. This custom held for both foreign and domestic shipping.

And so lighthouses during the pre-modern era were privately constructed and operated (with permission and authority to collect dues given by the Crown) because the state seldom had any advantage in building or running a commercial operation. As long as every ship required lights along the coast, light dues for services rendered were not difficult to determine. The system worked well. When lighthouses were sold off in the nineteenth century, many sold for hundreds of thousands of pounds, which demonstrates that lighthouses could be a profitable affair. As was the case with the army, the incentives of the Crown and of the entrepreneurs were compatible: the Crown wanted lights along the coast, and lighthouse entrepreneurs were willing and able to supply lights when they owned the lighthouses. More important, lighthouse owners could charge every ship for their light because the nature of coastline shipping meant that every ship required light.

With the Industrial Revolution of the late eighteenth century, the inventions of steam power, screw propulsion, and the chronometer changed shipping forever. The removal of sail power and the ability to know an exact location meant that ships could sail safely away from coastlines for the first time. The ability of ships to sail from London to New York or from London to Liverpool in open water reduced the demand for all of the lighthouses along the route. Every lighthouse served a purpose for its local port by marking dangers for ships close to that shore, but not every ship was close to that shore, and these ships did not require that lighthouse. Suddenly the ability to know who used the light became difficult to determine and the free rider problem developed. Starting in the historical record of the nineteenth century, we find the first complaints by shipowners that they were being demanded light dues for lighthouses from which they received no service. A particularly interesting complaint dealt with ships that were forced to put into a harbor due to poor weather. Shipowners complained that since they had not planned to visit that port, they should not be subject to light dues. Regardless of the merits of their argument, it points to the fact that in the nineteenth century, all ships did not use all of the lighthouses along a route.

Once it was possible for ships to move from one location to another without the use of every lighthouse along the way, it was possible for a given ship to claim that it received no benefit from particular lighthouses, even though it might have. Thus a more costly monitoring system was required, and the optimal amount of light was no longer easy to determine. The invention of the chronometer created a problem for lighthouse operators: now they needed to know which ships were requiring light service in order to provide the correct amount and to determine who to charge what dues. The solution for the lighthouse operators, at the time, was to claim that every ship needed the light and demand dues accordingly. This position was fought hard by the shipowners, who ultimately won the argument. It was only when innovations in shipping came along, which allowed ships to move off the coast, that a conflict arose. Private provision was no longer compatible with Crown interests in navigation, and the result was an end to private light along the British coastline.

Private Roads and Turnpikes

Mr. Oudant, secretary to the late Princess of Orange, did discourse of the convenience as to keeping the highways from being deep, by their horses, in Holland (and Flanders where the ground is as miry as ours is), going in their carts and, wagons as ours in coaches, wishing the same here as an expedient to make the ways better, and I think there is something in it, where there is breadth enough.

Samuel Pepys, *The Diary of Samuel Pepys*, November 1, 1662

Nothing is more ordinary than a road, and today almost nothing is more naturally thought of as being within the realm of public provision. Although toll roads are periodically found in various places, especially for new bridges and large highways, and although the innovations of electronic payment devices might increase the number of tolls in the future, in almost all Western countries road development and maintenance is a matter of government supply. Public provision was not always the case, and the history of roads is marked by an ebb and flow of tensions between private and public interests.

In medieval times, the "King's Highway" was an easement, or right of way, across another's property. A manorial lord would have been responsible for looking after the right of way within the manor by keeping it free of debris and other major obstacles. When the way became impassable from muck and water, various materials like stones, wood, or even rubbish, would simply have been placed on top to work their way into the soil. These tasks would have fallen upon the lord's tenants, the very people who most likely used the highway. A highway was not a road in any modern sense, but if used enough, it would become a beaten path for foot and animal traffic. The road was a rather local, informal affair, and travelers had every right to "go upon the corn" in order to avoid muck, logs, and other impediments in their way.[6] The first attempt to legislate roads above more than a pathway came with the Statute of Winchester (1285), although it called for little more than landowners to maintain a clear path. Prior to the pre-modern era, if the path involved more than simple routes across a manor, much of the work was done by religious orders, although merchants, private guilds, and the gentry would often construct roads and bridges and see to their repair when it suited their private interests. The Roman Catholic Church required roads for rotations of ministers, religious pilgrimages, and ceremonies. Towns were better off with roads to trading centers. And local lords often built roads for mineral exploitation or for the movement of grains and animals. It was a hodgepodge system that apparently worked well enough for the local needs, but as populations and trade routes grew, the inadequacies became more apparent.[7]

In the early years of the pre-modern era, just after the dissolution of the monastic orders and the confiscation of monastic lands, the Statute for Mending of Highways was passed in 1555. This watershed legislation would be the backbone of the British road system for the next 300 years. Under this act, the responsibility for road maintenance rested with the local parish. Members of the parish would appoint or elect a "surveyor of highways" who worked, gratis, to monitor road quality. The job of surveyor was not held by the local gentry but rather by yeoman farmers and local merchants. The surveyor was required to inspect roadways and to announce at the local church any problems with the roads. He had the power to assess fines, and he picked the time when members of the parish were required to devote six days of labor to the physical maintenance of the roads. This statute labor changed considerably over time, with allowances for substitutes, and eventually payments rather than labor in kind. Throughout the seventeenth century, some parishes attempted to impose a highway tax among the parish members to finance maintenance but without much success. As long as the roads were used for local foot and animal traffic, the system worked reasonably well. However, by the end of the seventeenth century, routes located near larger centers or between major trading towns were in considerable disrepair.

The disrepair was caused by several factors. First, the amount of traffic on roads continued to grow over time. Pack horses, loaded with wares, moved goods from one town to another. Although an exception outside major towns, wheeled vehicles started to use the roads as well. Second, much of the increased traffic was not local but consisted of merchants, wholesalers, postal contractors, officials, friars, and other travelers. This new traffic led to a conflict between the locals in charge of repair and the major users of the roads who did not pay for upkeep. Finally, these roads were never intended for such use. "The parish highway often consisted . . . of a mere horse track across a miry common, or a watery hollow lane twisting between high banks and overhanging hedges . . . such a highway was practically impassable for wheeled vehicles, and sometimes even for a horseman, for half the year."[8] As noted by Pepys, the increase in wheeled traffic over the dirt roads often made the ruts deep and impassable during bad weather. In principle, the parish system might have worked if parishes had the authority to charge through-users of the road, but they could not. Further problems arose because parishes often controlled only small portions of a road, which led to coordination problems with other parishes over maintenance and investment.[9] Thus parishes often did nothing to improve road conditions, resulting in impeded trade.

By the middle of the seventeenth century, a new institutional development for road maintenance and construction emerged to deal with these problems: the turnpike trust. The turnpike trusts were private, nonprofit firms formed by local groups, and granted charters from the

Crown to oversee the construction and maintenance of sections of road. Slow to emerge, the initial trusts were intended as temporary supplements to the parish system. Initially, Parliament granted local magistrates the power to charge tolls along certain roadways. However, by the middle of the eighteenth century, they were being created at a rate of twenty per year and had evolved into private enterprises in all but name. The trusts set up tollgates along the route to charge non-foot passengers for the right to use the road. These tollgates were often sold to private individuals who paid the trust a lump sum and kept the revenues for themselves. In order to maintain the roads, the trusts established limits on the type and width of carriage wheel, the weight of load, and the number of horses in a team that could pass along their stretch of road. The trusts were independent of one another and scattered across the country. Trusts varied in size: the largest one controlled 148 miles, whereas in another case, one section of road 194 miles long had twenty-three separate turnpikes controlling it.[10] Over the course of the eighteenth century, they steadily controlled more roads, and they were credited for improving the roads by 1800.[11] Bogart estimates that the turnpike trusts contributed to a 20 percent fall in freight charges and that they had their largest impact around the major urban centers.[12] By 1838, over 1,100 different trusts controlled 22,000 miles of turnpike roads, as compared with over 15,000 parishes that controlled 106,000 miles of roads. On average, the turnpike trusts spent almost five times more on maintenance per mile than did the parishes.[13] The turnpikes controlled the busier and larger roads close to London and other major cities; the parishes controlled most of the side roads used only by locals.

Still by the beginning of the nineteenth century, it was clear to many reformers that most roads were inadequate given the increased traffic and trade, and movements toward a centrally organized, professionally administered system began. The postal service and the board of agriculture pushed hard to eliminate the turnpike system and demanded that the roads "accommodate the traffic, rather than the traffic accommodate the roads." In a House of Commons committee hearing in 1819, John MacAdam, an early road reformer and the person for whom "macadam" paving techniques are so named, asked: "Is it not time to enquire whether the system of road-making now is in use good? . . . to consider the making, the form and surface of roads, scientifically?"[14]

The nineteenth century saw dozens of highway acts, but the General Highway Act of 1835 saw the end of the parish system and ultimately the end of the turnpikes as well. This act repealed all of the previous acts and established the foundations of the modern road administration—although it would take until the end of the century to complete it. Ironically, the new system would be more similar in structure to the parish system of administration than to the trusts. Local geographic areas would control their own roads, levy compulsory taxes or rates, have permanent salaried professional officials, and employ wage labor. Gone were the surveyors, gratuitous common service, and the forced labor.[15]

Why Parish and Turnpike Roads?

Two systems existed side by side in the provision of roads in Britain during the pre-modern era. On the one hand, the parish system was a form of public provision, but one laced with medieval service requirements. On the other hand, the turnpike system was a form of private ownership that charged users prices for road services. Both were replaced with modern road systems at the end of the pre-modern era. The two systems had coexisted because each provided a solution, given extant technologies, to the need to monitor in a high-variability setting.

Roads are a classic example of "market failure." The bulk of road expense is a fixed sunk cost, but the additional cost of accommodating travel along a path is quite low. As a result, economic efficiency dictates that the price for using a road should be low as well, in order to induce the optimal amount of traffic. However, when only the additional cost is covered, the road is never built in the first place because of the high initial investment. During the pre-modern era this investment was less of an issue for the small parish "road." A local parish could support a local road simply because it amounted to little more than a private pathway.[16] Local lords and individuals had a strong private interest to provide paths for their own local use, and the cost of such a path was minimal. To the extent that these paths were used for purposes other than what they were intended, they were clearly underprovided, but this concern was often trivial. It was only when heavy, nonlocal traffic increased that the quality of the local roads began to diminish and became inadequate.

Turnpike trusts were the response to the failure of parish administration to provide roads required by nonlocals. Turnpikes were located along the major trade routes. Later, they became the roads used by the carriage services. The parish provision was inadequate to provide these roads, not just because the locals were unwilling to pay for the harder road surfaces, straighter routes, and smaller grades, but because the parish had no means to collect fees from the nonlocals. The turnpike system was the pre-modern solution to the payment and monitoring problem. As long as they were protected from competition from other roads, they could charge prices above the marginal costs of running the road in order to cover total costs. The roads were poor by future standards, but the turnpike system did improve roads and adapt the latest technology. When, in the nineteenth century, engineers began developing roads through use of materials, surveys, and leveling grades, the trusts exploited these advantages. The result was a steady improvement in carriage times between destinations. The trusts lasted almost 200 years, during which they were at least adequate in providing some financial incentive for keeping roads in workable order.[17]

It is ironic that the system of road maintenance went from public (parish) provision, to private (turnpike) provision, and then back to public (the highway authority) provision. The reason for this return to public administration was the ability of the local government to monitor the work of the roads. When highways involved nothing more than making a clear path for locals, monitoring by the local users was trivial; thus the parish system worked. In contrast, the turnpike system allowed for the benefits of an entrepreneurial system, in light of the costs of monitoring performance in a highly variable world. The trust would do the work as long as the expected revenues from better transport were greater than the costs. Those groups who thought they could build and provide road services best were the ones most likely to be successful in lobbying the Crown for road grants. In this way, the system of private roads was similar to the provision of other services through private offices.

Had the Crown or even the parish been able to specify the attributes of a road and then measure and monitor its construction and performance, it seems unlikely that private roads would have existed. As it was, no such ability existed. Roads were made from local materials, and these, along with the terrain, varied considerably. Local weather conditions affected the quality of the roads, as did the nature of the traffic. It was difficult to separate out the contributions of a road builder from the role of nature. Of course the problems were exacerbated by the lack of standard measures for grades, materials, and distances.

With the development of road science in the nineteenth century came a change in the ability to measure and monitor. Standards were developed for uniform methods of roadbed construction, for screening materials to remove dirt and other materials that affected a road's performance, and for specifying road surfaces and profiles.[18] Together, these innovations allowed the Crown, through local administrations, to monitor paid staff to build and maintain the roads. Modern roads are, in fact, an excellent example of science overcoming nature. Whereas a beaten path follows the contours of the land, is subject to flooding, and wears depending on the natural soil quality, a modern road cuts through these random elements. Surveyors, bedding materials, and engineered tops could be identified and looked after with some reasonable expectation. Perhaps the strongest piece of evidence for changes in the ability to monitor road construction comes from the elimination of road restrictions. Prior to the development of road engineering, the only means of controlling road quality was not through a specification of the road materials and construction, but through limits on who could use the road. Once a given quality of road could be specified and monitored, the roads became open to everyone.

Of course, improvements in monitoring worked for the trusts as well. The trusts took advantage of road science and subsequently grew in the latter eighteenth and early nineteenth century. Where the trusts failed was in their pricing. The social problem with trusts was that they charged a price above marginal costs for road services, yet once a road was built it should be provided for free. Hence it was socially beneficial for the roads to be provided through general rates and used for free. Historically this course of action had not been possible because of the inability to build and maintain roads without enormous amounts of embezzlement. Once the monitoring problem was solved, the Crown eventually took over the roads. By the end of the nineteenth century, the process was complete.

THE TREASURY

Taxes are intimately associated with the state, and it is hard to believe that any government or ruler would "outsource" their collection. Yet, like so many other pre-modern offices, "tax farms" were initially purchased from the Crown and run privately. It is interesting that the ability to monitor and measure tax collections through innovations in bookkeeping, combined with the central importance of tax revenue collection, led to the evolution of tax farming into professional, civil service appointments much earlier than other offices.

Tax revenues for the English Crown were flat and low from 1490 to 1670.[19] Throughout this time, Parliament placed restrictions on the types of revenues the Crown could raise. Hence the Crown could sell off state lands and offices, manipulate the currency, or impose import taxes. Most notably, until Cromwell's Commonwealth in the middle of the seventeenth century, the state was not allowed to tax internal trade through excise taxes on produced commodities.[20] So limited, the Crown was never able to raise significant revenues on its own through customs (taxes on imported goods) and land taxes. Throughout the seventeenth century, the reign of the Stuarts was characterized by desperate measures to secure funds: from Charles I's infamous confiscation of gold stored in the Tower, to France's Louis XIV's secret subsidies to Charles II and James II.[21] As O'Brien and Hunt state: "Decade after decade, the Tudor and Stuart regimes tried, but failed, to collect higher levels of taxation."[22] Yet following the Glorious Revolution in 1688, tax revenues increased so much historians have labeled the following hundred years the "financial revolution."[23] As one measure of this change, consider that in the 1660s, with an approximate population of 5.5 million, the Crown had difficulty raising £2.5 million, whereas by 1763, with a population of 8 million, public expenditures of £20 million produced no Parliamentary alarm. The reason lay in the concomitant growth in tax revenue over the same period, a growth that far exceeded the growth in economic productivity.[24]

As it turned out, the treasury's change in fortune corresponded with changes in its internal organization. Until the mid-sixteenth century, tax collection was mostly performed by the Crown through a hodgepodge of public agents. In 1568, Elizabeth I began a system of tax farming whereby the rights to collect taxes within a given jurisdiction from specific sources were leased to individuals or consortiums. Tax farmers were often bankers, financiers, or wealthy peers who basically paid the Crown a lump sum of money in exchange for the tax revenues. These financiers then hired agents to do the actual collecting. Hence, tax farmers would pay the Crown a flat fee for the right to collect a specific tax, often for a specified time. If they collected more funds than the fee, then they made a profit. If they failed to collect enough, then they sustained a loss. Like all private enterprises, the tax collector had a strong incentive to minimize the costs of doing business. Contracts with tax farmers included the tax rate, location, and items to be taxed. Tax farms, unlike other offices, were not sold for life but rather were leased subject to renewal.

On the surface, tax farming seems the most reasonable case in which sale of public office might work. There was no particular reason why the Crown should have a comparative advantage in tax collection. In addition, competition among bidders for leases should have allowed the Crown to extract the tax farm rents, as bidders would raise the amount they would pay close to the amount of net tax revenue they could generate. It was unfortunate for the Crown that the incentives of tax farmers did not always align with those of the Crown. Serious information and incentive problems existed on both sides. Throughout the tax farm era, the Crown struggled with its ignorance of prices, volumes of trade, amounts of smuggling, and the potential for tax. The Tudor monarchs attempted to address these issues by taking oaths from merchants on volumes and prices of goods traded. They also created "books of rates" that attempted to establish formal prices to base their taxes on. Oaths tended to be unreliable, and book rates were often out of date and irrelevant. The bottom line: the Crown had to rely exclusively on the competitiveness of the bidding market to ensure a reasonable share of the rents available. However, evidence indicates that the Crown was unable to extract the full value of the tax farms. For example, Kindleberger notes an instance where James I sold the right to collect taxes to a particular group of seven peers, who then immediately turned around and sold "the taxes to merchant contractors for a net return to the peers of £27,500."[25]

There were opportunism problems on the Crown's part as well, since the Monarch used both implicit and explicit methods to extract more, ex post, from tax farmers. First, it was not beyond the Stuarts to change the terms of the lease midway through the contract.[26] Second, tax farming in customs dues only worked well when foreign trade was not interrupted by war, pirates, or privateers because the ability to collect sufficient customs depended on uninterrupted trade. Of course the decision to wage war and protect merchant ships rested in the hands of the monarch who received a fixed revenue from the tax farmers. Because the monarch's tax revenues did not benefit directly from improved trade, his decision to engage in trade-disrupting behavior did not reflect the costs he imposed on the tax farmers. This opportunism exacerbated the incompatible incentive problem that existed between the Crown and tax farmers.

Finally, an information problem existed within the tax farms themselves. Bankers and financiers who hired collection agents possessed no special abilities in monitoring the agents who became notorious for colluding with the merchants and accepted bribes to reduce the amount of tax paid. The general historical consensus suggests the entire system was rife with corruption. Thus the inability of the Crown to know the value of its tax base, the bad incentives on the part of the monarch, and the failure of bankers to monitor collectors led to a tax system incapable of raising large sums of money for the state. It is not too surprising that strong pressures and inducements to create a better system came from the perspective of the Crown, and these ultimately came from improvements in bookkeeping. These innovations took place in the mid-seventeenth century, and the demise of the tax farms soon followed. The customs tax farms, begun in the middle sixteenth century, were gone by 1671. The excise tax farms, begun only in 1643, mostly to tax spirits, were terminated in 1672. Finally, the older hearth tax farms ended in 1683.[27]

England was unique in finding a professional bureaucratic solution to the tax-farming problem, based on detailed record keeping and reporting. The transition was certainly not immediate, and in the earlier years the collection of tax revenue continued to be laced with patronage appointments and venal offices. However, by the middle of the eighteenth century, the staff became salaried and were hired on merit, especially in the case of excise taxes where most of the increases in revenue arose. The continental powers clung to tax farming until the late eighteenth century. The increased efficiency of the English system is evident given that by the mid-1700s the English tax revenues per capita were three times those in France.[28] From the 1680s onward, the lion's share of revenues came from land, customs, and excise taxes. Over time, the importance of land taxes fell, and that of excise taxes increased. Customs taxes were always constrained by the ability of smugglers to avoid taxes when rates increased. The excise department became the example of an efficient government department. Brewer notes: "One reason why Hanoverian ministers were so eager to rely on excise taxes was because they knew that they would be collected by a body of men widely regarded as the most proficient revenue officers in government."[29]

As always, trust and purchase were used in situations where measurement was costly, relative to the costs of monitoring employees. It is ironic that in the case of professional tax collecting, what made the system so effective was a simple form of monitoring that contained strong economies of scale.[30] By 1770, the system was organized as follows: throughout the country, trained "gaugers" would assess taxes at specific establishments. These men were monitored by supervisors who would randomly inspect the gaugers' work. Next came the actual tax collector, who was accompanied by a clerk and a trainee, whose job it was to carry supplies and guard the money.

The system seems designed around what might be called "the rule of three," which exploited the old saying that "three men can keep a secret if one of them is dead." With multiple individuals keeping records of the tax accounts, the Crown was able to minimize collusion among tax collectors. Indeed, the system was reminiscent of the information-reporting structure in the navy: captain, lieutenant, and master. If the tax collector corresponded to the captain, then the trainee's position resembled that of a ship's lieutenant and no doubt the trainee acted as a watchdog for the central office, who had improved chances for advancement when a corrupt officer was removed from the system. The clerk's role, like that of a ship's master, provided an independent third assessment. Used together, the treasury had some confidence that corruption was sufficiently mitigated.

The collectors took the revenues to the central office in London. The central office was divided into four tasks: receiving funds, accounting, auditing, and inspecting excise officer journals. Thus, aside from having separation in tasks and multiple people in charge of the money, elaborate journals were kept. Three sets of journals were kept by all officers. One was a ledger kept at the local office outlining the daily schedule, a second was a journal carried with the officer to record his actual movements, and the third was a journal of minutes left with the trader. Entries were made in ink, absolutely no alterations were allowed, and all journals were turned into the central office every six weeks for inspection. Brewer tells the humorous story of John Cannon, an excise man who made an error in his journal and decided to scrape it with his knife. Not satisfied with the result, he attempted to correct it several more times until he managed to put a hole in the paper. Panicking, he then tried to cover the hole with wax. In the end he made matters worse since "by my so often visiting this page I had made the book so pliable that it would open itself at the very page where my folly was done as if it had vowed to be a witness against me to discharge me."[31]

On top of these measures, officers were periodically "removed" to different locations and were not allowed to serve in the location where they grew up in order to avoid collusion with merchants. Brewer notes that as many as 41 percent of officers were removed in any one year.[32] Officers were required to take written and practical tests and to complete a period of probation. The "examination was not a formality."[33] It took a long time to become a supervisor, and promotion was not automatic. A supervisor would earn as much as two and one half times that of a gauger.

This complicated public system was no doubt expensive, and no evidence exists that private tax farmers were governed by anything of similar magnitude. The centralized checking of journals no doubt had considerable economies of scale, and these procedures would have been prohibitive for individual tax farms, which were given a single port or commodity to tax. But this fact points to the fundamental incentive incompatibility of tax farming: whereas tax farming required small, competitive farmers to generate competitive bids, these small farms were incapable of achieving the economies of policing the books to avoid the collusion among merchants and collectors. It is clear that the professional system was successful in raising substantial revenues after two centuries of no growth in taxes collected.[34]

Direct government tax collection existed prior to Elizabeth I and during the Interregnum, yet the level of total tax revenue for the two centuries prior to 1688 shows little change over the entire period. The mere presence or absence of tax farming cannot explain the final success of in-house collection. The key would appear to be bookkeeping and auditing innovations that evolved from 1660 to 1670 within the context of an independent treasury. It was during this time that the treasury "introduced the bookkeeping procedures which were to remain standard Treasury practice into the nineteenth century."[35] Furthermore, the treasury came under the authority of Parliament. In 1665, an act was passed by parliament that granted Charles II £1.25 million for the running of his government in exchange for the treasury's right to receive and disburse the money. Ordinary citizens who advanced money to the treasury would receive signed orders, numbered chronologically, for their repayment. Thus this act allowed Parliament to back public credit rather than the personal credit of the monarch.[36] In 1667, a second act extended this principle to ordinary revenues from customs, excise, and hearth taxes. Centralizing control of finances led to "the great blossoming of Treasury records into systematic series— Order Books, Warrant Books, Letter Books and, above all, the Minute Books which stretch in an almost unbroken series until their cessation in the mid nineteenth century. Bold 'No. I's' upon the covers of the 1667 volumes still testify to this novel initiative."[37] Thus the transfer of control over finance from the King's Household to Parliament brought about by the unique conditions of the Restoration, required the innovation of stringent bookkeeping to monitor performance. These monitoring innovations reduced the role of nature in tax collection and allowed Parliament to raise taxes through a professional treasury without the "leakage" experienced by royal attempts at tax collection.

CHAPTER EIGHT

The Courts, Criminal Law, and Police

Thus not only assaults, but virtually all thefts and even some murders were left to the general public. That meant that responsibility for the initial expense and entire conduct of the prosecution was thrown on the victim or his or her family.

DOUGLAS HAY AND FRANCIS SNYDER,
"Using The Criminal Law, 1750–1850"

Venal offices in pre-modern Britain were a common, ordinary, part of everyone's daily experience, and considered normal and natural to people at the time—despite how odd they appear to moderns. Perhaps nowhere was the oddness more striking than in the judicial system where, at least for most parts of it, the use of fees, private offices, and profit incentives for the provision of what is now a bureaucratic public service was common. Of all the institutions examined thus far, those in the legal realm were perhaps the most complicated—in part because of the different types of English courts but also from the sheer number of offices involved: judges, court officials, sheriffs, and the various prison offices. In these offices the difference between revenues and costs policed (pardon the pun) the behavior of the service provider. Here too, changes in monitoring brought about by the Industrial Revolution modified the old institutions into the modern ones we know today.[1]

Prior to the middle of the nineteenth century, justice was mostly a private affair. In fact, 544 years passed between the Statute of Winchester (1285), which established private policing of criminal activity in England, and the Metropolitan Police Act (1829), which created a public police force in London. A public police force did not arise out of nothing but evolved out of a hundred years of criminal law reform and experiments with various forms of quasi-public policing efforts, especially during the latter half of the eighteenth century. After a span of almost 600 years, the final emergence of public police and courts appears relatively sudden, but the institutional changes were gradual. Significant changes to criminal law and the emergence of early types of police began in the beginning of the eighteenth century as Parliament dealt with increases in property theft rates.

Of course the emergence of police and public justice has been a subject of research. Among social historians, these innovations are often seen as methods used by the wealthy to usurp the traditional customary rights of the working poor and enforce social control based on bourgeois values.[2] Older, Whiggish historians saw the arrival of the police as a "logical" and "rational" progression toward a modern world, mostly because they saw the older, pre-modern institutions as inefficient and corrupt.[3]

Each of these explanations is incomplete. It is true that customary rights of workers were eliminated, but it was due not to bourgeois values but instead to changes in measurement that made customary rights too expensive to maintain. It is also true that the pre-modern institutions became inefficient, but the inefficiency was due to changes brought about by the Industrial Revolution. The transitions from private to public police and from civil to criminal law were brought about by the reduced role of nature. In this particular instance, it was the reduced role in determining the final composition of goods in terms of quality. When nature played a large role in production, the result was a large variance in output quality. As nature's role was reduced, goods of the same name became more similar to each other. This shrinking variance in the quality of goods—the emergence of common standardization—played a major role in the evolution of justice.[4] Standardization was like the current of a great river—slow and barely noticeable at the surface but deep, powerful, and capable of profound changes underneath. During the first quarter of the nineteenth century, as this process increased, the river grew in size and the impact was felt everywhere.

Standardized goods caused a problem because they were often mismatched with earlier legal institutions that were designed to handle more artisan, nonstandard, goods. As standardization developed, the gains from anonymous exchanges increased; however, along with these gains the losses due to theft and embezzlement increased, and the evolving law and police were responses to this. In other words, one result of improved standardization was increased theft and a subsequent demand by manufacturers and property owners for institutional change. Hence the growth of criminal law and the emergence of public police were tied together by the emergence of uniform, standardized goods that developed during the Industrial Revolution.

THE PRE-MODERN LAW COURTS

The pre-modern court system was complicated. In effect, the court offices were held through a combination of purchased offices and patronage appointments. Judges were always appointed through some type of patronage, which has changed remarkably little over time; whereas other court offices were sold until the middle of the nineteenth century, when those offices became professionally occupied.

Modern English courts can be traced back to medieval times where the feudal lord acted as judge and jury for disputes within his jurisdiction. The office of the court, during this time, was inseparable from the ownership of the land. In England, the office of the court thus developed into a form of property called a "freehold". As the demand for legal decisions increased, these offices were generally sold to individuals who specialized in the provision of legal services.[5] By the pre-modern era, dozens of oddly named offices existed within the various courts. For example, in 1740 the Court of King's Bench had 43 offices, which included the lord chief justice, the king's coroner and attorney, clerk of rule, clerk of the affidavits, all the way down to tipstaffs and the turnkeys of the King's Bench Prison. Throughout time, efforts were occasionally made to legislate these offices, and restrictions on fees and positions were put into place.[6]

English court judges, whether of Chancery, King's Bench, Common Pleas, or Exchequer, never acquired their positions through purchase. These offices were not for sale; the positions were filled through patronage appointments made indirectly by the Crown. Technically, most judges were appointed by the lord chancellor (who was appointed by the monarch) in consultation with the prime minister and the Crown.[7] Judges were chosen only from members of the bar and almost always based on performance. Unlike the other departments of the government, "the law was a competitive profession even prior to the introduction of a system of entrance exams."[8] Hence, the judiciary provides an interesting example of office acquisition that changed relatively little from pre-modern to modern times.

Yet, the working environment of pre-modern judges was different from that of their modern counterparts. Although judges were paid salaries, the bulk of their income came from fees, the sale of offices within their courts, and other sources of proprietary income. Judges were often advanced to the peerage and given incomes attached to offices in the House of Lords. Also, higher court judges were given ownership over various income-generating offices outside their particular court.[9] Duman, who examines the salaries and investments of the 208 judges in England between 1727 and 1875, found personal estate values ranging from £2,000 to £300,000, with a median value of £60,000, toward the end of the period. When including land values in the estates as well, some judges amassed vast fortunes through the effective management of their courts. For example, Lord Eldon (d. 1838) was the richest, with an estate of £1,300,000 at his death. Although judges generally came from landed aristocratic families and thus their estate values would include inherited wealth in addition to acquired wealth, inheritance was not a major factor in final wealth levels because most judges were not eldest sons.[10]

It is important to highlight that judges were not paid in terms of their decisions or the number of cases they heard. For their judicial work, they were always on a salary. Basing judicial remuneration on some type of piece rate that links judicial decisions to judicial incomes would have resulted in perverse incentives. Paying by the case leads to short cases, paying by the number of convictions leads to too many convictions. The importance of independent judicial decisions hardly needs elaboration, and any type of output-based reward system would have caused a serious incompatibility of incentives between the Crown and judge. Justice requires judges to have no financial interest in the case outcome.

Furthermore, judges were never allowed to resell their position or otherwise decide who would replace them. Nor were they allowed to hire deputies to sit in their place, which stands in sharp contrast to the freehold officeholders in their courts. The reasons for these rules are obvious: individuals willing to pay the most for a position on the bench would be the very ones who should be prevented from becoming judges because those willing to pay the most would seek to manage the court to maximize their incomes and not necessarily to provide the best legal decisions.

These rules did not apply to the lower offices. The incomes of these other positions resulted from fees regulated by Parliament. The Royal Commission reports of 1818–1822 list the fees and duties of all officers in the legal administration. Some positions, such as the king's coroner and attorney, charged for over 100 different services. Others had much more limited duties. Clerks and other court officials managed these offices to generate profits, and they were allowed to sell their positions to the highest bidder. In these offices the private profit motives aligned well with the interests of the court and created no incompatible incentives.

Here we see a major departure from modern institutions: these fees were charged to those using the court services. In the pre-modern era, apprehension, investigation, and prosecution of criminals was done by the victim through services purchased at the court and marketplace. Indeed "the central feature of the old system was that the main responsibility for investigating and above all prosecuting crimes rested with the injured party."[11] Similarly, Hay and Snider note: "In England in the eighteenth century apprehension was the task of the victim of crime, aided (where he could get such help) from a parish constable or town watchman."[12] The victims might have taken this task on themselves, hired private firms, or belonged to a private association to investigate and prosecute, but in any case, public police service was not an option.

The use of venal court offices and private police was not without its problems. In 1730, a Royal Commission was formed to investigate alleged abuses found within the system. The commission completed its task in 1740, and found the interests of officeholders often conflicted with the interests of the court. Judges created redundant offices and sinecures for sale, clerks lengthened the requirements for court submissions when paid by the page, trials were lengthened and delayed by court officials paid by the number of days of the trial, and bribes were taken over and above fees to move cases along or even release prisoners.[13] These problems extended to the police service provided by and around the courts as well. Parish constables and watchmen were supplemented by "thief-takers." A thief-taker was essentially a bounty hunter, and the system of rewards often created incentives incompatible with justice. Paley tells the tale of two young men on trial in 1754 for highway robbery.[14] It turned out the two had been unknowingly recruited by a thief-taker to take the fall in a staged robbery. The two were convicted, but before the thief-taker could collect the £120 reward, the plot was uncovered. Paley concludes: "It is difficult to escape the conclusion that the major effect of the provision of £40 rewards was to provide an incentive not to the detection of crime but to the organization of thief-making conspiracies."[15]

It is tempting to think that the system was entirely corrupt, but work got done and, overall, the system functioned adequately until the middle of the eighteenth century when high rates of property crimes and embezzlement began to emerge. Experiments with different institutional solutions began, but it was not until 1860 that all of the court offices had been eliminated and only two classes of officials were attached to the common law courts: masters and associates, both paid exclusively by fixed salary and hired based on civil service exams.

The end of the predominantly private judicial and police system came about because the nature of goods stolen changed. As goods became more standardized, they became more difficult to identify with their legal owners. As a result, the ability of private individuals to cost-effectively investigate, prosecute, and generally produce justice declined significantly. The linkage between the changing role of nature and the organization of justice through public courts and police was complicated by the effect that increased standardization had on theft and the role of criminal law.

INCREASED STANDARDIZATION, THEFT, AND EMBEZZLEMENT

Prior to the Industrial Revolution, life involved a large natural component that led to high variability in product quality everywhere. Efforts were made to reduce variation in quality by aggregating commodities, sorting them into different classes, or making guarantees. Attempts were also made to use more homogeneous inputs, employ better tools, and develop instruments of measurement. However, the ability to successfully take such actions rested on the fundamental variability that arose in nature, which in the pre-modern era was enormous.

This variability meant it was practically impossible for different workers to produce identical goods. Sources of power were seasonal and varied considerably across space. Tools of measurement were often crude, and the hand tools used led to an artisan form of production and nonuniformity in final output. Inputs were local and varied from one jurisdiction to another, leading to wide-ranging variation in output. Production supervision was minimal and small scale, leading to less specialization and less uniform products. No refrigeration, no dependable transportation, no standard measures, and no reliable means of knowing where you were resulted in outputs that were highly variable and artisan.

This artisan characteristic of production significantly changed with the Industrial Revolution, during which a steady stream of innovations and new tools increased the amount of standardized goods, even in industries where craftsmanship prevailed. Tools that allowed for finer measurement, stamps and jigs, and higher-quality hand tools improved the ability to make standardized products such as cutlery, furnishings, and hardware, even though these products were not initially mass produced.[16] Development of special milling machines, turret lathes, and other instruments within the machine tool industry led to precision in general manufacture.[17] Steam power, continuous supplies of coal, and new methods of production allowed some industries to free themselves from the rhythm of natural power sources.[18] As a consequence of increased travel and road safety, markets became bigger, supplies more regular, and inputs more consistent across long distances. Improved uniformity enhanced the use of machines, which in turn created even smaller variances in output. High volume of production complemented standardization because "standardization and uniformity demanded a special kind of quality control, which required continuous supervision and thus factories."[19] Large volumes made investments in jigs and dies worthwhile, and these contributed to standardization.

Standardization allowed firms to alter their marketing methods and changed the way they organized their workforce to improve performance. For example, standardized goods were marketed and sold anonymously or by third parties.[20] Early in the eighteenth century, sales by contract were uncommon and manufacturers traveled with their artisan wares to sell directly to buyers. By the end of the eighteenth century, a national network of common carriers had developed that allowed producers to sell at a distance by sample and by taking orders.[21] The increased sale of goods at farther distances required standardization.[22] In this manner, the initial and subsequent forces of standardization reinforced each other and accelerated the trend.

Thus the increased division of labor, the increased use of machines, the use of nonseasonal sources of power, the better roads, the changes in marketing, and use of standard inputs all led to increased standardization of products throughout the Industrial Revolution. The variance in the quality of just about any commodity shrank dramatically.

On the one hand, this change from artisan to standard products greatly increased the wealth of society. Having standardized goods reduced the costs of measurement for identifying the various attributes of a product and therefore lowered the costs of exchanging goods. In this regard, standardization had enormous value for the emerging modern economy and opened the door for large gains from anonymous market exchange—the type we engage in so much today.[23] Prior to widespread standardization, goods were more difficult to measure and were often evaluated subjectively. Thus exchanges tended to be enforced informally through personal reputations. Disputes regarding such agreements had to be resolved directly by the parties to the agreements, as the courts were unlikely to know what the parties agreed to. For example, when a buyer who purchases ten one-pound bags of sugar claims that the sugar is not up to specifications and the seller disagrees, the courts are reasonably able to adjudicate the dispute. However, when a buyer who commissioned a painting is displeased about its quality, he is unlikely to be helped by the courts and his only recourse is to tarnish the painter's reputation.[24]

On the other hand, standardization brought with it new problems. New opportunities for theft arose because the very feature of standardization that lowered the costs of exchange through markets and contracts also lowered the cost of fencing stolen goods and increased the costs of protecting goods from theft—including theft by employees. Standardization lowered the cost of fencing stolen goods for thieves because the thief selling a standardized good can transact anonymously and reduce his exposure. Standardized goods make those fencing and purchasing stolen goods less vulnerable to being caught.

Legal owners of standardized goods then have higher costs in discovering, investigating, and prosecuting theft for several reasons: First, uniform quality of goods slightly hinders the owner from discovering a theft but drastically hinders him from investigating it. Second, when the transportation costs of standardized goods are low and their markets wide, owners are hindered because they have little knowledge of distant markets. Third, preventing the theft of standardized goods involves, at least in part, a collective action problem. Any private effort to reduce theft and black-market sales of standard goods provides a benefit to all owners of standardized goods, but the costs of this action are borne by the private party. Hence efforts to privately reduce theft will be underprovided.

Contrast these liabilities with the protection and theft of nonstandard artisan goods. Nonstandard goods are often identified with their owner, and certainly are likely to be identified by their owner; that is, the owner has a comparative advantage in identification. This advantage holds true for both intermediate and finished goods. Thus the legal owner of artisan goods tends to be the efficient "protector/investigator" of the goods. Artisan owners are familiar with their goods; they know more than anyone else about their legal status, are best able to determine when and what has been stolen, and are best able to recognize their goods when possessed by others. These factors make them the efficient owners of the protection rights of the good. This comparative advantage of the artisan owner is enhanced when the markets for these goods are more local due to high transportation costs.[25]

Two major institutional changes resulted from the increased costs of identifying stolen goods brought about by increased standardization. First, standardization led to changes in the definition of crime and personal freedom. Past practices that had not been criminal were made so, and the form of punishment changed. Second, standardization indirectly led to the formation of public police. By converting actions into crimes it became easier to address the theft and embezzlement brought about by increased standardization. However, criminal law removed restitution, or repayment, that came from a civil suit and thus reduced the owner's incentive to investigate and prosecute crime, which further led to a demand for public police. The advantage of police arose over investigating and prosecuting theft, especially as markets broadened beyond the scope of any individual. All other things being equal, when goods became more standardized, then it was efficient for theft to be resolved by police. When goods were less standardized, then private theft resolution by the individual owner was more efficient.

THE EVOLUTION OF CRIMINAL LAW

What constitutes a "crime" is a matter of state definition. Prior to the Industrial Revolution, offenses were generally civil matters. An individual violating the property rights of another would most often be privately arrested; brought to a court to be privately prosecuted before a judge who owned the court offices; and if found guilty, would generally pay restitution and court expenses. This system of torts—that is, injuries or harms—dating back to before the Norman invasion, slowly and steadily evolved as many torts became classified as crimes against the Crown, punishable by a fine, a beating, incarceration, transportation, or death. This evolution significantly accelerated throughout the eighteenth century—especially with respect to property crimes: the state increased its ability to search and arrest, offenses that had historically been torts began to be classified as crimes, and the number of capital offenses on the books increased.[26]

Criminal Law Evolution Examples

The practice of gleaning provides an example of eighteenth-century legal evolution from civil law (which if excessive could be tortious) to criminal. "Gleaning" often refers to the custom of peasants collecting grains and stalks in a field after harvest, but in the pre-modern era this term had a wider meaning. During this time, it was common and lawful for workers to glean scrap material from production and either use or resell it. Mates on ships were allowed to keep the sweepings from cargoes of sugar and coffee in the hold. Millwrights were allowed the scraps of wood and metal left over. The practice of gleaning extended beyond the employment relation. Peasants had gleaning rights to grazing (common of pasture), hay after harvest (common of shack), wood from forests (common of estover), and peat and turf (common of turbary), to name a few.[27] In every endeavor, workers could reap the bits and pieces of materials "lost" in the act of production.[28]

Gleaning had historically been acceptable to employers, as it was hard to finely distinguish or monitor between normal and deliberate waste.[29] If manufacturers could have reduced the gleanings at no cost, both real wages and gains to the manufacturer would have increased. But of course eliminating gleaning involved a transaction cost, and so it was tolerated and considered part of the compensation to workers. If an employer felt the gleaning was carried too far, his remedy was to dismiss the worker and sue for damages in a civil trial for breach of trust. A breach of trust was not an easy thing to prove because the mere possession by a worker of a manufacturer's material did not constitute a breach.

The problem was that gleaning too easily became embezzlement when goods became standardized and difficult to identify once off the production floor. Ashton puts it this way: "In each case the workers saw to it that the crumbs from the masters table were ample. Casks were handled not too gently; sacks were liable to burst open. . . . The line of demarcation between the extension of established rights and barefaced robbery is difficult to draw."[30] The artisan nature of goods prior to the Industrial Revolution limited these embezzlements to tolerable levels, but as production started to change throughout the eighteenth century, they grew in size. Whether in textiles, cutlery, needle production, ironwork, or nails, "in some of England's major industries, the embezzlement of raw materials was a serious and growing problem."[31] Knight discusses this problem in the context of a naval shipyard during the American War of Independence: "The next difficulty was to prove the stores were in fact the Kings, and also that they had not been legally bought at a dockyard sale of old stores. Cordage made for the King was to have a white thread . . . canvas had a 'blue streak,' and all metal goods had the broad arrow stamped on to them. However, these marks could easily be removed."[32]

As the eighteenth century wore on, manufacturers lobbied and were successful at getting these practices defined as crimes and made illegal.[33] This legislation bypassed the complication of gleaning issues and matters of trust between masters and servants.[34] For example, during the eighteenth century, the legal status of gleaning evolved into pilfering or embezzling and was called "clicking," "bugging," "scraping," "chippings," "vails," "sweepings," or even "cabbage," depending on what industry was being referred to. These names often appear as the titles to legislation that criminalized the behavior. During the eighteenth century, fourteen acts covering fifteen industries were enacted to convert gleaning to embezzlement.[35] The Clicking Act of 1723 allowed a magistrate or agent to search the premises of a leather shoe-making journeyman who was suspected of clicking—taking excessive bits of leather. Thus "clicking was criminalized."[36] The Bugging Act of 1749 criminalized the practice of substituting inexpensive fur for beaver pelts in hat making and introduced prison punishments for the crime. This act and the Worsted Act of 1771 further increased the powers of search and made "ordinary tasks of the labour process such as sweeping out the room, snipping weft ends . . . potentially criminal offences."[37] Elsewhere, Linebaugh points out that "the Bugging Act, like the Clicking Act preceding it or the Watch Scraping Acts following it, was designed to put an end to the customarily acknowledged appropriations of workers who had not yet been fully alienated from the means and materials of production."[38] In other words, these acts were designed to end gleaning in situations where workers had access to production materials. Indeed, eight different embezzlement statutes were enacted related to the woolen industry alone that extended criminal sanctions to what had earlier simply been normal practice or the civil wrong of breach of trust.[39] Other acts were more general: the Truck Act of 1831 outlawed payment of wages in goods rather than cash. By the early nineteenth century, most embezzlement was prosecuted criminally as larceny.

And so, rights of custom were removed and made illegal (turned into wood theft, poaching, trespass, larceny, embezzlement, etc.) through the parliamentary acts of the eighteenth century. As a result, many workers found themselves in the criminal court for doing things that previously had been legal. What had once been called a perquisite was now redefined as theft and larceny, which allowed easier means of prosecuting workers.[40]

Gleaning was not the only previously legal act criminalized. Prior to 1692, it was not a crime to possess stolen goods.[41] Throughout the eighteenth century, penalties were increased for "receivers" of stolen goods, and in 1827 possession of stolen property became a felony. Similarly until 1799 it was the civil wrong of breach of trust, not a criminal offense, for a servant to "convert to his own use money for goods received from a third person for his master."[42]

By 1855, the Criminal Justice Act allowed a summary trial of indictable thefts of small value; this act further extended the prosecution of embezzlement, which was often of small individual values. Parliament eliminated the grounds of proving discovered materials were actually stolen. This legislation further allowed property owners to attack the practice of embezzlement.[43] Styles notes that during the eighteenth century, the burden of proof was often shifted to the accused.[44]

Criminality was also extended to a long-standing common-law doctrine in master-servant relations called "possession immunity." According to Fletcher, immunity meant "transferring possession of an object conferred immunity from the criminal law on the party receiving possession, for subsequent misuse or misappropriation of the entrusted object."[45] This doctrine meant that a servant could hold the property of his master without fear of arrest. In other words, ownership of a good was separated from the mere possession of it. The embezzlement acts of Parliament of the eighteenth century removed immunity in various industries and Parliament finally eliminated it in 1857.[46]

Criminal Law and Standardization

This remarkable evolution of criminal law was the consequence of the massive emergence of standardized goods everywhere in society. When stolen goods were idiosyncratic, the legal owner was the low-cost identifier of these goods, and the task of retrieving them, along with the civil procedures allowed for restitution, were assigned to the owner.[47] With increased standardization, the ability of workers to steal improved, while the ability of employers and owners to privately investigate and prosecute the theft of standardized goods fell. As a result, black markets increased, and owners were unable to civilly litigate because identification was no longer possible. Embezzlers would sell purloined goods to networks of black-market dealers, known in the wool industry as "slingers." Unfortunately, given the inability to identify the standard goods to a producer, it was difficult to prosecute these slingers.[48] Because standard goods were profitable to steal and embezzle because they were difficult to trace, their mass arrival called for extensions to the criminal law.[49]

Consider the effect of standardization on the matter of gleaning. Historically, workers were limited in their ability to glean too much by the owners' ability to identify stolen merchandise. Once inputs and outputs became standardized, however, stolen goods became easier to fence and the costs of gleaning to the manufacturer increased considerably.[50] Thus, "embezzlement was rife in the manufacturing industries of eighteenth- and early nineteenth-century England."[51]

Or consider standardization's role in possession immunity. When goods became standardized the legal separation of "possession" and "ownership" caused problems. Because owners of standardized goods are unable to identify one specimen from another and thus are unable to identify goods sold legitimately or stolen, possession tends to be synonymous with legal ownership. That is, if someone is in possession of a standardized good, he will be the presumed legal owner. Today possession and ownership are usually bundled together, and we know the phrase "possession is nine tenths of the law." This layman's phrase arose in the English setting between the seventeenth and nineteenth centuries.[52] Prior to this time, the popular notion of ownership did not immediately follow from possession.

The opposite is true about an artisan good. Someone in possession and claiming ownership of a nonstandard good will be required to have some type of proof of ownership beyond mere possession. Proof may be in the form of a title, registration, receipt, or perhaps local specific knowledge of ownership. Ownership is less likely to be linked to possession of artisan goods because individuals are known to be matched with particular assets. Hence possession immunity worked with artisan inputs because a worker could receive possession of working material, knowing that the owner could not lay criminal charges of theft. Possession immunity formalized in law the fact that ownership could be separated from possession in a time when goods were easily identified with their owner.[53] With standardized goods it was efficient to have possession identified with ownership, and thus it made no sense to maintain the immunity provision.

Taken all together, the evolution of criminal law can be understood as a response to the falling role of variability in product quality. Because criminal law evolution reflected the rising difficulty in prosecuting civil cases against embezzlers and other property thefts due to increased standardization, it is not too surprising to find a change in the pattern of court cases over the eighteenth century. Measuring the frequency of crime and civil disputes is never simple, and doing so in the eighteenth and nineteenth centuries is even more problematic. However, studies have been conducted and some generalizations are possible. For example, Brook comprehensively surveyed civil litigation in England between 1640 and 1830 and found a dramatic fall in litigation in both the Court of King's Bench and Court of Common Pleas (cases not involving the Crown) until the end of the eighteenth century, followed by an increase.[54]

Some see this fall in litigation as evidence that trust was increasing among Englishmen during the period.[55] This interpretation is difficult to reconcile with the increased legislation regulating thefts at places of employment and the steadily increasing amount of crime over the same period. Although criminal statistics were not kept at this time, Beattie conducted an enormous study of indictments in Surrey and Sussex over this time period and concluded that property crime experienced "a gentle rise over the course of the [eighteenth] century."[56] An alternative to the "growing trust" explanation follows from the changes that took place on the criminal side. The steady increase in standardization meant that former civil law institutions were incapable of handling the rise in property violations. Local constables and magistrates were less effective, and individual property owners less able to identify stolen goods. The result was less prosecution of "crimes" through civil courts. As the criminal law was adapted, theft was dealt with in criminal courts; this transition is reflected in the growth in criminal indictments. Thus the criminal courts essentially substituted for the civil litigation.

Policing in the Black Country: An Example

Further evidence for the evolving role of criminal law and the reduced emphasis on private investigation and prosecution comes from Philips's detailed account of virtually all indictable offenses brought to trial between the years 1835 and 1860 in an area known as the Black Country. The Black Country, so named because of the intense coal mining and iron works of the area, stretches across 100 square miles just northwest of Birmingham. It held a population of 211,323 in 1831 and grew to 473,946 by 1871.[57] Philips's study begins before the introduction of public police and prosecution, during the time when parish constables assisted private individuals in the investigation and prosecution of crime. He generally finds the constabulary effective in dealing with crimes where the "victim either knew, or had a fairly strong suspicion who the offender was."[58] However, he finds that parish constables were relatively inefficient at "finding the perpetrators of crimes of which the victims could not name the offenders."[59] In the early days of the Black Country, Philips states that most larcenies were of the former type and that "all the constable had to do in such cases was take into custody the offender caught red-handed, or search the belongings of the suspected offender and, if the stolen property was found, arrest him."[60] Presumably, the victim was able to identify the stolen goods because they had an artisan character.

Criminal activity in the Black Country changed with the continued growth of factories and larger mines. With the industrial growth came an increase in industrial theft. Philips reports that property crimes without violence accounted for 85 percent of the indictable offenses handled by the new police, and that 80 percent of these cases were larceny. Industrial theft, consisting of inputs like coal, iron, and tools, was the most common, accounting for 28.2 percent of all offenses. The second highest category was theft of clothing, which accounted for 17.2 percent of offenses.[61] Of the industrial thefts, Philips notes that the increase over time in this category stemmed from "the expansion of large-scale capitalist mining and manufacturing production."[62] "This offensive continued to gather momentum; over the period 1835–60, there was a continual and marked increase in industrial theft prosecutions—in absolute numbers, as a ratio per 100,000 population, and as a percentage of all prosecutions brought for any indictable offence and of all larceny prosecutions brought."[63] A major problem with industrial thefts and clothing theft was the inability of the original owners to identify their goods. Philips notes that these items were "easy to get at, easy to carry away, and *relatively difficult for the owner to identify with certainty*."[64]

The same thing was taking place in the woolen industry.[65] Local constables could search the home of a spinner or weaver suspected of embezzlement but were ineffective at dealing with the network of black-market dealers. This black-market trade was only stopped with the introduction of police. Philips concludes "the system continued to work until the 1840s without any serious breakdown of law and order in those communities that relied on parish constables."[66]

The Watchmen and the Improvement Commissions

The case of the Black Country reveals more than just a reduced role of private citizens and an increase in property crimes. It shows the role of a new, modern institution: the public police. Police were not a premodern institution, but one that arose out of changes brought about by standardization; the early roles of the police were dominated by solving crimes of theft and embezzlement in situations where goods had become standardized and difficult to identify with or by a specific owner. But before the police arrived on the scene, other institutional attempts at protection took place.

One primary form of providing security came from watchmen. Defined by the Statute of Winchester (1285), they were "the only general public measure of any consequence enacted to regulate the policing of the county between the Norman conquest and the Metropolitan Police Act, 1829."[67] The watch and ward system was made up of as many as sixteen men who patrolled and guarded the gates of walled towns during the night. These duties were called the "ward" when conducted in the daytime. All men of the town were on the roster to volunteer their turn, and all were privately armed. Their chief duty was to arrest strangers when "they find cause for suspicion," and deliver the stranger to the parish constable in the morning. If a stranger resisted arrest, then a hue and cry was made and everyone in the town was to assist in the arrest. This system was in place until the end of the eighteenth century.

The watch was useful only to prevent theft of artisan goods and patrol for strangers and strange activity because watchmen could effectively police when they could identify goods in the possession of strangers—a horse, for example—or suspicious activity of known individuals. The watchman was neither an investigator nor a detective, and with the coming of standardized goods (including the increased use of money payments rather than barter), the watchman was relatively ineffective in identifying stolen property. With the arrival of standardized goods beginning in the late eighteenth century, the watchmen, along with the walls they patrolled, ceased to be effective.

Another eighteenth-century attempt at regulating order on the streets came from the "improvement commissioners." During the eighteenth century, the urbanization of England began in earnest and created problems for the maintenance and safety of new, small streets and roads. Neither the parish system nor the turnpike trusts were suitable for dealing with the new, small streets being developed in new suburbs. The results were streets laced with manure, impeded by signage and encroaching buildings, barely passable for muck holes, and dangerous due to the darkness and open cellar doors at the base of buildings. At night, matters were only worse. The solution was found in the creation of "improvement commissions," which were special statutory bodies with limited powers to collect taxes to pay for paving, lighting, regulating, and watching of the roads in their jurisdiction.[68]

An improvement commission was created by a specific parliamentary statute for the specific purpose of making a town or suburb run better, and its focus was almost always at the street level. Between 1748 and 1835, almost 300 commissions were created, and of these 100 in the greater metropolis of London. Commissioners were individuals of some stature who often sat for life. Some were elected by a small franchise, but most were not. These commissioners would collect taxes and hire individuals to maintain and look after the streets. After the Municipal Act of 1835, they were amalgamated into the new elected bodies. From the historical record, it appears that the bulk of their activities were devoted toward paving the streets; however, every legislation mentioned some provision for establishing a street watch. The watch functioned along the lines of the traditional watch and ward system.

It is well agreed among historians that the commissions were a response to the problems of increased population and urbanization pressures on unowned roads, and that any policing done involved duties "required to keep a place functioning" rather than "anti-crime activities."[69] Within any given jurisdiction governed by an improvement commission, watch duties evolved over time. For example, in the county of Chester, the first watch was established in 1625, and the first permanent and paid watch in 1703. In 1762, Chester was granted an improvement act that allowed for sixty watchmen with no change in duties from the past. In 1803, a second improvement act was passed with increased tax authority. Still the watch was engaged in dealing mostly with strangers, petty theft, and fire duties. In 1835, the Municipal Act terminated the commission, and police duties began to expand into inspection and detection of crime.[70]

However, the improvement commissions were poor versions of modern police. They could not investigate or pursue criminal activity. Instead, they merely copied the watch and ward system that had been around for centuries, and even with this, their attentions were more directed at the civil and mechanical matters of street maintenance than at crime. By the early nineteenth century, strong pressures existed to develop a public policing institution that could handle the problems that had arisen over the increased standardization of the Industrial Revolution.

THE EMERGENCE OF PUBLIC POLICE

Today police are invariably linked to violent crime, but their history would suggest otherwise. England, in the thirteenth century, was a rather violent country: the homicide rate was 18–23 per 100,000 population, and violent deaths accounted for 18.2 percent of all criminal indictments.[71] However, the trend in violence from this period until World War I was steadily downward. By the seventeenth century, homicide rates had fallen by half, and the fall continued throughout the eighteenth century. By 1890, "only three people in all of England and Wales were sentenced to death for murder committed with a revolver."[72] All of this was done in the context of private provision of police and justice. It was not until the nineteenth century that policing in England became publicly provided. The steady decline in violent offenses from the Middle Ages on is evidence that the emergence of the public police in the first half of the nineteenth century was not in response to a sudden increase, or continuing high levels, in violent crime.[73]

Instead of violence, the rise of police resulted from the role of standardization already discussed. First, as more acts increasingly became recategorized as criminal, demand for public police increased. With crimes, those found guilty were punished or fined, and the fine went to the treasury. A crime required a public official to investigate and prosecute because the absence of restitution removed the major incentives for the private investigation and prosecution of a theft. In addition, private policing of standard goods was a "public good," meaning that these efforts benefit other owners of these goods as well. Because private individuals do not reap all of these benefits, private policing generates too little enforcement. Second, the reduced ability of private individuals to deal with the theft of standardized private property led to a demand for public police. Larger markets—both legal and black—and more goods difficult to identify by owners hindered private policing. Finally, the mere logistical problem of finding offenders was exacerbated with the improvement of roads in the eighteenth century because "many property-owners had great difficulty finding and arresting offenders against them in the days before organized professional police forces—particularly if the offenders had traveled any distance from the scene of the crime."[74]

Styles provides an interesting examination of the public good aspect of criminal investigation: the dissemination of information on the incidence and character of offenses. The eighteenth century saw an "information explosion" in the form of advertisements, newspapers, and handbills to replace the ancient "hue and cry" of the local watch. Despite these media, private efforts at criminal prevention and prosecution did not exploit the new technology. Styles points to four information problems with private investigation: criminals could easily "escape discovery by flight," local magistrates were "profound[ly] ignoran[t] . . . of places and people . . . in distant parts of the country," finding information was expensive and inconvenient, and an "official facility for distributing information" was lacking.[75] It was not until the publicly funded magistrate, John Fielding, of the Bow Street office, instituted his General Preventative Plan in 1772, that any attempt to forward criminal information was made. When his funding was cut, the practice was not taken up again until later in the next century when it was publicly paid for.

The Transition to Public Police

Prior to the nineteenth century, preventing crime was not exclusively an act of individual private citizens. As mentioned, private individuals were often aided by owners of venal offices in the local court. Three common officials used in this capacity were the constable, the sheriff, and the watchman.[76] Hay and Snyder note how these officials were more dependent on the justices and private citizens than the future police:

> Both constabulary and watch were far more dependent on the justices for direction than the new police were to be, and that activities were usually limited to patrolling and assisting private citizens in the immediate apprehension of offenders. The enforcement of the law, in the sense of bringing offenders before the courts and convicting them there, depended primarily on the activities of the bench, and of the private prosecutor.[77]

Larger firms employed security guards and organized their firms to prevent theft. Groups within a community would form prosecution associations, hire private police patrols and investigative services, and use systems of rewards for capture. These private efforts dealt with the entire spectrum of criminal activity. For example, assaults, thefts, and even murder were left to the victims or their families to investigate and bring to trial.[78] More common though, private crime prevention was often organized around horse theft, since horses were valuable and easy to steal.[79]

Although the parish constables, watchmen, and justices of the peace were quasi-public offices who assisted private individuals, in the eighteenth century it often fell on them to enforce the growing number of criminal offenses, the increase in no small part due to the changing classification of activities.[80] Because they were often inadequate to deal with the growth and changes in crime, efforts were made to enhance these positions or find complementary means to assist in their police function. For example, the 1777 Worsted Act allowed an employers' association to organize an industrial police force that could "regulate virtually every aspect of the production process. But their chief function was to detect and prosecute acts of embezzlement."[81] Prior to the Worsted Act, various private organizations attempted to police embezzlement. In Yorkshire, for example, a group formed a voluntary association in 1764 to reduce "short and false reeling" (embezzling yarn). The voluntary force was funded through subscriptions based on enterprise size. Soderlund notes: "Despite its success, however, the Yorkshire manufacturers' undertaking remained vulnerable. In the end it failed, victim of inter-capitalist rivalry."[82] In other words, individual firms were reluctant to pay for policing that benefited their competitors. By 1776, it was finished, since "the inspectors failed to fundamentally challenge the pattern of workplace appropriation practiced by thousands of woolcombers and handloom weavers."[83] In addition, for a period in the 1760s, London magistrates were paid out of treasury funds to investigate crimes. The Bow Street magistrates office formalized this process into a force known as the Bow Street Runners, often considered London's first professional constables. Though similar in function to private police and thief-takers, they were paid by the magistrate with government funds. Although not well funded toward the end of the century, the office kept criminal records and made public horse patrols to guard London roads.[84]

The creation of the public police, an institutional revolution, can best be explained by the increased role of standardization. Since violent crime was decreasing, violence was not the source of the increased demand for protection. Rather, as the ability to privately police declined and as the level of property theft rose, the role of criminal law increased.[85] Public police forces were officially created through several pieces of legislation: the Metropolitan Police Act (1829) that established a paid police force in London, the Municipal Corporations Act (1835) that required all incorporated boroughs to have a police force, the County Police Acts (1839 and 1840), and the County and Borough Police Act (1856) that ultimately required all jurisdictions to be publicly policed. By the end of the nineteenth century, the system of public police, courts, and prosecutors had become completely entrenched. The transition was quite fast. In 1830, most counties had no police forces, but by 1860, the police had become common.[86] After generations of no public police, the transformation must have seemed revolutionary to the people of the time. And yet the new institution, once introduced, was accepted quickly. Indeed, the police existed on the "moral assent of most of the population to the role of a police force as enforcer of law and order."[87]

Factory Colonies

The arrival of modern police played a fascinating role in a short-lived institutional experiment of the early nineteenth century. In the face of rising difficulties in preventing theft and embezzlement in the late eighteenth century, producers sought a private solution outside of the law. They created "factory colonies" during the early years of the Institutional Revolution.

Prior to the Industrial Revolution, most production took place in family-operated cottage industries. When larger volumes of output were required, work was "put-out"—what today we call outsourced—to independent subcontractors. As such, the boundaries of the firm were not always hard and fast. Contracts between the employer and the subcontractors could be very informal, and work was often intermittent. The arrangement was loose, and even though hundreds of workers might be involved in the production of a final product, they would generally have no contact with each other. At times throughout the eighteenth century, artisan workers were even brought together "under one roof" into "proto-factories" in an effort to minimize transport costs.[88] As Ashton ironically notes: "The notion that the coming factories meant a 'depersonalization' of relations in industry is the reverse of the truth."[89] Although the products produced in both of these cottage industries—and the inputs used to make them—were artisan in nature, a slow transition was taking place. More and more goods were gradually being standardized as tools and methods were refined and as nature's role was reduced. By 1830, the factory system we know today was well under way, and by the end of the nineteenth century, it was common in many parts of Britain.

These factories exacerbated the problem of theft and difficulties of proving it because they used and created unprecedented levels of standardized products. Given the lack of public police and the limitations of private methods of investigation under the law, industry owners were left with carrying the burden of enforcement and prosecution. They formed associations, hired private guards and inspectors, and subscribed to agencies to help prevent theft.[90] They also searched workers on site and took care to watch their pockets while on the job.[91] A major part of this problem was that factory authorities had no jurisdiction outside their yard, and as a result, resale markets could flourish. That lack of jurisdiction represented a major problem for the factory system. Evidence for this is found in the testimony of manufacturers who lobbied throughout the eighteenth century for criminal sanctions against the barter system.[92]

Of course these private efforts to lower general theft levels often helped one's competitors as well, leading to the classic collective action/free rider problem previously discussed. The result was that prevention and enforcement were undersupplied because no single firm could reap all the social benefits. Thus although companies attempted to privately organize policing, the coalitions they formed were unstable, and parliamentary testimony suggests they were ineffective.[93] Consequently, as the gains from specialization and exploiting the new technological developments were increasing and driving capitalists to bring workers more and more together, an alternative private response was required to deal with the immediate rise in theft and embezzlement. The immediate, radical solution was to create factory colonies. In a factory colony, workers and their families moved to an isolated part of the countryside where they could work and live together.[94]

For example, consider cotton factories, which were among the first associated with the Industrial Revolution. Although these and other factories eventually dominated the industrial cities of England, the first factories were located in remote and isolated parts of the country. Collier, in her detailed study of several early factories, notes: "The factory system first made its appearance not in the large towns where it later became concentrated, but in the country districts."[95] Fitton and Wadsworth note that the locations of many of the surviving buildings of these early factories are still remote.[96] The Burrs Mill, established in 1801 in Bury, was nine miles north of Manchester; the Styal Mill, built by Samuel Greg in 1784, was in a location "with a very scanty population."[97]

The owners of these private communities erected houses, shops, churches, schools, and other amenities for their workers in these isolated settings. Chapman notes how common the building of colonies was:

> Experience soon showed that big wage packets were not the only solution [to attract workers], particularly where it was necessary to attract workers to isolated mill sites. At Cromford, Arkwright found it necessary to offer employment to whole families, and to build houses before they could be induced to move from Nottingham, Derby or Manchester. By 1790 he was providing a public house, a weekly market and garden allotments to retain his workforce. The Strutts at Belper, David Dale at New Lanark, the Evanses at Darley Abbey, the Gregs at Styal, and other factory colony builders had to offer comparable incentives.[98]

Fitton and Wadsworth emphasize the private nature of these towns: "They were, it is easy to forget today, a deliberate creation, without assistance from the State or local authority and with no public services. The factory, the weirs and dams, the machine-shop, the roads and bridges, the inn, the truck-shop, the church and chapel, the managers mansion all were devised by and grew up under the owner's eye."[99]

Within these communities, friction occurred among both skilled and unskilled workers, not just over long shifts and wages but also over the "insistence on close and continuous supervision of work by overseers."[100] Szostak notes: "The individual factory labourer was almost always supervised by someone . . . supervision of production workers by foreman and capitalists, developed simultaneously with the shift to factories."[101] Wages in the mill were generally higher than agricultural wages, but the workers surrendered a certain amount of civil liberty to work there. Behavior within and outside the mill was monitored. Workers would sign contracts that committed them to work at the factory for several years, and often an apprentice contract in the colonies would last for seven years.[102] Failure to stay could lead to bounties advertised in local papers and to prosecution. Factory owners also instituted local forms of justice in the form of fines or "forfeits." In the Strutt Mills, these were issued for such offenses as "absence from work without leave," "destruction of mill property," "failure to do work as required" (the largest category), "misconduct outside working hours," and "theft of mill property." In Fitton and Wadsworth's reporting of these forfeits, the theft category includes "stealing packethread; having waste found on body; stealing candles, yarn, rolers, nails, pincers, etc.; and making good yarn into waste and pockiting [*sic*] it."[103]

Not all types of manufacture were able to move to remote locations. For example, a factory colony was not possible for the navy. Instead, they attempted to deal with the problem in other ways. For example, the navy began selling scrap wood directly and used the funds to supplement wages. In 1767, the British navy earned £100,000 doing this, "twice the cost of the wage increase."[104] The navy also denied wives (who could steal material under garments) permission to come on site to collect chips and deliver food to the workers. Finally, by 1805, the practice of chips (gleaning) was completely eliminated. This measure exploited the benefits of the factory system while containing the problem of embezzlement. Most interesting is that the navy, not being a colony, never had the degree of supervision during nonworking hours found in the colonies.

The factory colony was an extreme form of what historians call "factory discipline." Quite incongruent with labor practices of our day, this discipline has been noted in every fiction novel of factory life in the nineteenth century. From an economic point of view, Gregory Clark points out that "a puzzling aspect of factory discipline was that instead of rewarding workers according to their output, it used behavior of workers as a measure of performance."[105] Clark concludes that firms had to act as a social coordinating device because workers lacked self-control when they had personal freedom. However, in light of the problem of embezzlement and the lack of public police, perhaps the factory colony is better viewed as a "voluntary prison." Workers accepted the higher wages in exchange for a reduction in their civil liberties, which reduced their ability to embezzle the firm. The loss of civil liberties and ease of interacting with outsiders was a constraint on employee theft and one that some workers were willing to exchange for higher pay.

Though the factory colonies lasted well into the nineteenth century, evidence does not support the idea that factories made money on community development. Factory owners had no special cost advantages in building schools and churches. Indeed, "they found that the establishment of a new community was an expensive and often frustrating experience, and labour turnover continued at a very high rate."[106] Collier notes: "It seems hardly credible, however, that a firm of the dimensions of Peel, Yates and Peel in 1801–1802 would trouble itself with the minute details of retail shop keeping, solely because of the profit that could be made."[107]

The gain must have been in the ability to supervise workers and prevent the sale of property stolen from the factory. The remote locations, the monitoring of behavior outside of working hours, the supply of shops, and the removal away from open markets all would have reduced the ability and benefits of individuals within the firm to steal. These drastic measures were necessary because the factory system gave workers access to large supplies of standardized inputs and outputs. Once beyond the factory gates, possession of the standardized good would have amounted to de facto ownership. Without modern institutions to prevent theft, isolation was the best method of protection.

As effective as factory colonies must have been in reducing theft, the costs would have been enormous. These costs represent a minimum measure of the gains from the new organization of production and thus illustrate the eventual advantage of moving to cities. As a result of these costs, this colony form of organization was relatively sparse and short-lived. By the middle of the nineteenth century, urban manufacturing had begun to dominate.[108]

From 1820 to the 1860s, factories moved back to the city—a move that coincides with the emergence of police. The critical difference between the urban factory and its colony predecessor was its organization. Long-term contracts and indentured apprentices were gone, labor generally became less skilled and less family related, and the entire colonial community disappeared. Large plants were more likely to pay their workers in money than in kind. In particular, the paternalism shown by the colonies had started to wane: "The scale and intensity of the textile masters involvement in the patronage of philanthropy and culture changed widely from the 1840s. . . . Elsewhere the change came later. . . . In all this, the factory owner was no longer confined to the role of patriarch superintending the welfare of his immediate band of workers."[109]

Technical changes increased the optimal scale of the factory as well as the number of low-skilled workers required. To continue the colony system under the larger scale, given the emergence of the police, simply proved too costly. Huberman states: "For many firms the apprenticeship system proved costly to maintain, and by the turn of the [nineteenth] century it was breaking down."[110] At the same time, increased mechanical production was creating more and more standardized outputs, which, as argued, increased embezzlement opportunities.

The presence of a public police force that could investigate and reduce theft outside the factory gates allowed the factory to move back to the city. With the changes to the criminal law, the police could crack down on public markets where stolen property could be resold. Laws on search, the criminalization of gleaning, and cash payments over barter all helped to reduce theft problems at work and facilitate the modern urban factory to come into existence.

The suggestion that factory colonies were an expensive attempt to mitigate embezzlement is a contentious idea because historians have commonly believed an alternative explanation: early factories moved to remote locations simply for the water power. These factories were large and required large amounts of water power. According to this theory, once steam was effectively introduced as a power source, the factories moved back to cities. Although this theory does explain the movement out and back into the city, it has several problems. First, towns often grew up around the best sources of water power, which had been used since the time of the Romans. As a result, the urban centers were already often located with excellent water power. Second, although sources of water power would have played a role in colony location, water power alone fails to account for all of the other institutional details and discipline of the colonies and for their removal when the factories moved back to the cities. Why were workers limited in movement to town centers while colony workers but not when the factory moved back to the city? Why were workers required to enlist for periods of time on the colony but not in urban factories? Why were nonworking hours and nonworking members of the household supervised on the colony but not in the city? Heckscher provides a nice description of these restrictions (even though his example is from France): "They . . . remind one more of a workhouse or a barracks or a prison than of a modern factory. . . . This mill employed at different periods between 1200 and 1700 workers. . . . It was surrounded on two sides by walls, and on the other two sides by moats filled with running water and fenced in. Keepers in royal livery guarded the entrances."[111] It is clear that there had to be more to colony existence than a source of water power. Without modern institutions to prevent theft, isolation was the best method of protection.

CHAPTER NINE

Conclusion

The great evil of this year . . . is the fall of My Lord of Sandwich whose mistake about the Prizes hath undone him.

SAMUEL PEPYS, The Diary of Samuel Pepys, December 31, 1665

And so we return full circle to our friend Samuel Pepys, that talented, nuanced, and conflicted diarist and administrator caught between the institutional apparatus of the pre-modern world and his own desires to be a modern man. In 1665, Pepys was just 32 years old, but he had already proven himself a master of naval logistic minutiae. His abilities as part lawyer, part accountant, part statesman and part politician, combined with his great intelligence, made him a rising star and contributed to his abhorrence of sloth and incompetence . . . in others.

And there's the rub: though Pepys was a man of great merit, he played by the rules of the time. He aligned himself with important nobles and persons of influence (including the king and his brother, the Duke of York); he accumulated a substantial amount of wealth through legitimate and questionable (though undetected) means; he sought positions through his personal connections, and was appointed on occasion even when he had no talent for the job; he made darn sure his nephew and benefactor, John Jackson, received an appropriate grand tour of the Continent; he used his positions to place his friends in various offices; and when his early patron Sandwich fell from favor, he made certain to distance himself just far enough to save his own skin.

The Earl of Sandwich, who until December 1665 had been a great servant of the state, should have known better than to make a "mistake about the Prizes." In this particular instance, he had been involved in a great naval victory over the Dutch, and was bringing home prizes worth up to £400,000.[1] Prizes were to be assessed at a prize court, and then distributed. Sandwich, out of impatience or vice, decided to "break bulk" and opened the holds ahead of time to sift through the cargo—a clear violation of the institutional rules regarding prizes. Although for a man of Sandwich's influence this act amounted to having one's hand in the proverbial cookie jar, he was caught and his "mistake" effectively put an end to his long and distinguished career.[2] In Pepys's world merit certainly counted for something, but in the world of patronage reputation counted for more, which is why honor was so important and worth paying such a high price to obtain and protect. Remaining a faithful servant in all matters was necessary for success and longevity in service. A slight infraction could not only lead to one's removal but also threatened the lesser servants in other offices.

Indeed, although Pepys's anxiety at Sandwich's troubles no doubt rested on a fondness for his friend, benefactor, and cousin, it also reflected the vulnerability he faced with Sandwich removed from favor. Pepys's ability to improve his lot was intimately associated with the standing and reputation of his patrons, and he worried about this constantly. Almost a year after Sandwich had been sent into exile as the ambassador to Spain, Pepys's diary records that he and his colleagues looked upon the situation "with horrour [sic], and gives us all for an undone people. That there is no such thing as a peace in hand, nor possibility of any without our begging it, . . . Lord Hollis [a friend] . . . wept to think in what a condition we are fallen."[3] In this particular case Lord Hollis wept too soon for Pepys, who survived Sandwich's fall. Later in his life, when Pepys's great patron King James II lost the Crown in the Glorious Revolution of 1688, Pepys's days in office were numbered, and at the height of his authority he had a forced retirement. It is a testament to the power of Pepys that it took the removal of a monarch to oust him from control over the navy.

Today the elements of patronage work basically the same, and the politics of Pepys's life have a familiar ring. Yet there is something quite distinct. In the pre-modern world patronage was accepted and respected, whereas today it is considered inappropriate and often is illegal. The difference results from our ability to measure merit and to award positions to those who can do the job. Pepys lived in a world dominated by the large role of nature, which in many contexts precluded the measurement of merit. This uncertainty was true of the political situation, where an unexpected change of events could shift alliances and power very quickly. In the Glorious Revolution, Pepys was in control of naval logistics, well prepared, and aware that William of Orange was planning an invasion. The admiral in command of the substantial British naval defenses was Lord Dartmouth, who took up a position at the mouth of the Thames. As fate would have it, some exceptionally unusual weather in late November allowed William to cross the channel, prevented Dartmouth from engaging, and . . . well, the rest is history. King James II was dethroned, William and Mary became co-regents, and a new relationship was established between Parliament and the Crown.[4] Ironically, neither James nor Pepys could blame Dartmouth for his failure to defend the country, given his reliance on wind.[5] It is easy to take for granted, from our modern and Western perch, the regularity and predictability of government because so much of nature has been removed from our lives. Pepys's world was rather different.

What truly remains the same over time is the tension between "getting a job done" and "doing it within an institutional framework." The institutions societies use depend on the role of nature, its variability, and our ability to measure and separate out natural from human inputs in any activity. In the pre-modern world, one could never escape from nature, and as a result institutions had to be designed to deal with this basic fact of life. The goal then, as now, was always to accomplish some type of production, but to do it in such a way that the problems of cheating and malfeasance were mitigated in a way that led to a high level of net wealth. What has always mattered is getting the rules right where the rubber meets the road, that is, providing a specific set of well-defined rules that create incentives targeted on the behavior of interest.

Life is filled with examples of institutions that get the job done. Look around. Grand and broad systems such as "the rule of law" and written constitutions exist, as do firms, churches, tribes, universities, societies and clubs, aid agencies, professional associations, unions, consumer's groups, political parties, condominiums, cooperatives, and so on. But many more informal examples abound of social systems that can be just as binding and often more interesting: families, friendships, social networks, peer pressures, customs, social norms, mores and religious values, and the like. All of these social factors—these collections of economic property rights that affect an individual's scope and ability of decision making—work together to make people behave a certain way: it is hoped in order to create a community that is prosperous, regenerating, and competitive. Not all societies are successful at achieving this end and often institutions are chosen that fail to meet the regularity of behavior that is desired. Stagnation is common for a period of time, but in the competitive environment of institutions, successful ones often win out.

This general line of reasoning applies to all types of circumstances other than services provided by the state in the pre-modern era. For example, the same issues arise in market situations or other private arrangements such as charities, firms, or agriculture.[6] Consider the organization of the family. Nature has historically played a critical role in family structure given the goal to produce high-quality children.[7] Fertility is a complicated natural process in which it is difficult to know of infertility beforehand, where fathers do not know paternity with certainty, and where mothers make massive hostage investments through childbirth early in the marriage and fathers do not. Within such an environment, finding the right spouse is difficult, mothers can be abandoned, and men can end up raising another male's offspring. Marriage has been the universal institution designed to handle these and other transaction-cost problems. It is interesting that nothing during the Institutional Revolution or Industrial Revolution changed the role of nature with respect to families. Factories, urbanization, and standardization all altered the role of women in the workforce, but left the biological roles of men and women unchanged. As a result, the marriage institution remained unchanged as well. It was not until the middle of the twentieth century, when technical innovations allowed some control over pregnancy and disease prevention, that the role of nature in sex and procreation was curtailed. It is not surprising that the nature of the family subsequently changed dramatically: marriage is now considered more of a "love"-based relationship; divorce is easier; grounds for divorce, child and spousal support, and property division are now legislated with rules that allow less discretion in family court; and marriage has begun to be extended to same-sex partners.

Also consider the organization of workers in general. Prior to the Institutional Revolution, labor was often managed through the doctrine of "master and servant." Workers often held similar status to dependent children. They were responsible and obedient to their master, but at the same time they were subject to the protection of the master. The relationship went both ways, and the relationship extended over multiple dimensions. Again, the concept of individual liberty is so tied to our modern identity that it seems hard to believe that just 200 years ago masters had an ownership interest in their servants. But they did. The period from 1750 to 1850 was marked by a dramatic change in the ability to measure time, resulting in the ability to use hours simply and cheaply as the basis of pay for the first time. This simple change allowed for a new relationship between the employer and employee, where a focus could be placed on the dimension of interest to the firm owner: a specific, actual output. The result was the "creation of free labor" in the nineteenth century. Today free labor is the normal state of affairs, and it is hard to imagine a Wendy's burger flipper having anything more than a wage-rate relationship to the franchise owner. The science of burger making and our ability to measure everything from temperature to condiment volume allows fast food to be produced and sold with little fear of botulism through a simple employment relation.

If the micro-institutional examination of family and free labor point to other applications, perhaps a more important extension would be an institutional reexamination of the Industrial Revolution. The term "Industrial Revolution" refers to the growth in output between 1750 and 1850. Over the course of these 100 years, per capita income grew at just less than 1 percent per annum. The increase was so small that major economic figures like David Ricardo and John Stuart Mill missed it. Still it continued until, by 1860, per capita income in England had doubled, along with a doubling of the population. Not much compared to modern growth levels, but after several thousand years at virtually zero growth, it was remarkable indeed.[8] The Industrial Revolution has presented two puzzles: why did it happen, and why was the takeoff in growth so slow initially?

The traditional view held that the Industrial Revolution was solely driven by technology. It was an easy story to tell because throughout the eighteenth century, a steady stream of high-profile innovations greatly increased production possibilities. The correlation is very seductive, but most economic historians take issue with the traditional story.[9] First, the Industrial Revolution was not entirely industrial; growth was widespread. Second, there was a long lag—fifty to eighty years—between the development of technologies and their discernible effects on aggregate output. Third, drastic changes happened to small firms in small industries, and should have led to a small change in total output.[10]

If technology cannot explain this growth, then what can? Many economic historians look for "feedbacks" or "dynamic" effects to account for the Industrial Revolution.[11] Here an alternative case for the role of institutions in growth is suggested. This explanation relies on the time it takes institutions to catch up to technological advances and the subsequent spillovers that result from institutional changes.

Large roles of nature and large opportunities for cheating often led to institutions designed mostly to deal with large and specific transaction-cost issues. Early in the pre-modern period, the old institutions matched the large role of nature. By the time the modern world was well under way in the nineteenth century, new and modern institutions had evolved that matched the reduced role of nature. During the transition, however, the switch from pre-modern to modern institutions was slow, leading to a delay between the reduction of nature's role and institutional change. As a result, throughout the Institutional Revolution numerous circumstances would have existed where the old institutional apparatus was inappropriate for the new order of things. This mismatch would have acted as a brake on economic growth.

The problem was that the evolution of institutional responses, which allowed for the full exploitation of the technical innovations, took time to develop—which is why Ricardo and Mill missed it. As a result, the full benefits of technological change could not be exploited until the full arrival of the modern institutions that came into being during the nineteenth century. For example, the physical tools necessary for factory production were available in the late eighteenth century but were unavailable for complete exploitation until the criminal law and police were fully developed. Thus the delay in per capita income could have resulted from the fact that technical innovations by themselves created institutional problems at the same time they solved engineering ones. Because the institutions took time to adjust, the full benefits of the technical changes took a long time to be felt.

Once new institutions come along, they can have spillover effects on other sectors of the economy. These spillovers can magnify the effect of the physical innovation that started the process to begin with. Consider the role of standardization. Standardization and the reduction of nature in every aspect of life had broad and general effects. Unlike any specific innovation, these changes affected the economy as a whole. As the institutional apparatuses of the country started to adjust to these fundamental changes, they also had similar widespread effects. Thus the innovation of the public police and the evolution of criminal law not only helped factories focus on production, but also had the complementary benefit of reducing other crimes. Moreover, the presence of police further encouraged innovations that led to more standardization.

Or consider the technical innovations. Steam and reliable clocks not only allowed for increased output, but allowed scheduling of ships, trains, and goods, which lowered the requirement to rely so much on trust and hostage capital. As the role of trust and hostage capital fell, modern democratic institutions developed, voting was extended to larger franchises, and modern bureaucracies arose. With enhanced ability to measure the role of nature, the entire system of civil administration was overhauled. Rather than a Crown-appointed justice of the peace to rule over a county and maintain the various service obligations through such appointments as church wardens, overseers of the poor, constables, and surveyors of the highways, new bureaucratic administrations arose employing salaried staff under supervision. These new institutions did not just affect a single industry such as cotton but every sector of society.

At this point it is only a conjecture, but if institutions are going to provide any explanation for the growth of output, then the analysis must be done on the microlevel where actual transaction-cost problems are created and solved by specific institutions. The existing studies of the Industrial Revolution have only begun to explore the transition of the Institutional Revolution, and it seems that further study is warranted.

Further study is not just a moot academic point. A better understanding of the role played by institutions in the Industrial Revolution would also help modern economists in their policy recommendations on matters of current economic growth and development. One of the perennial topics that drives interest in economics is the source of the wealth of nations. From Adam Smith to Jared Diamond, continual interest has centered around the question: "why are some countries so wealthy and others not?" Many, many theories have been proposed, and although some are able to explain some of the variation, much remains unexplained. Prior to the fall of the Soviet bloc, it is fair to say that most economists believed strong capital markets, well-running courts, and markets free from government interference were the main sources of wealth. And when the Berlin Wall came down and the Western consultants rolled in, this triad was the prescription given. The result surprised most experts at the time: rather than a unified rapid growth to Western wealth levels, some Eastern European countries grew, others stagnated, and some actually had negative growth. It became clear that economic development required more than capital, courts, and laissez-faire.

Since the reformation failures of Eastern Europe, Haiti, and other World Bank projects of the past fifteen years, it has become fashionable to focus on "institutions" as the missing remedy for economic development. Great efforts are afoot to try to measure transactions costs and social capital. In 2000, Hernando de Soto—the economist, not the explorer—wrote the international best seller *The Mystery of Capital: Why Capitalism Triumphs in the West and Fails Everywhere Else,* in which he argues that the institution of "secure property rights" is the key to economic development. He claims these rights lead to individual independence, clear and standardized information on ownership, increased trust, written contracts, better access to credit, and easier transferability. In many ways, however, it comes across as similar to the economic advice given to Romania. Is growth merely a matter of transplanting a singular modern Western property-right institution to an alien environment, in the same way a motor can be moved from one car to another?

The claims that the source of wealth and prosperity lie within a nation's institutions are intuitive enough. After all, the West gives the third world cash, and they remain poor. We transfer technology, and they remain poor. All that seems left is to provide the "institutions." Unfortunately, the institutional solution is often based on a simplistic reading of Ronald Coase; that is, if only rights could be secured, then bargaining could take place that would lead to the efficient level of output.

But something is missing. Return, for a moment to the key Coasean idea articulated in Chapter 1: every institution—by rewarding some actions and punishing others—not only determines what actions will be taken toward producing good outcomes but also what actions will be taken for bad behavior. Every greedy individual, even though he is likely to be better off when the size of the pie increases, can also benefit by taking a larger piece for himself—anyone exploits others if he can get away with it. Of course, others anticipate this behavior and try to stop it. The costs involved in attempts to engage and prevent bad behaviors are transaction costs.

And that's what is missing in modern discussions of development: the establishment of "secure property rights" is not free. Nor is there a unique method to do so. Every institution designed to create "secure property rights" comes at a cost and depends on the circumstances faced in a given situation. Failure to understand the microlevel circumstances—which would include the role of nature—means that successfully plopping a Western institution onto another environment would only be a matter of luck.

Consider the following taken from a recent study of Ethiopian grain trade:

> Grain is highly differentiated because there is no formal standardization and classification system, contracts are oral and nonstandardized

grain shipments are not inspected or certified officially, and there are very limited means of legally enforcing contracts. . . . These constraints cause grain traders to be highly vulnerable to being cheated with respect to market prices, quality and quantity of the delivered grain, and other contractual terms such as the timing of delivery and grain spoilage or loss during transport.[12]

The report goes on to conclude that if only the grain could be standardized and classed in a way similar to how it is done in Kansas, then wealth would increase. It is unfortunate that the problem for grain markets in Ethiopia is not whether they can copy Western capital markets or not. The problem is that in their entire institutional environment a Western capital market would do worse. It is only their current low-gross-production arrangements that produce the highest net wealth in their high-transaction-cost environment. Merely transplanting an inappropriate institution, even if it works well in a modern, low-variance economy, will only lower their net wealth. What is needed is a change in the microenvironment that is causing the large transaction-cost problem.

It is interesting to note how the grain market being described is remarkably similar to English markets (such as yarn) prior to the Industrial Revolution. In the opening chapter, it was suggested that if people could teleport back in time to 1704, then they would not recognize the institutions around them. What if we moderns could teleport our modern institutions back to 1704 and have them imposed on England? Perhaps the modern Scotland Yard or a professional army could be imposed. Would we really expect the Industrial Revolution to happen sooner, or that the standard of living would respond positively? Of course not. Indeed, the outcome would be similar to experiments in which the U.S. Constitution was imposed on Indian reservations or democracy upon Iraq. Why, then, should we expect Ethiopian grain markets to imitate the Minneapolis Grain Exchange if only a few Western institutions are imposed? The problem is that Ethiopia is not Minnesota.

The theory of this entire book rests with the idea that institutions are chosen and designed to maximize the wealth of those involved, taking into account the subsequent transaction costs.[13] Every institution produces a different level of wealth and a different level of transaction costs, and therefore generates a different level of "net wealth." The institutions that survive are the ones that maximize net wealth over the long haul—

even in Ethiopia. Failure to recognize this characteristic of institutions means that attempts to improve the wealth of others by transferring institutions will be doomed to failure.

SUMMING UP

We must understand that an institution is a complicated collection of expectations, norms, and constraints that work together to influence the way people interact with each other. As a "collection," it is necessarily difficult to understand. An institution can change—for better or worse—over time. Sometimes the purpose and function of an institution changes, while the institution itself remains in place: lords and ladies still exist but not powers of lordship. Other times an institution is replaced completely by another, and all the while the social function being provided carries on: roads have always been provided but through different authorities. An institution is created by people, sometimes quite deliberately and at other times rather spontaneously. Institutions both arise out of the storms of revolutions and evolve peacefully through ordinary human interactions. Institutions can be prone to adaptation, and they can be incredibly inert. They can generate wealth or lead to stagnation and decline. An institution is not a social "add-on" or afterthought but rather an integral part of any culture. Often the movement of an institution is the subtle driving force in history.

Without an understanding of the economic rationale of institutions, we often find them puzzling, unconnected, and inefficient. The connection between dueling and a public office appointment is hardly apparent upon first glance. The connection between turnpike trusts and purchased commissions is no more so. Venality and patronage seem corrupt, and private enforcement of rights harkens back to a tribal society. By using economic theory as a guide, we may organize the various nitty-gritty details of any institution to a point where they can be seen as part of an overall logical system.

An institution is a "system" of several factors that work together toward some type of goal.[14] One way to think about such a system is through the idea of economic property rights; that is, an institution is essentially a system, or collection, of economic property rights. Within an institution, individuals are able to carry out certain decisions (to some extent) but not others. The economic property rights may be derived from formal contracts, private information and opportunity, or the force of a personality. The result of all these decisions is some type of outcome—a "regularity of behavior."

Starting with the grand idea that efficient institutions are designed to mitigate transaction costs and arguing that during the pre-modern era these forces manifested in a system of patronage and purchase, this book has shown how a vast array of behavior and institutional rules were connected. All the elements of aristocratic life—the parks, the duels, the concept of honor, the education, the port, the seat, the estates, the occupations—were connected through the function of hostage capital as a method of generating trust. Furthermore, within any one of these categories, say dueling, the institutional details were further connected: rules for random lethality, participation rules, roles of seconds, etcetera. Alternatively, all of the private offices—for roads, prison and port officials, postal services, tax collectors, lighthouse operators, and army officers—were also connected through the compatible incentives the owners had with the Crown. Each system had its problems but survived for hundreds of years because each avoided the enormous measurement costs that were required for direct supervision, given the huge role of nature. Once fundamental measurement problems were solved—involving time, distance, weights, and power, among others— it became possible to cheaply measure worker performance, input and output quality, and the role of nature in areas of life that were unheard of before. This ability to cheaply measure ushered in the world of modern institutions. The ability to measure time brought about a more efficient method of payment to workers based on the hour. The ability to measure talent, knowledge, and expertise resulted in a selection process for employment based on exams, training, and performance. The increased standardization of inputs and outputs transformed the state into the efficient enforcer of private property through extended criminal law and public enforcement. And the general removal and limitation of nature in production led to greater and greater specialization and full-time employment within a given activity. The seasons of nature play little role in the modern world of production.

Throughout this book the hypothesis speaks with one voice: a logical, economic connection exists between a wide range of bizarre pre-modern rules and customs, and the evolution of these institutions into the modern world. What on the surface seem to be archaic, inefficient institutions created by people who just did not know any better, turn out to be ingenious solutions to the measurement problems of the day.

Notes

Chapter One

1. Other positions included clerk of the acts, clerk of the privy seal, Tangier commissioner, treasurer for Tangier Commission, surveyor-general of Victualling, governor of Christ's Hospital, and deputy lieutenant for Huntingdonshire (Ollard 1984, 362–365). All of these positions, in the words of Ollard, allowed Pepys to earn riches "hand over fist."

2. Rodger 2004, 97.

3. See, for example, North 1990; Acemoglu, Johnson, and Robinson 2005a; Mokyr 2010.

4. Glete 1993, 16.

5. Marx and Engels 1976 (1848), 82.

6. Trust and venal institutions do not, of course, capture all institutions—as mentioned, many institutions such as firms and markets are not puzzling and existed before and after the Institutional Revolution.

7. Most modern institutions, such as bureaucratic governments, rely heavily on the ability to measure individual contributions. Hence they were inappropriate in the premodern era and, for the most part, did not exist.

8. Plumb 1963, 50.

9. Aylmer 1961, 69.

10. Plumb 1963, 41.

11. Swart 1949, 47.

12. Pepys 1970, 6:100 (May 12, 1665).

13. Doyle 1996, 201.

14. Aylmer 1980, 92.

15. A similar view of the state is articulated in Barzel (2000, 2001). There, he explains why absolute monarchs find it in their self-interest to continually transfer rights to their subjects. Acemoglu, Johnson, and Robinson (2005a) provide another theory of the state based on political and economic institutions. Here, I ignore this evolution and concentrate on the structure of the transfer.

16. Still, a theory of growth in empire is beyond the scope of this book. The interested reader should see North and Thomas (1973) for an early articulation of this hypothesis, and North (1990), Barzel (1997, 2001), or Acemoglu, Johnson, and Robinson (2005b) for later versions. Brewer (1988) exploits this hypothesis in great detail and claims Britain's ability to extract taxation and create wealth at the same time was the necessary condition for its successes in wars throughout the eighteenth century.

17. Elias 1983, chapter 1.

18. Duman 1982, 17. See generally Morris 1999.

19. This argument was first laid out in Allen (2005).

20. The question might arise: can these questions in Figure 1.2 be asked today? For the offices and occupations analyzed here, the answer would be no. Today, there is a cheap way to monitor worker performance. However, there are many activities today for which performance is still difficult to measure, and in those cases some form of private ownership or patronage exist.

21. Coase 1959, 25.

22. Coase 1960.

23. Aside from Coase (1960), Davis and North (1971), Hayek (1973), North and Thomas (1973), North (1981, 1990), Grief (1989, 1993, 2006), Milgrom, North, and Weingast (1990), and Barzel (1997) all made major contributions to this hypothesis.

24. Allen 1991, 2000.

25. Understanding that institutions are chosen to maximize wealth net of transaction costs has two important implications. First, wealth is generated not just by the traditional sources of technology and exchange, but also by lowering transaction costs. When an institutional innovation is made that reduces transaction costs, net wealth is higher even if there is no change in the total amount produced. Second, the social goal is not to minimize transaction costs. Minimizing transaction costs can easily be done by eliminating social interactions, but doing so would lead to even greater losses of output. This understanding is critical in discussing the Institutional Revolution that took place between 1780 and 1850. Often, technical changes took place that made the old institutions inefficient and created incentives to replace them with modern institutions. These new institutions could, and often did, have extremely high transaction costs as well, given that they often increased the division of labor, were used across wider geographic areas, and put more time and space between trading individuals. Still, the modern institutions were better because they allowed for an even larger gain in output. The social goal is to design institutions to maximize wealth net of transaction costs, not to minimize these costs.

26. But not all. See Elias (1983) for a complementary view.

Chapter Two

1. Consider the following comment regarding the production of a simple product like yarn before the Industrial Revolution: "It is well nigh impossible to secure uniformity of yarn. The clothier asked for a definite standard when giving out the wool to be spun, but the tendency would be for each house and each spinner to vary a little in the thickness and firmness of the yarn; some sent in hard-twisted, others soft-twisted, and it was very difficult to reduce the work to one standard" (Heaton 1965, 335). This was just yarn! The same could be said of virtually all production prior to 1750: standardization was uncommon.

2. Allen 2006.

3. Of course, Washington would have had his own powered vehicles as well, and so who knows what the actual outcome would have been. All we can say for sure is that the result would not have depended on the wind, and the loser would more likely have been held personally responsible.

4. Allen and Lueck 2002.

5. This section is based on the excellent book by David Landes (1983).

6. David Landes (1983, 187) notes that "the unification of time, of course, enormously enhanced the value of time measurement, for it eliminated all manner of confusion and of pretext for inexactitude and made possible a far more efficient ordering of activity. Watches became that much more necessary to everyday life."

7. See Alder (2002) for the fascinating account of the trials, tribulations, error, and cover-up that is the story of the meter.

8. Zupko 1977, 20.

9. Ibid., 32.

10. Tavernor 2007, 132. Serious attempts to find an invariable and imperishable standard of weight and measure began in the eighteenth century, and in Britain were related to the development of the clock, where attention was given to the distance a pendulum would swing within a second. By 1824, the Imperial System of measures was established in Britain. The standards were well defined and independent of nature. They were not always easy for the average person to understand, however. For example, a yard was defined in 1824 to be 360,000/391,393 of a pendulum beating seconds in a vacuum, at the latitude of London, at sea level (Tavernor 2007, 129).

11. Mokyr 2010, 139. Libecap and Lueck (2010) show that when land is surveyed based on a rectangular grid, as opposed to metes and bounds, the land is more valuable and traded more often.

12. Although the Spanish Influenza outbreak of 1919 was significant in this regard.

13. Pepys, August 16, 1665. Pepys's diary points to more than just outbreaks of viruses; he is consumed by general health matters and their effect on day-to-day activity (Ollard 1984, 53).

14. Hopkins 2002, 35.

15. Ibid., 37.

16. Ibid., 41–42.

17. Magner 2005, 363.

18. Ibid., 364.

19. Rodger 2004, 484–487.

20. Berg 1994, 269–270.

21. Rosenberg (1963) provides a detailed discussion of the machine tool industry.

22. Mokyr 2010, 135–136.

23. See Kurlansky (2002) for an entertaining history of salt.

24. Szostak 1991, 13–15, 168–169.

25. Sir Thomas Smith, c. 1560, quoted in Sternfeld 1991, 98.

26. Steinfeld 1991, 56.

Chapter Three

1. This chapter is based on Allen (2009b).

2. Asch 2003, 12.

3. Taken from Guttsman (1969, 60).

4. Dewald 1996, 5, 194–197.

5. Orwell 1968, 70.

6. Doepke and Zilibotti 2008, 747–748. Mokyr (2010, 384) suggests many were "idle and useless drones." It is not that these sentiments are completely wrong, but they do mischaracterize aristocrats.

7. Stone and Stone 1984, 15; Dewald 1996, 91.

8. Clark 2007.

9. Doepke and Zilibotti 2008.

10. Acemoglu, Johnson, and Robinson 2005a.

11. Dewald 1996, 92; Zmora 2001, 4.

12. James 2009, 41.

13. Acemoglu, Johnson, and Robinson 2005a argue that the final transfer was not voluntary but was a response to the threat of force. I take this topic up at the end of the chapter.

14. Habakkuk 1967, 2–12; Clark 1995, 18–19.

15. Beckett 1986, 27.

16. Ibid., 35.

17. Ibid., 35–40.

18. Habakkuk 1967, 2; Dewald 1996, 2.

19. English aristocrats, by the pre-modern period, held few special legal rights. Contrary to this, on the Continent many minor nobles held rights that freed them from certain taxes, granted them special hunting privileges, and the like (Zmora 2001, 2–4; Asch 2003, 43–44).

20. Dewald 1996, 68–69.

21. This transformation took place across Europe (Elias 1983, chapter 1).

22. Dewald 1996, 37–38.

23. Harris 1986, 103.

24. Gunn 1988, 2–7.

25. Asch 2003, 51.

26. It is notable that the pre-modern aristocrats were not members of the bourgeoisie. This class was made up of lawyers, other professionals, skilled artisans, and successful merchants and industrialists. At the beginning of the pre-modern era, the bourgeoisie was insignificant in size, wealth, and power, but they would grow over the next 300 years and eventually overtake and intermarry with aristocrats at the end of the nineteenth century. Indeed, they would even play a significant role in the two English revolutions of the seventeenth century (Acemoglu, Johnson, and Robinson 2005a, 453–457). None of the constraints in behavior that applied to aristocrats ever applied to the bourgeoisie. They would grow in wealth and power through trade, production, and thrift in the marketplace—a much different path than the aristocrats.

27. Stone and Stone 1984, 295.

28. One might wonder how an individual became wealthy without land or membership in the aristocracy to begin with. But the fact is that there were always options outside the aristocracy for gaining wealth (e.g., merchant trade, professions, industry). The aristocratic monopoly was over the provision of high public office, not accumulated wealth.

29. Beckett 1986, 92.

30. Stone and Stone 1984, 349.

31. Jane Austen (2003 [1813], 36–37) captures the social considerations of marriage in *Pride and Prejudice*. This novel provides another interesting fictional account of the

difficulty of love crossing social class boundaries when Lord Bingley develops feelings for the eldest daughter Jane. Lord Bingley, his sisters, and Mr. Darcy are in a discussion of the marginally gentry Bennet family. One of the sisters starts off: "'I think I have heard you say, that their uncle is an attorney in Meryton.' 'Yes; and they have another, who lives somewhere near Cheapside.' 'That is capital,' added her sister, and they both laughed heartily. 'If they had uncles enough to fill all Cheapside,' cried Bingley, 'it would not make them one jot less agreeable.' 'But it must very materially lessen their chance of marrying men of any consideration in the world,' replied Darcy. To this speech Bingley made no answer; but his sisters gave it their hearty assent, and indulged their mirth for some time at the expense of their dear friend's vulgar relations." And we think lawyers are maligned in modern times! To have a relation in the vulgar legal profession during the pre-modern era was enough to eliminate almost any chance of upward social movement.

32. Cannon 1984, 74; Beckett 1986, 103.

33. Stone and Stone 1984, 290.

34. Bush 1984, 68.

35. Crouzet 1985, 70.

36. Doepke and Zilibotti 2008, 776.

37. On the Continent the feudal rights of aristocrats tended to last longer. Moving from west to east the rights increased and were often called "lordship" rights. This title referred to feudal rights governing peasants living on the lord's land. Many Continental nobles had little political power (Dewald 1996, 68–69).

38. Acemoglu, Johnson, and Robinson 2005a, 459.

39. Churchill 2002, 344. It was because of his role in the Hudson's Bay Company that the northern Manitoba town and river were named after him.

40. Cannon 1984, 64.

41. See Brewer 1988, 404–406.

42. Churchill 2002, 409.

43. The Crown had its own issues with being honest toward the aristocrats, but for most of the pre-modern era it was seriously constrained in this regard. Although the Crown after 1500 took some time to work through the new relationship with the pre-modern aristocrats, culminating in the two revolutions of the seventeenth century, after 1688 the Crown was in no position to act as an absolute sovereign and was constrained by its constitutional relationship with the aristocrats. This prevented blatant confiscation and reneging on agreements by the Crown (North and Weingast 1989; Acemoglu, Johnson, and Robinson 2005a, 456).

44. In economics, models based on trust have been well worked out. Early papers included Klein and Leffler (1981), Camerer (1988), Coleman (1988), Iannaccone (1992), and Berman (2000). Models of trust are essentially variations of sustaining cooperation in repeated game settings. See Mailath and Samuelson (2006) for a summary of game-theoretic results. One piece of evidence for a trust system comes from the fact that there were always more aristocrats than high offices available (Stone 1965, 465–468 estimates that there were between two to three times as many peers as major offices). Bush (1984, 54) notes the same thing.

45. See Dasgupta and Serageldin (1999) and François (2002) for formal models of hostage social capital.

46. Economics calls such situations ones of "imperfect public monitoring" because everyone observes the same noisy outcome, but the actual action taken by the aristocrat is not known with certainty. See Green and Porter (1984) for the details of public monitoring games.

47. Ibid.

48. Dewald 1996, 37–38.

49. Stone and Stone 1984, 101.

50. Asch 2003, 56–61.

51. Perhaps the matter of patience requires further elaboration because some have argued that aristocrats lacked patience and indeed have argued aristocrats were taught by their parents not to hold this virtue. Doepke and Zilibotti (2008) argue that because aristocrats engaged in much leisure-consuming activities, it made sense for their parents to encourage and develop human capital investments that would be useful in leisure. In particular, they argue that aristocratic families would not instill the virtue of patience, which is useful if interested in the long-term financial returns that accompany success in the business world. Although they provide no direct evidence for this claim, even if true, it would be consistent with the theory presented here because it is the founding members of the aristocracy that require patience.

52. Churchill 2002, 48.

53. Ibid., 414.

54. Dewald 1996, 48–49; Asch 2003, 33–38.

55. Once again we see a slight difference on the Continent, where aristocrats were more likely to dabble in commerce and banking (Dewald 1996, 94).

56. There were occasional instances throughout the pre-modern period when the entrance requirements of the aristocracy were violated. For example, during the early Stuart reign, James I (1603–1625) attempted to raise funds by selling knighthoods. As a result, the position of knighthood became "a title without social distinction, and therefore meant nothing in terms of social integration" (Stone and Stone 1984, 241). And so it should have become if the role of the aristocracy was one of "trustworthy servant."

57. The best discussion of the family settlement is Bonfeild (1986).

58. Stone and Stone 1984, 78.

59. The strict family settlement explains why, in speaking of others, aristocrats would refer to the income per year (i.e., the flow) they earned rather than their wealth (the stock or present value of their earnings). When all assets are unrestricted, as they mostly are today, then speaking of income or wealth is a mere matter of choice. However, when much of the stock of wealth is restricted in terms of use, wealth levels are not a good measure of the ability to consume. The income flow represented an aristocrat's ability to engage in consumption.

60. Stone and Stone 1984, 73.

61. Ibid., 72.

62. Ibid., 101.

63. Smith 1994 (1776), 415.

64. Ibid., 417.

65. It is interesting that on the Continent things worked slightly differently. All of the children of an aristocrat retained some type of title and remained nobles, even when they did not inherit the estate. This greatly increased the number of titled individuals

and watered down the hostage capital role of titles because they no longer signaled a large level of other capital attached to them.

66. Dewald 1996, 51.

67. Beckett 1986, 102.

68. Locke 1692, section 164, part X.

69. Cannon 1984, 34.

70. Ibid., 41.

71. Beckett 1986, 102.

72. The modern Olympics were begun through the efforts of Pierre de Coubertin, the son of a French baron who was influenced by sport at Rugby School. See Hill (1992).

73. Stone and Stone 1984, 185.

74. Dewald 1996, 92.

75. Bush 1984, 75.

76. Austen 2003 (1813), 333.

77. Beckett 1986, 50.

78. Ibid., 288.

79. Soltow 1968, 19.

80. Rubinstein 1981, 196.

81. Ibid., 193; Asch 2003, 25.

82. Rubinstein 1981, 71.

83. Ibid., 204–205.

84. Clark 1995, 145.

85. Asch 2003, 27.

86. Dewald 1996, 60–65.

87. Ibid., 62.

88. Asch 2003, 49.

89. Acemoglu, Johnson, and Robinson 2005a, 458–462.

90. Stone and Stone 1984, 425.

91. Cannadine 1990, 54.

92. Ibid., 111.

93. Ibid., 119.

94. Ibid., 125–136.

95. Cannon 1984, 19.

Chapter Four

1. This chapter is based on Allen and Reed (2006).

2. See Baldick (1965, 104–106) for a discussion of the whole affair.

3. Billacois 1990, 9.

4. Kiernan 1988, 102.

5. For example, see Kiernan 1988 or McAleer 1994.

6. Nye 1998, 85. See also Elias 1983, 240.

7. Lessig 1995, 969–970.

8. Posner 1996, 1736–1740.

9. See Allen and Reed (2006) for a formal model that shows the specific conditions for the duel to work.

10. Frevert 1998, 41.

11. However, the dead dueler might have a family, and participation in a duel leading to death would likely maintain the family's status.

12. Clark 1995, 168–169, 342.

13. Halliday 1999, 3.

14. The *Morning Herald*, reflecting the sentiments of everyone, stated in part: "The city was thrown into a great ferment this morning by a report which seemed utterly improbable, that at first few people believed it . . . the Duke of Wellington, the conqueror of a greater conqueror than either Alexander or Caesar, the first warrior of his day, the victor of a hundred battles, the Prime Minister of Britain, . . . placed himself in a position where it was probable that he might have become a murderer . . . And all this risk was run . . . merely because a noble lord, in a fit of anger, wrote a pettish letter" (Baldick 1965, 106).

15. For example, see Steward 2000, 6.

16. One final and interesting aspect regarding dueling participation was that qualified duelists were expected to duel in every legitimate duel. The condition of repeated dueling participation existed to prevent staged or fake duels because success in a fake duel did not prevent further dueling. Indeed, a staged duel likely attracted the attention of other duelists in the competitive court life.

17. Schwartz, Baxter, and Ryan (1984, 345) is the only source, to my knowledge, with this point of view.

18. McAleer 1994, 47.

19. Parker 2001, 8–9.

20. Pepys 1970, 8:364 (July 29, 1667).

21. Kiernan 1988, 117.

22. Cochran 1963.

23. Ibid.

24. Ibid.

25. McAleer 1994, 47.

26. Cochran 1963.

27. Ibid., 61.

28. Frevert 1998, 39.

29. Schwartz, Baxter, and Ryan 1984, 337.

30. Murray 1984, 4.

31. Pepys 1970, 3:157 (August 6, 1662).

32. Johnson and Libecap 1994a, 1994b.

33. The first reported duel in America was between two servants of a Massachusetts gentleman in 1621 (Baldick 1965, 115).

34. Kline 1973, 401.

35. Burr was, however, charged with "willful murder" by a New York coroner (Parmet and Hecht 1967, 227).

36. Of course, Burr did kill a hero of the American Revolution, and Hamilton supporters ever since have painted him with a demonized brush. Immediately after the duel stories circulated that he had spent hours practicing and even had a special suit made to deflect bullets (Parmet and Hecht 1967, 217).

37. Other parts of the story recount that both men had been involved in duels

before, Hamilton forgave Burr on his deathbed, and most members of the ruling elite sought to treat Burr like "any other man who killed another in a duel" (Parmet and Hecht 1967, 215).

38. Steward 2000, 126. Lincoln was to duel against Illinois state auditor James Shields in Missouri, near Alton. Shields had challenged Lincoln over some mocking letters published in the *Sangamo Journal*, an Illinois newspaper. Although Lincoln had written some of the letters under the name "Rebecca," his future wife wrote some as well under the name "Cathleen." Lincoln took the blame for all of the letters. The duel was avoided at the urging of the seconds but not on any grounds of legitimacy. It is not too surprising then that Lincoln was ashamed of this event, and neither he nor his wife ever spoke of it. Later, when he was president an army officer asked him about it. His reply: "I do not deny it, but if you desire my friendship, you will never mention it again" (Donald 1995, 92). Lincoln was likely to be aware that avoiding the duel had been a dishonorable event in his life.

39. Tocqueville, as quoted in Baldick 1965, 115.

40. Steward 2000, 8.

41. Hughes (1998, 73) reports that the fatality rate for Italian duels in the late nineteenth century actually fell to half of 1 percent.

42. Peltonen 2001, 9–10.

43. Baldick 1965, 67–69.

44. Kiernan 1988, 94. He goes on to say that "in the Royalist camp steps had to be taken to curb it." This statement make sense because the Royal camps still revolved around the institution of patronage based on trust.

45. Aylmer 1973, 70.

46. Allen 2009a.

47. Aylmer 1973, 10.

48. Ibid., 61.

49. Rodger 2004, 112.

50. Aylmer 1973, 61–62; emphasis added.

51. Campbell 1965, 56.

52. Brewer 1988, 65.

53. Johnson and Libecap 1994b, 97–98.

54. McAleer 1994, 62.

55. Nye (1998, 88) claims that dueling was responsible for perhaps only two dozen deaths in Europe between 1875 and 1900.

56. Ibid., 83.

57. McAleer 1994, 18.

58. Ibid., 45.

59. Hughes 1998, 73.

Chapter Five

1. This chapter is based on Allen (2002).

2. Lavery 1998; Moorehouse 2005.

3. Rodger 1986, 11.

4. Rodger (2004) argues that command of the oceans was necessary for command of the world.

5. Glete 1993, 211–220.

6. A popular navy song written by Richard Leveridge in 1735, called "The Roast Beef of Old England," starts off: "When Mighty Roast Beef was the Englishman's Food / It ennobl'd our veins and enriched our Blood: / Our Soldiers were Brave and our Courtiers were Good. / Oh! The Roast Beef of Old England, / And Old English Roast Beef!" (Bryant 2000).

7. Rodger 2004, 458.

8. Ibid., chapters 1–4.

9. Ibid., 382–383.

10. Ibid., 54.

11. Ibid., 388.

12. Ibid., 122.

13. Wareham 2001, 93.

14. Allen 2002.

15. Benjamin and Tifrea 2007, 993.

16. Ibid., 996–1000.

17. Rodger 1986, 57.

18. Tunstall and Tracy 1990, 234.

19. Lewis 1960, 362.

20. Keegan 1988, 48.

21. Benjamin and Tifrea 2007, 976–987.

22. Rodger (2004) has an excellent comparison and description of rates, tonnage, displacements, and so on.

23. Henderson 1971, 9–10.

24. Lavery 1989, 317.

25. Palmer 1997, 692.

26. Forrester 1960, 29.

27. Lavery 1989, 317; Rodger 2004, 272.

28. Glete 2000, 23.

29. Henderson 1971, 3; Baugh 1977, 196; Whipple 1978, 23.

30. Rodger 2004, 411.

31. Ibid., 414, 424–425.

32. Ibid., 361.

33. Rodger 1986, 58.

34. Ibid., 60.

35. Rodger 2004, 17.

36. Glete 2000, 38.

37. Rodger 1986, 244; Rodger 2004, 202.

38. Rodger 2004, 460.

39. As quoted in Palmer 1997, 699.

40. Keegan 1988, 90.

41. See Lavery (1989, 318) for a long list of examples.

42. Rodger 2004, 321–326.

43. Pepys 1970, 7:394 (October 28, 1666).

44. Ollard 1984, 222–225.

45. Rodger 1986, 246.

46. Ibid., 256.

47. Palmer 1997, 697.

48. Glete 2000, 48–49.

49. Baugh 1977, 41.

50. As quoted in Rodger 2004, 123. See also Ollard 1984, chapter 16.

51. Rodger 1986, 38.

52. Ibid., 314–315.

53. Ibid., 314.

54. Rodger 2004, 320; Benjamin and Thornberg 2007, 323.

55. Benjamin and Tifrea 2007, 990.

56. Converting wealth levels across centuries is wrought with problems. This estimate is based on the work of O'Donoghue, Goulding, and Allen (2004).

57. Warner 1975, 74.

58. Ibid., 227.

59. Wareham 2001, 41.

60. Lewis 1965, 234.

61. Howarth 1974, 227.

62. Wareham 2001, 21, 26, 229; Rodger 2004, 517–523.

63. Henderson 1971, 31.

64. Baugh 1977, 44.

65. Lavery 1989, 40.

66. Ibid., 99.

67. Eaton and White 1983.

68. Glete 2000, chapter 2.

69. Tunstall and Tracy 1990, 96.

70. Corbett 1967, 76.

71. Keegan 1988, 48.

72. Palmer 1997, 679.

73. Ibid., 683.

74. Keegan 1988, 45.

75. Tunstall and Tracy 1990, 89; emphasis added.

76. Ibid., 225; Palmer 1997, 703–704. Nelson was not unlike other commanders in this regard.

77. Benjamin and Tifrea 2007, 976–987.

78. Rodger 1986, 218.

79. Rodger 2004, 59.

80. See Tracy (1991b) for a detailed discussion of the battle. It was fortunate for Calder that this event took place after the 1778 revisions and thus he was censured rather than executed.

81. Hattendorf 1984, 143.

82. Ibid., 143.

83. Rodger 2004, 122.

84. Ibid., 381.

85. Dandeker 1978, 304.

86. Wareham 2001, 20.

87. Henderson 1971, 144.

88. Baugh 1977, 41.

89. Rodger 1986, 124.

90. Rodger 1984, 245.

91. Royal Navy 1790, 94; emphasis added.

92. Ibid., 97.

93. Ibid., 3.

94. Rodger 2004, 106.

95. Royal Navy 1790, 159.

96. Hough 1973, 101.

97. Benjamin and Thornberg 2003, 204.

98. Andrews 1984, 24.

99. Rodger 2004, 59.

100. See Tracy (1991a) for a detailed discussion of privateers and attacks on maritime trade.

101. Andrews 1984, 282.

102. Lubbock 1948, 119.

103. As noted earlier, these men received a small share of any prize. However, the bulk of their income came from salaries and wages.

104. Benjamin and Thornberg 2007, 319.

105. Ibid., 321.

106. Ibid., 319.

107. Rodger 1982, 11.

108. Greenhill and Giffard 1994, 75. See also Dandeker (1978) for a discussion of the conversion in control over promotion and recruiting in the nineteenth century. He documents how the navy became a formal bureaucracy using impersonal procedures during the age of steam.

109. Keegan 1988, 72.

110. Benjamin and Tifrea 2007, 992.

111. Tunstall and Tracy 1990, 48.

112. "Its success was immediate and lasting. It was published in 1727 in its original form, and fifty years later was still a sound text-book" (Tunstall and Tracy 1990, 59).

113. Tunstall and Tracy 1990, 50–62.

114. Palmer 1997, 690–692.

115. Tunstall and Tracy 1990, 7.

116. Benjamin and Tifrea 2007, 987.

117. Parkinson 1977, 17.

118. Tunstall and Tracy 1990, 50.

119. Glete 1993.

Chapter Six

1. This chapter is based on Allen (1998).

2. Cooper 1963, 21.

3. Bruce 1980, 11.

4. As quoted in Parker 1988, 1.

5. Ibid., 7–24; Glete 2000, 9–16.

6. Glover 1977, 22.

7. Harries-Jenkins 1977, 69.

8. Bruce 1980, 86.

9. Barnett 1970, 138.

10. Harries-Jenkins 1977, 85.

11. Ibid., 85.

12. Some officers in the British Army did not purchase their commission. And some evidence indicates that when the system ended the Crown even compensated these officers!

13. Frey and Buhofer 1988.

14. Bruce 1980, 3–7.

15. Parker 1988, 15–17.

16. As quoted in Bruce 1980, 123.

17. Houlding 1981, 106.

18. Glover 1977, 79.

19. Harries-Jenkins 1977, 72.

20. Houlding 1981, 100. Glover, however, claims that the number of purchased commissions varied a great deal, and were as low as 20 percent of promotions in times of war (Glover 1977, 82).

21. Houlding 1981, 101.

22. Wellington, as quoted in Stocqueler 1873, 153.

23. It is true enough that a purchased commission could in principle be forfeited for misconduct, but an act of misconduct is hardly the path to demonstrate a bond for good behavior. Besides, in actual practice, forfeiture for misconduct rarely occurred. According to Harries-Jenkins: "Critics of the system argued that it was very unusual for an officer to forfeit the value of his commission through misconduct, since an individual who was to be dismissed from the army was 'invited to retire', a procedure which allowed him to sell out" (1977, 85). There is one other exception, mentioned later. Once an officer reached the rank of lieutenant-colonel, the commission could not be sold, and hence the purchase was a form of hostage capital. So for a very small few, the purchase system may have indeed been a route into the aristocracy.

24. It could have served to keep the army in the hands of men interested in maintaining the status quo. It could have reduced the incentive for officers to engage in looting. It could have been a source of retirement capital. None of these are satisfactory. Patronage would have been a better method of keeping the army in aristocratic hands if avoiding revolutions was the objective. The sale of commissions probably increased the incentive to loot, since officers were always interested in recouping their investment. And capital for retirement was no doubt better invested elsewhere.

25. Churchill 2002, 92–93.

26. McClure 1901.

27. Rogers 1977, 58.

28. Brennan and Tulloch 1982.

29. Marshall 1978 [1947].

30. Field 2009.

31. Tullock 1987.

32. Axelrod 1984.

33. Field 2009, 22.

34. Ibid.

35. Cooper 1963, 11–12; Harries-Jenkins 1977, 61; Bruce 1980, 8–9.

36. Montross 1960, 312–314.

37. Lord Barrington, as quoted in Bruce 1980, 174.

38. Glover 1980b, 46.

39. Ibid., 48–49.

40. Redlich 1964, 495–496.

41. Parker 1988, 59.

42. Glover 1977, 21.

43. Redlich 1964, 74. In current dollars this sum would be approximately $23 million.

44. Parker 1988, 59.

45. Even though the pyramid of ranks had relatively few colonels, this rule preventing sale explains why the largest number of retirements through sale of commission in the army came at the rank of colonel.

46. Redlich 1964, 496.

47. Glete 2000, 22.

48. Rodger 2004, 406.

49. Thomson 1994, 29.

50. Parker 1988, 59–60.

51. Writing of battles during the pre-modern era, about 300 years after the introduction of firearms, Parker (1988, 44) concludes that "in the age of the military revolution, the skill of individual governments and generals in supplying war often became the pivot about which the outcome of armed conflict turned."

52. Parker 1988, 58.

53. Glover 1980b, 14.

54. Ibid., 16.

55. Burke 1979, 203.

56. Shanahan 1966, 142.

57. Bruce 1980, 9.

58. Parker 1988, 32.

59. Glover 1980a, 51.

Chapter Seven

1. The naval administration of Pepys's day was tiny. It consisted of the lord high admiral (the Duke of York), the Navy Committee of the Privy Council, the Admiralty, and the Navy Board. The board was made up of three commissioners and four principal officers. These officers consisted of the treasurer, controller, surveyor, and the clerk of the acts (Rodger 2004, 95–96). Pepys, therefore, was very close to power.

2. Pepys 1970, 6:285.

3. Coase 1974.

4. This history is drawn from Coase (1974), and Hague and Christie (1975).

5. Hague and Christie 1975, 30.

6. Webb and Webb 1963b, 6.

7. Darby 1973, 174–175.

8. Webb and Webb 1963b, 143.

9. Bogart 2005b, 481.

10. Webb and Webb 1963b, 168.

11. Ibid., 160.

12. Bogart 2005b, 501.

13. Barker and Savage 1974, 120; Bogart (2005a) estimates a tenfold increase.

14. Webb and Webb 1963b, 172.

15. Although the 1835 act affected most of the roads in Britain, it left intact the turnpike trusts, whose days were numbered anyway. With the advent of train passenger travel, the "transfer of business was instantaneous and complete (Webb and Webb 1963b, 215). It was not surprising that people preferred to travel at thirty miles per hour rather then ten miles per hour, especially when it cost less. As rail moved into one route after another, the trusts went out of business. The last toll charged by a trust was issued in 1895, although the trusts were mostly finished by the 1860s.

16. Keeping in mind that these were rights of way for locals to move from one field to another, or from one building to another, rather solves the mystery.

17. Jackman 1965, 341–346.

18. Alberts 1972, 144.

19. O'Brien and Hunt, 1999.

20. Ibid., p. 67.

21. Churchill 2002, 74–77.

22. O'Brien and Hunt 1999, 67.

23. Dickson (1967) provides an exhaustive account.

24. Roseveare 1969, 2.

25. Kindleberger 1993, 159.

26. North and Weingast (1989) provide a series of examples.

27. O'Brien and Hunt 1999, 72.

28. Brewer 1988, 89.

29. Ibid., 101.

30. The following is taken from the fascinating account by John Brewer (1988).

31. Brewer 1988, 109.

32. Ibid., 110.

33. Ibid., 104.

34. What change allowed this financial revolution to happen? It is tempting to view the Glorious Revolution (à la North and Weingast [1989]) as the watershed moment when Parliament placed restraints on the Crown to prevent reneging on loans, leases, and other contracts. This event could have led to Parliament's willingness to subject itself to taxation and debt (Clark [1996] rejects this hypothesis). Perhaps the Glorious Revolution is best seen as part of a continuous transfer of power, from the Restoration onward, from Crown to Parliament. As previously noted, the timing of changes in tax farming do not fit the watershed view of the Glorious Revolution. Changes in the way taxes were collected and the creation of many binding restrictions on the Crown occurred prior to the revolution in 1688. Had the Glorious Revolution solved a reneging problem of the Crown, it seems likely that the Crown would have engaged in more tax farming, not less.

35. Brewer 1988, 92.

36. Roseveare 1969, 61.

37. Ibid., 62.

Chapter Eight

1. Most of this chapter is based on Allen and Barzel (2011).

2. See Linebaugh (2003) or Becker (1983) as examples.

3. See Radzinowicz 1948.

4. Although some standardized goods had existed earlier, the Industrial Revolution led to previously unparalleled reductions in the role of nature, which dramatically increased both the number of standard goods and their uniformity.

5. Holdsworth 1956, 246. Holdsworth, in his famous history of the common law, states: "The peculiar feature common to the history of the official staffs of the central courts is the idea that many of these offices were the freeholds or the properties of the officials" (1956, 246).

6. In England these efforts took place in 1551–1552, 1690, 1692–1693, 1740, and finally in a series of acts from 1818 through 1873 (Holdsworth 1956, 250).

7. Duman 1982, 79: "Regardless of which official actually chose the judges, the government and the Sovereign were consulted and their judgments influenced judicial appointments."

8. Ibid., 29.

9. Holdsworth 1956, 255.

10. Duman 1982, 50.

11. Davies 2002, 153.

12. Hay and Snyder 1989, 18.

13. See Aylmer (1980, 100–106) for details.

14. Paley 1989, 301–302.

15. Ibid., 323.

16. Berg 1994, 269–270.

17. Rosenberg 1963.

18. In reference to iron, "One of the major advantages of puddling and rolling was that it was capable of producing a homogeneous output" (Szostak 1991, 127). Changes in weaving, bleaching, and supplies of clay led to increases in the standardization of clothing, nails, and dishes (Szostak 1991, 127).

19. Mokyr 1999, 106.

20. Szostak 1991.

21. Szostak 1989, 13–15, 168–169.

22. Elsewhere Szostak states: "Of special importance here is the need for standardization. Selling goods face to face does not require a standardized product; selling by sample does. In order to take advantage of new and better methods of distribution, then, it was necessary to produce a standardized product" (1989, 355).

23. Greif (2006) generally argues that the emergence of widespread anonymous exchange is one of the key factors of modern growth.

24. See Barzel (2004) for a discussion.

25. Consider, for example, an extreme case of an artisan good: children. When a child is missing, the parent is the first to know. Likewise, seeing one's child in the

unauthorized possession of another adult is sufficient for the parent to know a theft has taken place. Parents, quite naturally, are still the primary "police" of their children because they have a strong comparative advantage in protection and because the value of their children to others is generally low. Third parties require much more information to identify a given stolen child and only become involved after the efforts of parents are unsuccessful or when the parents request their services. A paper currency is the opposite case for an extreme standardized good. Although counterfeits are not unheard of, the $20 bill in one wallet is identical (ignoring serial numbers) to any other $20 bill. Thus private individuals have no advantage in identifying stolen cash or in trying to recover it. Indeed, often private individuals take standardized goods and modify them in ways that make them unique in order to improve their ability to privately protect them.

26. This transformation has been thoroughly documented by Becker (1983) in the context of embezzlement statutes and by Fletcher (1976) in the context of larceny.

27. Ditton 1977, 40.

28. Ashton 1966, 208.

29. Linebaugh, in the context of silk production, states: "These customs, latitudes or cheats arose either between the merchant and the master to whom the silk was put out for work, or between the master and his workers. Allowance was made for waste, or negotiated in either case. The techniques of production appeared to be highly wasteful" (Linebaugh 2003, 264. See also Styles 1983a, 179).

30. Ashton 1966, 208.

31. Jones 1982, 131.

32. Knight 1975, 221.

33. See Fletcher (1976) and Becker (1983).

34. Philips 1977, 225.

35. Soderlund 1998, 647.

36. Linebaugh 2003, 234.

37. Ibid., 268.

38. Ibid., 239.

39. Becker 1983, 1499–1500, 1510–1511.

40. For example, see Philips 1977, 188–189; Hay 1980, 70–71.

41. Philips 1977, 221.

42. Ibid., 225. Philips goes on to note how the creation of the factory assisted in this changing relationship: "The development of the industrial system and the concentration in factories and workshops simplified the legal position on ownership and theft of raw material; there was no longer the legal problem which outwork posed, that while the ownership of the raw material remained with the master, the possession was with the outworker. Once all the material was worked up within the factory or workshop, this legal confusion disappeared" (1977, 189).

43. Becker 1983, 1487.

44. Styles 1983a, 195.

45. Fletcher 1976, 472.

46. Ibid., 483.

47. For example: "Occasionally it was possible for the victim of embezzlement to provide watertight evidence of fraud. Thus the wool bought from John Pobjoy by Thomas Blackburn, a small Bradford on Avon clothier, was readily recognized by its owner,

John Cooper, as wool stolen from his slubbing shop because it was a peculiar German wool, finer than was common, and used by no other clothier in Trowbridge" (Randall 1990, 208).

48. "Prosecution of the slingers, however, was more difficult since proof of ownership could not always easily be established. This had been a principal complaint of the clothiers to the 1774 committee. Cooper told them "that he had in searching of suspected persons' houses, found a large quantity of wool and yarn of various sorts, different colours, different wools, and in many small quantities, and *not being able to swear to the identity of any of it,* the persons could not be prosecuted" (Randall 1990, 207; emphasis added).

49. The theft of something like currency had always been criminalized, but currency was always a standard good—even if coins could be clipped and counterfeited. In contrast, goods that remained artisan had their disputes remain in the civil courts. Rather, it was the massive new standardization of the ordinary products of life that led to the changes in criminal law. Styles notes the relationship between standardization and the new criminal acts. "Another obstacle to detection was the difficulty of identifying embezzled materials. The 1749 act, the 1774 wool act and the 1777 general act created a range of catch-all offences out of mere possession of suspicious materials. The burden of proof was placed on the accused, reversing the normal relationship between prosecutor and defendant in later-eighteenth-century English law" (1983a, 195).

50. Jones (1982, 129) notes: "There seems to be a general consensus amongst both contemporaries and historians that the adulteration and embezzlement of raw materials constituted a major problem during England's Industrial Revolution . . . by the nineteenth century a regular trade had developed in embezzled yarn."

51. Randall 1990, 193. Randall documents the rise in complaints to Parliament between 1750 and 1840 and estimates that in the woolen industry embezzlement amounted to about 2 percent of the finished cloth's value (1990, 201).

52. Garner 1995, 674.

53. Artisan goods that were stolen or embezzled could be identified and recovered through civil actions. Although this process may not help with the detection of crime, it greatly simplifies proof of a crime because witnesses could persuasively testify that an object belonged to a particular party. In the case of an artisan good, a legal owner was able to identify a specimen, stolen or not, even though the specimen was in the possession of someone else. For artisan goods, ownership and possession could be easily separated. When goods became standardized, this separation was no longer possible, and possession became a signal of ownership.

54. Brook 1989.

55. Mokyr (2008, 73–74) remarks: "Whether eighteenth century Britain was really becoming a kinder and gentler place is a difficult issue, but at least within the circles of commerce, finance and manufacturing, trust relations and private settlement of disputes seem to have prevailed over third party enforcement."

56. Beattie 1974, 73–79.

57. Philips 1977, 25.

58. Ibid., 60.

59. Ibid., 1977.

60. Ibid., 61.

61. Ibid., 177.

62. Ibid., 180.

63. Ibid., 189.

64. Ibid., 196; emphasis added.

65. Randall 1990, 210.

66. Philips 1977, 62.

67. Critchley 1978, 7.

68. The best discussion of these commissions is found in Webb and Webb (1963a).

69. Williams 2000, 116.

70. Barrow et al. 2005, 28–35.

71. Malcolm 2002, 21.

72. Ibid., 91.

73. Although indictments for violent crime generally fell throughout the pre-modern era, property crimes rose (Beattie 1974, 61).

74. Philips 1989, 117.

75. Styles 1983b, 132–134.

76. Hay and Snyder (1989, 18) state: "In England in the eighteenth century apprehension was the task of the victim of crime, aided (where he could get such help) from a parish constable or town watchman."

77. Ibid., 16.

78. Ibid., 23.

79. Philips 1989, 125: "A number of the early societies were aimed specifically against horse thieves—horses being very valuable property which were easy to steal and easy to move away quickly."

80. See Jones (1983) for a discussion of early forms of police.

81. Soderlund 1998, 647.

82. Ibid., 654.

83. Ibid., 661.

84. Linebaugh 2003, 221–222.

85. Starting with Becker and Stigler (1974), several articles have discussed the merits or shortcomings of a public police force. For example, Landes and Posner (1975) argue that private enforcement is unlikely to be efficient, while Friedman (1984, 1995) argues that a private system can be efficient. Rather than see one system as better than the other, it seems more reasonable to view each as constrained efficient. The private system, efficient in its time, was replaced by a public one when standardization became common.

86. Philips 1977, 54.

87. Ibid., 54.

88. Berg 1994. Coordination between the various stages of production in these proto-factories was often limited to market transactions, and control between the stages was limited. These proto-factories were nothing like the factories to come; they lacked the vertical control and heavy supervision of a factory owner. The true factories were ones that controlled worker behavior to prevent embezzlement.

89. Ashton 1966, 102–103.

90. Becker 1983, 1511.

91. Szostak 1989, 354–355. See also Jones 1982, 129.

92. Becker 1983, 1510–1511.

93. Ibid., 1509–1512.

94. Williamson (1980) also views the factory as a method of reducing theft problems, but he is not concerned with colonies.

95. Collier 1964, 14.

96. Fitton and Wadsworth 1968, 106.

97. Collier 1964, 39.

98. Chapman 1972, 55.

99. Fitton and Wadsworth 1968, 98.

100. Chapman 1972, 54.

101. Szostak 1989, 343–344.

102. Huberman 1996, 29. See also Fitton and Wadsworth 1968, 233.

103. Fitton and Wadsworth 1968, 234.

104. Dobson 1980, 99.

105. Clark, 1994, 132.

106. Chapman 1972, 55.

107. Collier 1964, 30.

108. Chapman 1972, 57.

109. Howe 1984, 272.

110. Huberman 1996, 29.

111. Heckscher 1955, 188.

Chapter Nine

1. Ollard 1984, 145.

2. Sandwich was effectively removed from power through an appointment as ambassador to Spain. Later, during the third Dutch War he was allowed to return and served as vice-admiral of the Blue, where he died in battle. Considering the importance and position of Sandwich, his lifetime contributions, and the smallness of his offense, his banishment to Spain and return to a much lower rank were a large punishment, indeed.

3. Pepys 1970, 7:369–370 (November 14, 1666).

4. Pincus (2009) describes the Glorious Revolution as the first truly modern one.

5. Ollard 1984, 306.

6. Pincus (2009, 74) notes a number of other institutions that developed during the time period examined here: the Penny Post, fire insurance, deposit banking, and stage coaches, for example. Allen and Lueck (2002) provide an extensive analysis of organization in modern agriculture based on transaction costs.

7. Blankenhorn 2007.

8. Of course the real growth in per capita income was about to explode even more. McCloskey puts the basic fact of the Industrial Revolution this way: "The heart of the matter is twelve. Twelve is the factor by which real income per head nowadays exceeds that around 1780, in Britain and in other countries that have experienced modern economic growth" (1994, 242).

9. McCloskey (1994, 253) summarized that "industrialisation was not a matter of foreign trade, not a matter of internal reallocation, not of transport innovation, not investment in factories, not education, not science."

10. Crafts and Harley (1992) carefully documented the slowness of the Industrial Revolution and noted how earlier studies that created indexes of industrial growth had

placed too much weight on fast-growing sectors such as cotton. Cotton was initially a minor textile, mostly used in producing lady's shawls. Even though it was growing at a spectacular rate, it had little impact on the overall growth rate. The same was true about other industries where early technological change had a big impact on a given industry. They concluded: "It seems impossible to sustain the view that British growth leapt spectacularly in one generation as a result of innovations in manufacturing" (Crafts and Harley 1992, 705).

11. See McCloskey (1994, 2010), Clark (1996, 2007), or Mokyr (2007, 2010) for different theories. Others, such as Acemoglu, Johnson, and Robinson (2005a, 2005b) and Mokyr (2010) make the case that institutions played a significant role in the Industrial Revolution.

12. Gabre-Madhin 2001, 36–37.

13. This theory sounds rather Panglossian but allows for low-wealth-producing institutions to last for a long time from an individual perspective. North Korea appears to those in the West as an incredibly inefficient institutional structure. Those in power have sacrificed massive amounts of national wealth in order to maintain political control. The fifty-plus years of its existence, however, are short in the life of a political institution, and 200 years from now this period is likely to be a small blip in the history of the country. Still it is useful to think of those in control of North Korea as trying to do the best they can under the circumstances they face.

14. Of course this notion of an institution is Greif's, as pointed out in Chapter 1: "An institution is a system of social factors that conjointly generate a regularity of behavior" (2006, 30).

Bibliography

Acemoglu, Daron, Simon Johnson, and James Robinson. 2005a. "Institutions as a Fundamental Cause of Long-Run Growth." In *Handbook of Economic Growth*, vol. 1A, edited by P. Aghion and S. Durlauf, 385–472. Boston: Elsevier, North-Holland.

———. 2005b. "The Rise of Europe: Atlantic Trade, Institutional Change and Growth." *American Economic Review* 95: 546–579.

Alberts, William. 1972. *The Turnpike Road System in England: 1663–1840*. Cambridge: Cambridge University Press.

Alder, Ken. 2002. *The Measure of All Things: The Seven-Year Odyssey and Hidden Error That Transformed the World*. New York: Free Press.

Allen, Douglas W. 1991. "What Are Transaction Costs?" *Research in Law and Economics* 14: 1–18.

———. 1998. "Compatible Incentives and the Purchase of Military Commissions." *Journal of Legal Studies* 27: 45–66.

———. 2000. "Transaction Costs." In *Encyclopedia of Law and Economics*, vol. 1, edited by Boudewijn Bouckaert and Gerrit De Geest, 893–926. Cheltenham, UK: Edward Elgar.

———. 2002. "The British Navy Rules: Monitoring and Incompatible Incentives in the Age of Fighting Sail." *Explorations in Economic History* 39: 204–231.

———. 2005. "Purchase, Patronage, and Professions: Incentives and the Evolution of Public Office in Pre-Modern Britain." *Journal of Institutional and Theoretical Economics* 161(1): 57–79.

———. 2006. "Theoretical Difficulties with Transaction Cost Measurement." *Division of Labor and Transaction Costs* 2(1): 1–14.

———. 2009a. "Theocracy as a Screening Device." In *The Political Economy of Theocracy*, edited by Mario Ferrero and Ronald Wintrobe, 181–202. New York: Palgrave/Macmillan.

———. 2009b. "A Theory of the Pre-Modern British Aristocracy." *Explorations in Economic History* 46(3): 299–313.

Allen, Douglas W., and Yoram Barzel. 2011 (forthcoming). "The Evolution of Criminal Law and Police during the Industrial Revolution." *Journal of Law, Economics, and Organization*.

Allen, Douglas W., and Dean Lueck. 2002. *The Nature of the Farm: Contracting, Risk, and Organization in Modern Agriculture.* Cambridge, MA: MIT Press.

Allen, Douglas W., and Clyde Reed. 2006. "The Duel of Honor: Screening for Unobservable Social Capital." *American Law and Economics Review* 8: 81–115.

Andrews, Kenneth. 1984. *Trade, Plunder, and Settlement: Maritime Enterprise and the Genesis of the British Empire: 1480–1630.* Cambridge: Cambridge University Press.

Asch, Ronald. 2003. *Nobilities in Transition: 1500–1750: Courtiers and Rebels in Britain and Europe.* London: Hodder Arnold.

Ashton, Thomas S. 1966. *An Economic History of England: The 18th Century.* London: Methuen.

Austen, Jane. 2003 [1813]. *Pride and Prejudice.* New York: Penguin Books.

Axelrod, Robert. 1984. *The Evolution of Cooperation.* New York: Basic Books.

Aylmer, Gerald E. 1961. *The King's Servants: The Civil Service of Charles I.* London: Routledge & Kegan Paul.

———. 1973. *The State's Servants: The Civil Service of the English Republic 1649–1660.* London: Routledge & Kegan Paul.

———. 1980. "From Office-Holding to Civil Service: The Genesis of Modern Bureaucracy." *Transactions of the Royal Historical Society,* 5th ser., 30: 91–108.

Baldick, Robert. 1965. *The Duel: A History of Duelling.* New York: Clarkson Potter.

Barker, Theodore C., and Christopher I. Savage. 1974. *An Economic History of Transport in Britain.* London: Hutchinson.

Barnett, Correlli. 1970. *Britain and Her Army: 1509–1970.* New York: William Morrow.

Barrow, J. S., J. D. Herson, A. H. Lawes, P. J. Riden, and M. V. Seaborne. 2005. "Local Government and Public Service: Law and Order." *A History of the County of Chester: The City of Chester: Culture, Buildings, Institutions* 5(2): 28–35. Edited by Alan T. Thacker and C. P. Lewis. http://www.british-history.ac.uk/report.aspx?compid=57304 (accessed December 22, 2010).

Barzel, Yoram. 1997. *Economic Analysis of Property Rights.* Cambridge: Cambridge University Press.

———. 2000. "Property Rights and the Evolution of the State." *Economics of Governance* 1(1): 25–51.

———. 2001. *A Theory of the State: Economic Rights, Legal Rights, and the Scope of the State.* Cambridge: Cambridge University Press.

———. 2004. "Standards and the Form of Agreement." *Economic Inquiry* 42: 1–13.

Baugh, Daniel. 1977. *Naval Administration 1715–1750.* London: Navy Records Society.

Beattie, John M. 1974. "The Pattern of Crime in England 1660–1800." *Past and Present* 62: 47–95.

Becker, Craig. 1983. "Property in the Workplace: Labor, Capital, and Crime in the Eighteenth-Century British Woolen and Worsted Industry." *Virginia Law Review* 69(8): 1487–1515.

Becker, Gary, and George Stigler. 1974. "Law Enforcement, Malfeasance, and Compensation of Enforcers." *Journal of Legal Studies* 3: 1–18.

Beckett, John V. 1986. *The Aristocracy in England 1660–1914.* Oxford: Blackwell.

Benjamin, Daniel, and Christopher Thornberg. 2003. "Comment: Rules, Monitoring, and Incentives in the Age of Sail." *Explorations in Economic History* 40: 195–211.

————. 2007. "Organization and Incentives in the Age of Sail." *Explorations in Economic History* 44: 317–341.

Benjamin, Daniel, and Anca Tifrea. 2007. "Learning by Dying: Combat Performance in the Age of Sail." *Journal of Economic History* 67(4): 968–1000.

Berg, Maxine. 1994. *The Age of Manufactures, 1700–1820: Industry, Innovation, and Work in Britain.* London: Routledge.

Berman, Eli. 2000. "Sect, Subsidy and Sacrifice: An Economist's View of Ultra-Orthodox Jews." *Quarterly Journal of Economics* 115(3): 905–953.

Billacois, François. 1990. *The Duel: Its Rise and Fall in Early Modern France.* New Haven, CT: Yale University Press.

Blankenhorn, David. 2007. *The Future of Marriage.* New York: Encounter Books.

Bogart, Dan. 2005a. "Did Turnpike Trusts Increase Transportation Investment in Eighteenth-Century England?" *Journal of Economic History* 65(2): 439–468.

————. 2005b. "Turnpike Trusts and the Transportation Revolution in 18th Century England." *Explorations in Economic History* 42: 479–508.

Bonfeild, Lloyd. 1986. "Affective Families, Open Elites, and Strict Family Settlements in Early Modern England." *Economic History Review* 39(3): 341–354.

Boswell, James. 1980. *Life of Johnson.* Oxford: Oxford University Press.

Brennan, Geoffrey, and Gordon Tullock. 1982. "An Economic Theory of Military Tactics." *Journal of Economic Behavior and Organization* 3(2): 225–242.

Brewer, John. 1988. *The Sinews of Power: War, Money and the English State, 1699–1783.* Cambridge, MA: Harvard University Press.

Brooks, Chris W. 1989. "Interpersonal Conflict and Social Tension: Civil Litigation in England, 1640–1830." In *The First Modern Society: Essays in English History in Honor of Lawrence Stone,* edited by A. L. Beier, David Cannadine, and James M. Rosenheim, 357–400. Cambridge: Cambridge University Press.

Bruce, Anthony. 1980. *The Purchase System in the British Army, 1660–1871.* London: Royal Historical Society.

Bryant, Jerry. 2000. *Roast Beef of Old England.* Audio CD. ESS.A.Y. Music.

Burke, Peter, ed. 1979. *The New Cambridge Modern History.* Cambridge: Cambridge University Press.

Bush, M. L. 1984. *The English Aristocracy: A Comparative Synthesis.* Manchester, UK: Manchester University Press.

Camerer, Colin. 1988. "Gifts as Economic Signals and Social Symbols." *American Journal of Sociology* 94: 180–214.

Campbell, George A. 1965. *The Civil Service in Britain.* London: Duckworth.

Cannadine, David. 1990. *The Decline and Fall of the British Aristocracy.* New Haven, CT: Yale University Press.

Cannon, John. 1984. *Aristocratic Century: The Peerage of Eighteenth-Century England.* Cambridge: Cambridge University Press.

Carmichael, H. Lorne, and W. Bentley MacLeod. 1997. "Gift Giving and the Evolution of Cooperation." *International Economic Review* 38(3): 485–509.

Chapman, Stanley D. 1972. *The Cotton Industry in the Industrial Revolution.* London: Macmillan.

Churchill, Winston. 2002. *Marlborough: His Life and Times.* Chicago: University of Chicago Press.

Clark, Gregory. 1994. "Factory Discipline." *Journal of Economic History* 54(1): 128–163.

———. 1996. "The Political Foundations of Modern Economic Growth: England, 1540–1800." *Journal of Interdisciplinary History* 27: 563–588.

———. 2007. *A Farewell to Alms: A Brief Economic History of the World.* Princeton, NJ: Princeton University Press.

Clark, Samuel. 1995. *State and Status: The Rise of the State and Aristocratic Power in Western Europe.* Montreal: McGill–Queen's University Press.

Coase, Ronald. 1959. "The Federal Communications Commission." *Journal of Law and Economics* 2: 1–40.

———. 1960. "The Problem of Social Cost." *Journal of Law and Economics* 3: 1–44.

———. 1974. "The Lighthouse in Economics." *Journal of Law and Economics* 17: 357–376.

Cochran, Hamilton. 1963. *Noted American Duels and Hostile Encounters.* Philadelphia: Chilton Books.

Coleman, James. 1988. "Social Capital in the Creation of Human Capital." *American Journal of Sociology* 94: 95–120.

Collier, Francis. 1964. *The Family Economy of the Working Classes in the Cotton Industry: 1784–1833.* Edited by R. S. Fitton. Manchester, UK: Manchester University Press.

Cooper, Leo. 1963. *The Age of Wellington.* New York: Dodd, Mead.

Corbett, Julian S. 1967. *Fighting Instructions: 1530–1816.* New York: Burt Franklin.

Crafts, Nicholas F. R., and Charles K. Harley. 1992. "Output Growth and the British Industrial Revolution: A Restatement of the Crafts-Harley View." *The Economic History Review* 45(4): 703–730.

Critchley, Thomas A. 1978. *A History of Police in England and Wales.* London: Constable.

Crouzet, Francois. 1985. *The First Industrialists.* Cambridge: Cambridge University Press.

Dandeker, Christopher. 1978. "Patronage and Bureaucratic Control: The Case of the Naval Officer in English Society, 1780–1850." *British Journal of Sociology* 29(3): 300–320.

Darby, Henry, C. ed. 1973. *A New Historical Geography of England.* Cambridge: Cambridge University Press.

Davies, Steven. 2002. "The Private Provision of Police during the Eighteenth and Nineteenth Centuries." In *The Voluntary City*, edited by David Beito, Peter Gordon, and Alexander Tabarrok, 182–212. Ann Arbor: University of Michigan Press.

Davis, Lance, Robert Gallman, and Karin Gleiter. 1997. *In Pursuit of Leviathan: Technology, Institutions, Productivity, and Profits in American Whaling, 1816–1906.* Chicago: University of Chicago Press.

Davis, Lance, and Douglass North. 1971. *Institutional Change and American Economic Growth.* Cambridge: Cambridge University Press.

Dasgupta, Partha, and Ismail Serageldin, eds. 1999. *Social Capital: A Multifaceted Perspective.* Washington, DC: World Bank.

Dewald, Jonathan. 1996. *The European Nobility, 1400–1800.* Cambridge: Cambridge University Press.

Dickson, Peter G. M. 1967. *The Financial Revolution in England: A Study in the Development of Public Credit, 1688–1756.* London: Macmillan.

Ditton, Jason. 1977. "Perks, Pilferage, and the Fiddle: The Historical Structure of Invisible Wages." *Theory and Society* 4(1): 39–71.

Dobson, C. R. 1980. *Masters and Journeymen: A Prehistory of Industrial Relations, 1717–1800*. London: Rowman and Littlefield.

Doepke, Matthias, and Fabrizio Zilibotti. 2008. "Occupational Choice and the Spirit of Capitalism." *Quarterly Journal of Economics* 123(2): 747–793.

Donald, David H. 1995. *Lincoln*. New York: Simon & Schuster.

Doyle, William. 1996. *Venality: The Sale of Offices in Eighteenth-Century France*. Oxford: Clarendon Press.

Duman, Daniel. 1982. *The Judicial Bench in England 1727–1875*. London: Royal Historical Society.

Eaton, Curtis, and William White. 1983. "The Economy of High Wages: An Agency Problem." *Economica* 50: 175–181.

Elias, Norbert. 1983. *The Court Society*. New York: Pantheon.

Field, Alexander. 2009. "Behavioral Economics: Lessons from the Military." Working paper, Santa Clara University.

Fitton, R. S., and Alfred P. Wadsworth. 1968. *The Strutts and the Arkwrights, 1758–1830: A Study of the Early Factory System*. New York: Kelly.

Fletcher, George. 1976. "The Metamorphosis of Larceny." *Harvard Law Review* 89(3): 469–530.

Forester, C. S. 1960. *The Age of Fighting Sail*. New York: Signet.

François, Patrick. 2002. *Social Capital and Economic Development*. New York: Routledge.

Frevert, Ute. 1998. "The Taming of the Noble Ruffian: Male Violence and Dueling in Early Modern and Modern Germany." In *Men and Violence: Gender, Honor, and Rituals in Modern Europe and America*, edited by Pieter Spierenburg, 37–63. Columbus: Ohio State University Press.

Frey, Bruno, and Heinz Buhofer. 1988. "Prisoners and Property Rights." *Journal of Law & Economics* 31(1): 19–46.

Friedman, David. 1984. "Efficient Institutions for the Private Enforcement of Law." *Journal of Legal Studies* 13(2): 379–397.

———. 1995. "Making Sense of English Law Enforcement in the Eighteenth Century." *The University of Chicago Law School Roundtable* 2: 475–498.

Gabre-Madhin, Eleni Z. 2001. *Market Institutions, Transaction Costs, and Social Capital in the Ethiopian Grain Market*. Washington, DC: International Food Policy Research Institute.

Garner, Bryan. 1995. *A Dictionary of Modern Legal Usage*. Oxford: Oxford University Press.

Glete, Jan. 1993. *Navies and Nations: Warships, Navies and State Building in Europe and America, 1500–1860*. Stockholm: Almqvist and Wiksell International.

———. 2000. *Warfare at Sea, 1500–1650*. London: Routledge.

Glover, Michael. 1977. *Wellington's Army: In the Peninsula: 1808–1814*. Newton Abbot, UK: David and Charles.

———. 1980a. *Warfare from Waterloo to Mons*. London: Cassell.

———. 1980b. *Warfare in the Age of Bonaparte*. London: Cassell.

Goldsmith, Oliver. 1964. "The Deserted Village." In *Goldsmith's Poems and Plays*, 30. London: Everyman's Library.

Green, Edward J., and Robert H. Porter. 1984. "Noncooperative Collusion under Imperfect Price Information." *Econometrica* 52: 87–100.

Greenhill, Basil, and Anne Giffard. 1994. *Steam, Politics and Patronage: The Transformation of the Royal Navy, 1815–54*. London: Conway Maritime Press.

Greif, Avner. 1989. "Reputation and Coalitions in Medieval Trade: Evidence on the Maghribi Traders." *Journal of Economic History* 49(4): 857–882.

———. 1993. "Contract Enforceability and Economic Institutions in Early Trade: The Maghribi Traders' Coalition." *American Economic Review* 83(3): 525–548.

———. 2006. *Institutions and the Path to the Modern Economy*. Cambridge: Cambridge University Press.

Gunn, Steven J. 1988. *Charles Brandon, Duke of Suffolk: c. 1484–1545*. Oxford: Blackwell.

Guttsman, Willi L., ed. 1969. *The English Ruling Class*. London: Weidenfeld & Nicolson.

Habakkuk, H. J. 1967. "England." In *The European Nobility in the Eighteenth Century*, edited by Albert Goodwin. New York: Harper Torchbooks.

Hague, Douglas B., and Rosemary Christie. 1975. *Lighthouses: Their Architecture, History and Archaeology*. Cardiff: Gomer Press.

Halliday, Hugh. 1999. *Murder among Gentlemen: A History of Duelling in Canada*. Toronto: Robin Brass.

Harris, Barbara J. 1986. *Edward Stafford: Third Duke of Buckingham, 1478–1521*. Stanford, CA: Stanford University Press.

Harries-Jenkins, G. 1977. *The Army in Victorian Society*. Toronto: University of Toronto Press.

Hattendorf, John. 1984. "Benbow's Last Fight." In *The Naval Miscellany*, vol. 5, edited by N. A. M. Rodger, 143–206. London: Allen & Unwin.

Hay, Douglas. 1980. "Crime and Justice in Eighteenth- and Nineteenth-Century England." *Crime and Justice* 2: 49–84.

Hay, Douglas, and Francis Snyder. 1989. "Using the Criminal Law, 1750–1850: Policing, Private Prosecution and the State." In *Policing and Prosecution in Britain 1750–1850*, edited by Douglas Hay and Francis Snyder, 3–52. Oxford: Clarendon Press.

Hayek, Friedrich. 1973. *Law, Legislation, and Liberty*, vol. 1. Chicago: University of Chicago Press.

Heaton, H. 1965. *The Yorkshire Woollen and Worsted Industries*. Oxford: Oxford University Press.

Heckscher, Eli. 1955. *Mercantilism*. London: Allen & Unwin.

Henderson, James. 1971. *The Frigates: An Account of the Lesser Warships of the Wars from 1793 to 1815*. New York: Dodd, Mead.

Hill, Christopher. 1992. *Olympic Politics*. Manchester: Manchester University Press.

Holdsworth, Sir William. 1956. *A History of English Law*. London: Methuen.

Hopkins, Donald R. 2002. *The Greatest Killer: Smallpox in History*. Chicago: University of Chicago Press.

Hough, Richard. 1973. *Captain Bligh & Mr. Christian: The Men and the Mutiny*. New York: E. P. Dutton.

Houlding, J. A. 1981. *Fit for Service: The Training of the British Army, 1715–1795*. Oxford: Clarendon Press.

Howarth, David. 1974. *Sovereign of the Seas: The Story of Britain and the Sea.* New York: Atheneum.

Howe, Anthony. 1984. *The Cotton Masters: 1830–1860.* Oxford: Clarendon Press.

Huberman, Michael. 1996. *Escape from the Market: Negotiating Work in Lancashire.* Cambridge: Cambridge University Press.

Hughes, Steven. 1998. "Men of Steel: Dueling, Honor, and Politics in Liberal Italy." In *Men and Violence: Gender, Honor, and Rituals in Modern Europe and America,* edited by Pieter Spierenburg, 64–81. Columbus: Ohio State University Press.

Iannaccone, Larry. 1992. "Sacrifice and Stigma: Reducing Free-riding in Cults, Communes, and Other Collectives." *Journal of Political Economy* 100(2): 271–291.

Jackman, William T. 1965. *The Development of Transportation in Modern England.* New York: Kelley.

James, Lawrence. 2009. *Aristocrats: Power, Grace and Decadence, Britain's Great Ruling Classes from 1066 to the Present.* London: Little, Brown.

Johnson, Ronald, and Gary Libecap. 1994a. *The Federal Civil Service System and the Problem of Bureaucracy.* Chicago: University of Chicago Press.

———. 1994b. "Patronage to Merit and Control of the Federal Government Labor Force." *Explorations in Economic History* 31(1): 91–119.

Jones, D. J. V. 1983. "The New Police, Crime and People in England and Wales, 1829–1888." *Transactions of the Royal Historical Society,* 5th ser., 33: 151–168.

Jones, Stephen R. H. 1982. "The Organization of Work: A Historical Dimension." *Journal of Economic Behavior and Organization* 3: 117–137.

Keegan, John. 1988. *The Price of Admiralty: The Evolution of Naval Warfare.* New York: Viking.

Kiernan, Victor G. 1988. *The Duel in European History: Honour and the Reign of Aristocracy.* Oxford: Oxford University Press.

Kindleberger, Charles. 1993. *A Financial History of Western Europe,* 2nd ed. Oxford: Oxford University Press.

Kiser, Edgar, and Joachim Schneider. 1994. "Bureaucracy and Efficiency: An Analysis of Taxation in Early Modern Prussia." *American Sociological Review* 59: 187–204.

Klein, Benjamin, and Keith Leffler. 1981. "The Role of Market Forces in Ensuring Contractual Performance." *Journal of Political Economy* 89: 615–641.

Kline, Mary-Jo, ed. 1973. *Alexander Hamilton: A Biography in His Own Words.* New York: Harper & Row.

Knight, Roger J. B. 1975. "Pilfering and Theft from Dockyards at the Time of the American War of Independence." *Mariners Mirror* 61: 215–225.

Kurlansky, Mark. 2002. *Salt: A World History.* New York: Walker.

Landes, David. 1983. *Revolution in Time: Clocks and the Making of the Modern World.* Cambridge, MA: Harvard University Press.

Landes, William, and Richard Posner. 1975. "The Private Enforcement of Law." *Journal of Legal Studies* 4: 1–46.

Lavery, Brian. 1989. *Nelson's Navy: The Ships, Men, and Organization, 1793–1815.* London: Conway Maritime Press.

———. 1998. *Shipboard Life and Organisation: 1731–1815.* Aldershot, UK: Ashgate for the Navy Records Society.

Lessig, Lawrence. 1995. "The Regulation of Social Meaning." *University of Chicago Law Review* 62: 944–1045.

Lewis, Michael. 1960. *A Social History of the Navy: 1793–1815.* London: Allen & Unwin.

———. 1965. *The Navy in Transition: A Social History, 1814–1864.* London: Hoder & Stoughton.

Libecap, Gary, and Dean Lueck. 2010. "The Demarcation of Land and the Roll of Coordinating Institutions." Working paper, University of California, Santa Barbara.

Linebaugh, Peter. 2003. *The London Hanged: Crime and Civil Society in the Eighteenth Century.* London: Verso.

Locke, John. 1692. "Some Thoughts Concerning Education." Modern History Sourcebook. http://www.fordham.edu/halsall/mod/1692locke-education.html (accessed March 29, 2011).

Lubbock, Basil. 1948. "Seamen." In *The Trade Winds*, edited by C. Northcote Parkinson, 102–120. London: Allen & Unwin.

Magner, L. N. 2005. *A History of Medicine*, 2nd ed. Boca Raton, FL: Taylor & Francis.

Mailath, George J., and Larry Samuelson. 2006. *Repeated Games and Reputations: Long-Run Relationships.* Oxford: Oxford University Press.

Malcolm, Joyce L. 2002. *Guns and Violence: The English Experience.* Cambridge, MA: Harvard University Press.

Marshall, Samuel L. A. 1978 [1947]. *Men against Fire: The Problem of Battle Command in Future War.* Reprint, Gloucester, UK: Peter Smith.

Marx, Karl, and Frederick Engels. 1976 [1848]. *The Communist Manifesto.* London: Penguin.

McAleer, Kevin. 1994. *Dueling: The Cult of Honor in Fin-De-Siecle Germany.* Princeton, NJ: Princeton University Press.

McCloskey, D. 1994. "1780–1860: A Survey." In *The Economic History of Britain since 1700*, 2nd ed., vol. 1, edited by Roderick Floud and Donald McCloskey, 242–270. Cambridge: Cambridge University Press.

———. 2010. *Bourgeois Dignity and Liberty: Why Economics Can't Explain the Modern World.* Chicago: University of Chicago Press.

McClure, Col. Alexander K. 1901. *Lincoln's Yarns and Stories.* Chicago: John C. Winston.

Milgrom, Paul, Douglass North, and Barry Weingast. 1990. "The Role of Institutions in the Revival of Trade: The Law Merchant, Private Judges, and the Champagne Fairs." *Economics and Politics* 2(1): 1–23.

Mill, John Stuart. 1865. *Principles of Political Economy*, 6th ed. London: Longmans, Green.

Mokyr, Joel. 1999. *The British Industrial Revolution: An Economic Perspective*, 2nd ed. Boulder, CO: Westview Press.

———. 2008. "The Institutional Origins of the Industrial Revolution." In *Institutions and Economic Performance*, edited by Elhanan Helpman, 64–116. Cambridge, MA: Harvard University Press.

———. 2010. *The Enlightened Economy: An Economic History of Britain, 1700–1850.* New Haven, CT: Yale University Press.

Montross, Lynn. 1960. *War through the Ages*, 3rd ed. New York: Harper.

Moorehouse, Geoffrey. 2005. *Great Harry's Navy: How Henry VIII Gave England Seapower*. London: Orion Press.

Morris, T. A. 1999. *Tudor Government*. New York: Routledge.

Murray, Ellen. 1984. *The Code of Honor. Dueling in America: American Dueling Pistols and Related Ephemera from the Collection of Lt. Col. and Mrs. William R. Orbelo*. Washington, DC: Star of the Republic Museum.

North, Douglass. 1981. *Structure and Change in Economic History*. New York: Norton.

———. 1990. *Institutions, Institutional Change and Economic Performance*. Cambridge: Cambridge University Press.

North, Douglass, and Robert Thomas. 1973. *The Rise of the Western World: A New Economic History*. Cambridge: Cambridge University Press.

North, Douglass, and Barry Weingast. 1989. "Constitutions and Commitment: The Evolution of Institutions Governing Public Choice in Seventeenth Century England." *Journal of Economic History* 49: 803–832.

Nye, Robert. 1998. "The End of the Modern French Duel." In *Men and Violence: Gender, Honor, and Rituals in Modern Europe and America*, edited by Pieter Spierenburg, 82–102. Columbus: Ohio State University Press.

O'Brien, Patrick, and Philip Hunt. 1999. "England, 1485–1815." In *The Rise of the Fiscal State in Europe, c. 1200–1815*, edited by Richard Bonney, 54–92. Oxford: Oxford University Press.

O'Donoghue, Jim, Louise Goulding, and Grahame Allen. 2004. "Consumer Price Inflation since 1750." *Economic Trends* 604: 38–46.

Ollard, Richard. 1984. *Pepys: A Biography*. Oxford: Oxford University Press.

Orwell, George. 1968. "The Lion and the Unicorn: Socialism and the English Genius." In *The Collected Essays, Journalism and Letters of George Orwell*, vol. 2, edited by Sonia Orwell and Ian Angus, 56–108. New York: Harcourt, Brace & World.

Paley, Ruth. 1989. "Thief-takers in London in the Age of the McDaniel Gang, c. 1745–1754." In *Policing and Prosecution in Britain 1750–1850*, edited by Douglas Hay and Francis Snyder, 301–342. Oxford: Clarendon Press.

Palmer, Michael. 1997. "The Soul's Right Hand: Command and Control in the Age of Fighting Sail, 1652–1827." *Journal of Military History* 61: 673–776.

Parker, David. 2001. "Law, Honor, and Impunity in Spanish America: The Debate over Dueling, 1870–1920." *Law and History Review* 19: 311–341.

Parker, Geoffrey. 1988. *The Military Revolution: Military Innovation and the Rise of the West, 1500–1800*. Cambridge: Cambridge University Press.

Parkinson, C. Northcote. 1977. *Britannia Rules: The Classic Age of Naval History 1793–1815*. London: Weidenfeld & Nicolson.

Parliamentary Papers. 1818. *Reports of the Commissioners*. CIHM Digital Series no. 01653.

Parmet, Herbert, and Marie Hecht. 1967. *Aaron Burr: Portrait of an Ambitious Man*. London: Macmillan.

Peltonen, Markku. 2001. "Francis Bacon, The Earl of Northampton, and the Jacobean Anti-duelling Campaign." *Historical Journal* 44(1): 128.

Pepys, Samuel. 1970. *The Diary of Samuel Pepys*. 10 vols. Edited by Robert Latham and William Matthews. Berkeley: University of California Press.

Philips, David. 1977. *Crime and Authority in Victorian England: The Black Country 1835–1860*. London: Croom Helm.

———. 1989. "Good Men to Associate and Bad Men to Conspire: Associations for the Prosecution of Felons in England 1760–1860." In *Policing and Prosecution in Britain 1750–1850*, edited by Douglas Hay and Francis Snyder, 93–120. Oxford: Clarendon Press.

Pincus, Steve. 2009. *1688: The First Modern Revolution*. New Haven, CT: Yale University Press.

Plumb, John H. 1963. *England in the Eighteenth Century*. New York: Penguin Books.

Posner, Eric. 1996. "Law, Economics, and Inefficient Norms." *University of Pennsylvania Law Review* 144: 1697–1744.

———. 2000. *Law and Social Norms*. Cambridge, MA: Harvard University Press.

Radzinowicz, Leon. 1948. *A History of English Criminal Law*. London: Stevens.

Randall, Adrian. 1990. "Peculiar Perquisites and Pernicious Practices: Embezzlement in the West of England Woollen Industry, c. 1750–1840." *International Review of Social History* 35: 193–219.

Redlich, Fritz. 1964. *The German Military Enterpriser and His Work Force*. Wiesbaden: Franz Steiner Verlag.

Rodger, N. A. M. 1982. *Articles of War: The Statutes Which Governed Our Fighting Navies 1661, 1749, and 1886*. Hampshire, UK: Kenneth Mason.

———. 1984. "The Douglas Papers, 1760–1762." In *The Naval Miscellany*, vol. 5, edited by N. A. M. Rodger, 125–165. London: Allen & Unwin.

———. 1986. *The Wooden World: An Anatomy of the Georgian Navy*. New York: Norton.

———. 1998. *The Safeguard of the Sea: A Naval History of Britain, 660–1649*. New York: Norton.

———. 2004. *The Command of the Ocean: A Naval History of Britain, 1649–1815*. New York: Norton.

Rogers, Hugh C. B. 1977. *The British Army of the Eighteenth Century*. London: Allen & Unwin.

Rosenberg, Nathan. 1963. "Technological Change in the Machine Tool Industry, 1840–1910." *Journal of Economic History* 23(4): 414–443.

Roseveare, Henry. 1969. *The Treasury: The Evolution of a British Institution*. New York: Columbia University Press.

Royal Navy. 1790. *Regulations and Instructions Relating to His Majesty's Service at Sea*, 13th ed. London.

Rubinstein, William D. 1981. *Men of Property: The Very Wealthy in Britain since the Industrial Revolution*. London: Croom Helm.

Sanford John L., and Meredith Townsend. (1865) 1972. *The Great Governing Families of England*. Freeport, NY: Books for Libraries Press.

Schwartz, Warren, Keith Baxter, and David Ryan. 1984. "The Duel: Can These Gentlemen Be Acting Efficiently?" *Journal of Legal Studies* 13: 321–355.

Shanahan, William. 1966. *Prussian Military Reforms 1786–1813*. New York: AMS Press.

Smith, Adam. 1994 [1776]. *The Wealth of Nations*. New York: Modern Library.

Soderlund. Richard. 1998. "'Intended as a Terror to the Idle and Profligate': Embezzlement and the Origins of Policing in the Yorkshire Worsted Industry, c. 1750–1777." *Journal of Social History* 31(3): 647–669.

Soltow, Lee. 1968. "Long Run Changes in British Income Inequality." *The Economic History Review* 21(1): 17–29.

Soto, Hernando de. 2000. *The Mystery of Capital: Why Capitalism Triumphs in the West and Fails Everywhere Else.* New York: Basic Books.

Steinfeld, Robert J. 1991. *The Invention of Free Labor: The Employment Relation in English & American Law and Culture, 1350–1870.* Chapel Hill: University of North Carolina Press.

Steward, Dick. 2000. *Duels and the Roots of Violence in Missouri.* Columbia: University of Missouri Press.

Stocqueler, Joachim H. 1873. *A Personal History of the Horse-Guards.* London: Hurst and Blackett.

Stone, Lawrence. 1965. *The Crisis of the Aristocracy: 1558–1641.* Oxford: Carendon Press.

Stone, Lawrence, and Jeanne F. Stone. 1984. *An Open Elite? England 1540–1880.* Oxford: Clarendon Press.

Styles, John. 1983a. "Embezzlement, Industry, and the Law in England 1500–1800." In *Manufacture in Town and Country before the Factory*, edited by Maxine Berg, Pat Hudson, and Michael Sonenscher, 173–210. Cambridge: Cambridge University Press.

———. 1983b. "Sir John Fielding and the Problem of Criminal Investigation in Eighteenth-Century England." *Transactions of the Royal Historical Society*, 5th ser., 33: 127–149.

Swart, K. W. 1949. *Sale of Offices in the Seventeenth Century.* The Hague: M. Nijhoff.

Szostak, Rick. 1989. "The Organization of Work: The Emergence of the Factory Revisited." *Journal of Economic Behavior and Organization* 11(3): 343–358.

———. 1991. *The Role of Transportation in the Industrial Revolution: A Comparison of England and France.* Montreal: McGill–Queen's University Press.

Tavernor, Robert. 2007. *Smoot's Ear: The Measure of Humanity.* New Haven, CT: Yale University Press.

Thomson, Janice. 1994. *Mercenaries, Pirates, and Sovereigns.* Princeton, NJ: Princeton University Press.

Tracy, Nicholas. 1991a. *Attack on Maritime Trade.* Toronto: University of Toronto Press.

———. 1991b. "Sir Robert Calder's Action." *Mariner's Mirror* 77: 259–270.

Tullock, Gordon. 1987. "Jackson and the Prisoner's Dilemma." *Journal of Economic Behavior and Organization* 8: 637–640.

Tunstall, Brian, and Nicholas Tracy, eds. 1990. *Naval Warfare in the Age of Sail: The Evolution of Fighting Tactics 1650–1815.* Annapolis, MD: Naval Institute Press.

Voltaire. 1947 [1759]. *Candide.* New York: Penguin Books.

Wareham, Tom. 2001. *The Star Captains: Frigate Command in the Napoleonic Wars.* Annapolis, MD: Naval Institute Press.

Warner, Oliver. 1975. *The British Navy: A Concise History.* London: Thames & Hudson.

Webb, Sidney, and Beatrice Webb. 1963a. *English Local Government: Statutory Authorities for Special Purposes.* Hamden, CT: Archon Books.

———. 1963b. *The Story of the King's Highway.* Hamden, CT: Archon Books.

Whipple, Addison B. C. 1978. *Fighting Sail.* Alexandria, VA: Time-Life Books.

Williams, Chris. 2000. "Expediency, Authority and Duplicity: Reforming Sheffield's Police, 1832–40." In *Urban Governance: Britain and Beyond since 1750*, edited by Robert Morris and Richard Trainor, 115–127. Aldershot, UK: Ashgate.

Williamson, Oliver. 1980. "The Organization of Work." *Journal of Economic Behavior and Organization* 1: 5–38.

Zmora, Hillay. 2001. *Monarchy, Aristocracy, and the State in Europe, 1300–1800.* London: Routledge.

Zupko, Ronald E. 1977. *British Weights and Measures: A History from Antiquity to the Seventeenth Century.* Madison: University of Wisconsin Press.

Index